CURRICULUM BOOKS WITHDRAW

The First Eighty Years

William Henry Schubert

With Special Assistance from
Ann Lynn Lopez Schubert

UNIVERSITY
PRESS OF
AMERICA

LANHAM • NEW YORK • LONDON

Copyright © 1984 by

University Press of America,™ Inc.

4720 Boston Way
Lanham, MD 20706

3 Henrietta Street
London WC2E 8LU England

Library of Congress Cataloging in Publication Data

Schubert, William Henry.
   Curriculum books.

      Includes bibliographies and index.
      1. Education–United States–Curricula–
Bibliography. I. Schubert, Ann Lynn Lopez, joint author.
II. Title.
Z5815.U5S34]LB1570[016.375'00973   80–8275
ISBN 0–8191–1261–5
ISBN 0–8191–1262–3 (pbk.)

All University Press of America books are produced on acid-free
paper which exceeds the minimum standards set by the National
Historical Publications and Records Commission.

To those who would reflectively, imaginatively
and lovingly inspire human beings to seek greater
meaning and goodness;

therefore,

To my wife, Ann, and to my parents, Walter and
Madeline Schubert, whose influences do this for
the curriculum of my life.

ACKNOWLEDGEMENT

Most lovingly, I wish to thank my wife, Ann, for her constant encouragement of my work. Her unwavering assistance in research, typing, discussion of ideas, and reading made this work possible.

I also wish to thank a number of scholars at other institutions who have encouraged the work by their comments, suggestions, and sharing of information. They include: Michael Apple of the University of Wisconsin, George Beauchamp of Northwestern University, O.L. Davis of the University of Texas, John I. Goodlad of the University of California at Los Angeles, L. Thomas Hopkins of Columbia University, Paul R. Klohr of the Ohio State University, William Pinar of the University of Rochester, Gerald Ponder of North Texas State University, George Posner of Cornell University, J. Harlan Shores of the University of Illinois at Urbana, Edmund Short of the Pennsylvania State University, Charles A. Speiker of the Association for Supervision and Curriculum Development, Kate Strickland of the University of Texas at San Antonio, Daniel Tanner of Rutgers University, Laurel Tanner of Temple University, Ralph W. Tyler of Science Research Associates, Max van Manen of the University of Alberta, and George Willis of the University of Rhode Island.

Many colleagues at my current institution, the University of Illinois at Chicago Circle, are also acknowledged for their encouragement and suggestions, especially Maurice J. Eash, Harriet Talmage, David Wilson, Eugene Cramer, Robert Crowson, William Ernst, Susan Eskridge, John Frantz, Neal Gordon, Edward Haertel, Geneva Haertel, Coleman Hill, Joy Johnson, David Laske, Bodh Loomba, Julius Menacker, David Miller, Van Cleve Morris, Larry Nucci, Ernest Pascarella, Susanna Pflaum, Sue Rasher, Herbert Walberg, and Edward Wynne.

Appreciation is extended to Madeline Schubert for helpful comments on an earlier version of the manuscript. Many thanks are also extended to Elaine and Karen for being thoughtful during their visit when we worked on this book.

Two professional associations are thanked for helping to make this work known among fellow-scholars: The American Educational Research Association Special Interest Group on the Creation and Utilization of Curriculum Knowledge, and The Society for the Study of Curriculum History.

Evelyn Pope is thanked for her many hours of effort in typing the manuscript. I am particularly grateful to Catherine Terdich for her editorial assistance.

Special appreciation is extended to J. Harlan Shores for his gift of more than two hundred curriculum books and monographs. Finally, Pearl Kanaley, my great aunt and first grade teacher, is thanked most kindly for supporting this project.

TABLE OF CONTENTS

PREFACE

Many fields today realize the necessity of
searching for their historical roots. Disciplines
such as mathematics, biology, chemistry, and physics are increasingly curious about the ideas of
their intellectual ancestors. For too long it was
assumed that sciences and their technological
derivatives in medicine, industry, transportation,
communication, etc., were nearly perfect evolu-
tionary systems. That is to say, they automatic-
ally expurgated inert thoughts and perceived little
need to probe their archaic past. Today, this
position is recognized for its puerility. Much of
importance can be gleaned from the thought patterns
and techniques, if not from the substantive knowledge, expressed in works by those who forged the
origins of many a scholarly domain. To be ahistorical is indefensible.

This is the case for the study of curriculum
in the field of education. Curriculum scholars,
administrators, and teachers need to see themselves
as part of an evolving historical context. They
need to know about the insights, foibles, and
achievements of those who faced similar problems
in other times and circumstances. Many do recog-
nize this need. Yet, historical consciousness
cannot be achieved by desire alone. The centralization of literature about curriculum is a necessary
prerequisite to knowledge and analysis of its
origins. To know one's origins is to know one's
present and to be able to create one's future.

Purpose and Organization

This book provides a chronology of curriculum
books that appeared in America from 1900 to 1979.
Thus, it is designed for anyone whose interests
and professional pursuits deal with education.
It portrays a stream of books used to educate
school administrators, teachers, and educational
scholars about curriculum for over seventy-five

years. It is not a history book in a technical sense; rather, it is a chronology of books with commentaries. Each chapter treats a decade for which background of two kinds is provided. The first consists of reminders about and reflections on socio-cultural, intellectual, artistic, and scientific developments. The second is discussion of major curriculum movements, trends, books, and authors. These context-setting sections are followed by yearly bibliographies of curriculum books published in the decade.

As an attempt to provide a comprehensive resource on curriculum books published in English, this book is designed to ease curriculum scholarship that can lead to improved curricular decision and action. The categories used to discuss curriculum contributions in each chapter are not always uniform because events are quite different from decade to decade. Uniformity is, however, provided by continuing reference to schools of curriculum thought; namely, experientialists, intellectual traditionalists, and social behaviorists. These schools are characterized in Chapter I.

Since this work is an attempt to help the curriculum field become less ahistorical, I will now relate a bit of the history that prompted me to write it.

How the Book Developed

During my first year of doctoral study I pondered possible directions for my curriculum research. As I pursued my coursework, one need in particular became indelible in my mind. I experienced great difficulty in locating bibliographies of curriculum works. I suspected that other students had similar difficulty. Soon I realized that this difficulty was shared by scholars in the field, even eminent ones. I felt that this might well be a productive problem to remedy, especially since I already had started a citation collection. Early in my doctoral study at the University of Illinois my mentor, J. Harlan Shores, wisely suggested that as I study I should keep a card file of all sources encountered. At the conclusion of the program I had accumulated cards on approximately 600 books, articles, miscellaneous papers, etc.

Stocked with these cards, I estimated that I was in a position to propose a paper for presentation at the 1976 American Educational Research Association Annual Conference. Brashly, I proposed to centralize and categorize all of the curriculum development literature from 1900 to 1976. Thankfully, I had the sense to limit the kinds of citations by using a system of rules. Essentially, the rules confined the study to curriculum books written in English. The proposal was accepted, and as the task evolved it seemed increasingly insurmountable. Yet, it is surprising what one can accomplish when one intentionally over-commits oneself. I, at least, had to approximate the proposed task.

It was at that point that my travels began, both actually and figuratively. I toured major curriculum text books and their bibliographies. One need only sample the elaborate citations in Caswell and Campbell (1935), Smith, Stanley, and Shores (1950), Stratemeyer et al. (1947), Seguel (1966), Trillingham (1934), and Taba (1962) to empathize with the magnitude of the task.[1] Numerous other texts were surveyed as well. My paper, The Literature of Curriculum Development: Toward Centralization and Analysis, was presented in San Francisco in April, 1976.[2] It included a bibliography of 753 curriculum publications, mostly books. In the paper, citations were categorized in three ways: (1) their tendency to be prescriptive or descriptive treatments of curriculum; (2) disciplinary orientation of the authors; and (3) principal sub-areas of education that the books treated. Although tendencies emerged in these areas, I learned that productive analyses should be considerably more complex and often specific to historical situations.

Following the presentation, considerable positive commentary was received through letters and personal contacts, all of which encouraged continuation on a larger scale. Since sources listed in bibliographies of curriculum texts had a frequent habit of conflicting with one another, the next venture was to check citations with standard reference collections. The following were among the most helpful, both in checking citations and augmenting the bibliography:

> Books in Print (Past and present editions, particularly the subject guides). New York and London: R.R. Bowker Company.

> Broudy, H.S. et al. Philosophy of Education: An Organization of Topics and Selected Sources. Urbana: University of Illinois Press, 1967, 1969, and 1971 supplements (Curriculum Sections).

> Columbia University. Dictionary Catalogue--Teachers College Library. Boston: G.K. Hall, 1970 and available supplements from subsequent years.

> Harvard University Library, Widener Library Shelflist Service. Education (Two Volumes). Cambridge: Harvard University Press, 1968.

> Library of Congress Catalog--Books: Subject Indexes. Washington: Library of Congress, 1943 to present.

> United States Department of Health, Education and Welfare. Subject Catalogue of the Department Library (Volume Four). Boston: G.K. Hall, 1965.

Even these formative reference works proved incomplete and sometimes inaccurate. I, therefore, determined that libraries must be visited. During the next year several library collections were surveyed. This endeavor prompted a good deal of

study of curriculum literature, not merely citations alone. The following libraries are thanked
for their immense assistance, even though officials
from them likely have no remembrance of my being
there.

University of Illinois--Urbana, Illinois
Northwestern University--Evanston, Illinois
National College of Education--Evanston,
   Illinois
University of Illinois at Chicago Circle--
   Chicago, Illinois
University of Chicago--Chicago, Illinois
Chicago Public Library--Chicago, Illinois
Washington University--St. Louis, Missouri
Rochester University--Rochester, New York
Waterloo University--Waterloo, Ontario
Johns Hopkins University--Baltimore, Maryland
University of Houston--Houston, Texas
Teachers College, Columbia University--
   New York, New York
Pennsylvania State University--University
   Park, Pennsylvania
Stanford University--Palo Alto, California
Ontario Institute for Studies in Education--
   Toronto, Ontario

A presentation of the updated findings was made
at the 1977 American Educational Research Association Annual Conference in New York City.[3] This
resulted in the request by the AERA Special Interest
Group on the Creation and Utilization of Curriculum
Knowledge for permission to copy and distribute
the bibliography to its membership. The slightly
revised version, A Chronology of Curriculum Development Literature,[4] was thus disseminated in 1977.
The response from scholars from many parts of the
United States and world indicated the desire for a
more substantial publication that portrayed the
growth of curriculum thought during the Twentieth
Century. Hence, the impetus for this book. As the
book's final version took shape, guidelines for
inclusions and exclusions became defined. These
are discussed as follows.

Citation Selection

Explicating rules for citation selection is a difficult task. Using any set of rules, even rigorous legalistic ones, involves sizable portions of human judgment. That is the case here; nevertheless, rules enhance potential for replicability.

Inclusions are limited to curriculum books published in English, including monographs and yearbooks, but excluding dissertations, research reports, and curriculum guides having limited distribution, unless these are formally published and have national or international distribution. Journal articles are excluded, unless they appear in books of curriculum readings. In rare instances educational journals devoted entire issues to curriculum matters and are included. (Several issues of the Review of Educational Research are cases in point.) This does not refer, however, to curriculum journals: e.g., The Curriculum Journal, Educational Leadership, Curriculum Inquiry (formerly Curriculum Theory Network), the Journal of Curriculum Studies, The Journal of Curriculum Theorizing. These publications normally devote all space to curriculum matters.

The central criterion that guided my selection of citations was the question: What Twentieth Century books contributed substantially, directly or indirectly, to curriculum thought? My commentary sections were guided by the question: How do these books portray a saga or heritage of ideas and emphases in curriculum thought? Responses to these questions must, of course, be built upon certain clarifications in terminology and decision mechanics.

Books are judged as suitable for inclusion if they deal with curriculum, i.e., the substance or subject matter of educational activity. More specifically they are included if they describe, prescribe, and/or discuss questions such as the following: How do or how should people determine what to teach others? How do they defend or justify it?

xvi

What issues are involved in deciding what to teach or learn? How do we and how should we study such matters? Essentially, the root, curriculum, is honored: What is/should be the nature of the course or journey on which we take those whom we teach? Generally, such works pertain to schooling since the study of curriculum formally evolved to satisfy pressures for universal schooling. An author's own categorization as indicated by a work's title is accepted, i.e., if curriculum appears in the title, the book is included. However, books with curriculum in the title are usually excluded if they deal primarily with a specialized subject area, e.g., mathematics curriculum, physical education curriculum, special education curriculum. Certain books that do not have curriculum in the title do deal directly with the above questions and have exerted influence on books labeled curriculum; therefore, they are included.

Finally, it is emphasized that several excluded categories are not deemed irrelevant; they were eliminated from this listing because of the author's lack of resources, time, and expertise. Surely, for example, non-English curriculum writings are needed for thorough perspective on curriculum issues, yet many are not translated into English. Surely, too, excellent contributions are available in journal articles, dissertations, and narrowly disseminated research reports. Study of such works is imperative to the provision of defensible curriculum perspectives in the future.

Nevertheless, serious study of books will, I submit, provide quite thorough exposure to the heritage of curriculum literature. Most influential curriculum articles, reports, and papers eventually make their way into books. In compiling the bibliography, I attempted to be comprehensive and accurate. Both attempts are likely to be somewhat deficient. I am sure that I have not found some books. I suppose that errors exist in some citations, though I have checked them carefully. I suppose that some scholars will dispute my selection of inclusions and exclusions, even when

utilizing the guidelines described above. They
may also differ as to my choice of books for
commentary and the nature, classification and
scope of commentary. I invite interested others
to add information and interpretation. It is
only through collaborative efforts that consciousness of the curriculum heritage can grow.
Criticism as well as agreement can stimulate
serious study, speculation and research. To these
ends this book is offered.

Notes

[1]Books that are included in the Bibliography of
Curriculum Books section that concludes each
chapter are not listed elsewhere. Readers may
simply refer to year indicated for complete citations. Other references and appended commentaries
are listed in Notes sections at the end of
chapters.

[2]Schubert, W.H. The Literature of Curriculum
Development: Toward Centralization and Analysis
(Phase I), 92 pages. A paper presented at the
American Educational Research Association Annual
Conference, San Francisco, April 22, 1976. This
is now available from ERIC. Microfiche is listed
in Resources in Education, and document is available
from: ERIC Document Reproduction Service; P.O.
Box 190; Arlington, Virginia 22210. (ED 163 617).

[3]Schubert, W.H. The Literature of Curriculum
Development: Toward Centralization and Analysis
(Phase II). A paper presented at the American
Educational Research Association Annual Conference,
New York City, April 6, 1977.

[4]Schubert, W.H. A Chronology of Curriclum
Development Literature. Printed and distributed
by the American Educational Research Association
Special Interest Group on the Creation and
Utilization of Curriculum Knowledge, 1977.

INTRODUCTION

CURRICULUM STUDY: SETTING THE STAGE

The kinds of concerns that stir the interests and efforts of curriculum scholars and practitioners are immensely important concerns. Although differences of persuasion abound in the curriculum field, those who devote careers to curriculum share a common concern about the substance of education. They address directly the issue of what is learned and why it should be learned. To be quite literal, curricularists are concerned with the human journey that results in learning. What, they ask, are the life excursions that bring persons to certain feelings, knowings, and doings? What do students need? Why do they need it? Through what kinds of content or activity can they acquire experiences that result in productive growth? What is productive growth and how can it be recognized?

These considerations pertain to, but are deeper and more pervasive than, concerns about curriculum guides, courses of study, course syllabi, and daily lesson plans. At best, such documents reflect shadows of ideas, knowledge, feelings, attitudes, skills, concepts, behaviors, and interrelationships that are learned and prescribed for learning. Fundamentally, these domains are the focus of curriculum study. Such study can take many forms; it can probe the limits of meaningful inquiry and action.

An Informal Area of Inquiry

According to the above characterization, informal curriculum study has occurred as long as humans have sought ways to induct their young into an accumulated heritage. Adults in prehistoric tribes made decisions about what children needed to learn to become members of the social group. As civilizations evolved along major river valleys, individuals began to specialize. They no longer

1

needed, nor were they able, to amass all of the knowledge of the social group. As adult roles began to specialize, children could no longer glean a holistic sense of the ways of their culture by following parents in daily activities. Therefore, specialists or teachers were needed to introduce the young to essentials in their heritage. Specialists were also designated to teach knowledge of specific roles in which learners would later participate. Although many of the early civilizations provided education that was mainly technical and concrete rather than abstract and formal, their efforts were quite clearly curricular. They made decisions about what the substance of learning should be. Usually, these decisions were implemented in institutions akin to schools. Cultural histories, histories of education, and biographies reflect much about the form and impact of schooling from ancient times to present.

The advent of Western philosophy in ancient Greece issues in another phase in the evolution of curriculum thought. Philosophical discourse about the substance and contribution of education emerged, and subsequently appeared in great normative treatises for centuries. Writings by Plato, Aristotle, Plutarch, Quintillian, Saint Augustine, Luther, Bacon, Descartes, Locke, Rousseau, and Kant are prime exemplars. Such writings had profound impact on the curriculum promoted in schools for generations and upon educational thought as well.

One can turn to another source, the idealistic and existential portrayals of human experience in poetry, plays, novels, biography, journals, diaries, stories and the arts. These embody insight into ways humans respond to the learning substance of living, i.e., to the curriculum of life itself. Think of the portrayals provided by such authors as Homer, Sophocles, Aristophenes, Dante, Goethe, Milton, Shakespeare, Donne, Blake, Pope, Dickens, Tolstoy, Dostoevski, Twain, Chekhov, Cervantes, Balzac, Faulkner, Steinbeck, Hesse, Joyce, Kafka, Ibsen, Vonnegut, Chaucer, Whitman, Dickinson, and a host of others. They have taught and continue

2

to teach about the curriculum of learning from life's experiences. Such authors contribute as much to what Mortimer Adler calls the "Great Conversation"[1] as do philosophers, scientists, and social scientists. In all of their writings great literary figures address the sources and substances of human knowledge, feelings, and actions. Sometimes they critically portray schools as systematic attempts of societies to reproduce and dispense their heritage of values, beliefs, skills, and alleged facts. In the richness of their art lies a seldom tapped reservoir of illumination about the substance of learning amid the tragedies, comedies, predicaments, and glories of human experience. Those who want to study curriculum should not pass by these portrayals of the curriculum of humankind.

In both the philosophical and the literary sources, however, curriculum is treated as an outgrowth or side effect of something larger. Curricular recommendations, for example, are offered as minor parts of elaborate philosophical systems. Curricular criticisms are offered as episodes in a character's action and feeling or as an author's personal commentary. These are useful to the study of curriculum, but alone do not legitimate curriculum as a professional area of study in its own right.

Such legitimation began to evolve with the advent of scholars who wrote almost entirely about the subject of education, e.g., Comenius, Herbart, Froebel, and Montessori. Curriculum, however, remained conflated with the whole topic of education. It was a consequence of the educational ideology advanced by a given scholar. Educational scholarship evolved rather fully as a separate academic domain in the early to middle 1800's. Pestalozzi's famed demonstration center at Yverdon, begun in 1804, exemplified a zenith in the European tradition of teacher education. Even Tolstoy was influenced by Yverdon. His travels to learn about schooling in Switzerland, France, and Germany resulted in his liberal redesign of elementary

3

schools in his Russian hometown of Yasnaya Polyana
in 1861. Horace Mann, noted initiator of universal, non-sectarian, free, public education,
organized the first three normal schools for the
education of American teachers in 1839-40. Not
only teacher education, but the specialized study
of education as a separate academic domain, spread
across the United States and Europe in the second
half of the Nineteenth Century. In 1902, John
Dewey published The Child and the Curriculum. This
represented a synthesis of his scholarly work in
establishing the Department of Pedagogie at the
University of Chicago with his practical experience
in developing the Laboratory School there. It also
represented an initial appearance and legitimation
of curriculum as an area of study. In the same
decade, the study of curriculum started to form as
a distinct sub-field of educational scholarship.

A Formal Area of Inquiry

No longer was all curriculum study a mere
offshoot of philosophy, literature, social science,
and recently education. In the beginning of the
Twentieth Century the attention of certain educators centered directly on curriculum questions.
In time, they came to be known as curriculum scholars. Shortly, too, administrators in schools
began to differentiate line and staff positions as
curriculum supervisors, coordinators, and consultants. Both scholars and practitioners geared
their attention to the question of what should be
taught in schools. Proposed and actual activities
of schooling became their direct concern. This
was due in no small measure to the ever-evolving
emphasis on universal schooling. With increased
focus on schooling, alternative curriculum viewpoints were aired and debated. The assumptive roots
of alternative arguments were explored more deeply.
Curricularists had, perhaps unwittingly, carved out
a new version of the perennial question about the
substance of education. In essence, they now
wanted to know how curriculum should be developed
for schools. Thus began the era of curriculum

development as a separate sub-area of specialization within the study of education.

Two aspects of this emphasis are worth noting in a bit more detail. Macro and micro perspectives both have their merits and demerits in any scholarly domain. So, too, in curriculum. Prior to the Twentieth Century, curriculum was treated indirectly as a rather small portion of a larger scheme that was dominantly philosophical, sociological, historical, psychological, and literary. As such, curriculum was examined in a broad contextual framework or macro perspective, rather than with the kind of microscopic detail that frequently accompanies specialized study. Macro perspectives, particularly those of a literary nature, probed into the substance of learning without necessarily relating it to schooling. Demerits of macro-perspectives obviously reside in lack of detailed analysis of topics for study within a delimited field. As education became differentiated from literature, social sciences, and philosophy, certain hazy boundaries began to identify educational inquiry during the Nineteenth Century. Curriculum study developed a similar differentiation in the Twentieth Century. Thus, a micro-perspective appeared and persisted. Curriculum was studied in more detail relative to schooling, but less as the journey of life's education.

Books identified by their authors as curriculum books were virtually non-existent prior to 1900. Exceptions did occur; to wit Claude Fleury's The History of Choice and Method of Studies (1695),[2] perhaps the earliest curriculum book. A case may also be made that Frank and Charles McMurry and other Herbartians wrote about curriculum in the late 1800's, though they usually called it method. This point is not argued; the evolution of the curriculum field was gradual, not abrupt. Twenty-four citations are quite evenly distributed from 1900 through 1917. These books pre-dated the 1918 appearance of Bobbitt's The Curriculum and the Cardinal Principles of Secondary Education, two sources most frequently recognized as the Adam and

5

Eve of curriculum works.

Thus, the early Twentieth Century brought a gradual growth in curriculum books that portrayed the evolution of curriculum as a separate sub-field [3] within the overarching study of education. With this evolution came the emergence of unwritten standards for becoming a legitimate member of the expanding curriculum coterie. For example, to have a curriculum scholar as one's mentor enhanced one's chances of becoming a recognized curriculum scholar or practitioner. One became known as a curriculum authority if one published books or articles with <u>curriculum</u> in the title. In 1929, the <u>Curriculum Journal</u> emerged and flourished until 1943, when it joined forces with <u>Educational Method</u> forming <u>Educational Leadership</u>, the curriculum journal having widest distribution today. Questions about the substance of education became increasingly specific in books and articles that focused on schooling. Emulation of methods of inquiry that fostered successes of natural sciences occurred in the social sciences and education, and concomitantly in curriculum. Detailed analyses of curriculum ideas took place. This is not intended to indicate that uniformity of language resulted. On the contrary, there were perhaps as many languages as curriculum scholars, a problem that has plagued the field throughout its existence. With analysis, however, came the propensity of curricularists to seek causes and to provide defensible explanations. The latter took the form of attempts to provide justifiable bases for curriculum inquiry and proposals.

At least three dominant schools of thought vied for supremacy. I shall call them the <u>intellectual traditionalists</u>, <u>social behaviorists</u>, and the <u>experientialists</u>. Disagreement might exist about the terms, but they are convenient categories for early curriculum thought, as well as for many of the variations that evolved during the first eight decades of the Twentieth Century. More will be said about each in Chapter One. In addition to the emphasis on scientific analysis, another feature of the micro-perspective should be noted. As specialization increased, and as pressures to perpetuate universal education mounted, the study of curriculum became relegated to the substance of schooling. Schooling became the emphasis rather than education at large. It had been the latter under the macro-orientations of previous centuries. In the conclusion of this book I argue that the study of curriculum will not productively survive if it does not directly embrace several non-school spheres of learning that profoundly influence the growth of children and youth in pluralistic cultures: e.g., homes, peer cultures, media, and work. The kind of inquiry needed is both macro and micro, an integration of specialized perspectives that focuses directly on curricular problems.

In the relatively short time that curriculum study has existed, a great deal has been written and too much has been lost or obscured in dark corners of university libraries, tattered and scattered bibliographies, and fading memories. Much that makes up the heritage of curriculum study in the Twentieth Century is well worth studying, both for relevance to current problems and for historical illumination. During the past twenty years perceptive curriculum scholars admonished members of the curriculum field to become increasingly conscious of their historical ancestors. Surprisingly, curriculum writers of the 1950's and 1960's seldom cited sources of works that were written between 1900 and 1940, with the exception of a dozen or so of the field's classics.[4] In 1974, Ponder[5] used the term ahistorical to characterize this state of the field. The sentiment was not without precedent.[6] During the 1970's the number of articles, professional papers, and portions of curriculum texts devoted to curriculum history increased. To this end, The Society for the Study of Curriculum History was established in 1977 under the guidance of Laurel Tanner and other founding members. The Society meets each year prior to the Annual Meeting of the American Educational Research Association. Its members engage in the presentation and discussion of contributions to curriculum history.

This book is offered to further historical consciousness for curriculum inquiry. It is primarily an attempt to whet curricular appetites and inspire further study. Such study may corroborate or it may dispute commentary contained herein, but the major point is to augment curriculum as a scholarly enterprise grounded solidly in its history. Therefore, the book is provided as a resource for anyone who wishes to learn more about the richness of curriculum literature. Thus, it is offered as a companion reference to facilitate the work of students who pursue advanced graduate degree programs in curriculum.[7] It is offered to scholars whose necessary, but seemingly endless library searches could, in part, be avoided. Of utmost importance is the hope for indirect value that this book might have for children and youth, the new members of societies who must be inducted into the social life that has evolved from the dawn of humankind. As I look at W.E. Smith's moving photograph (on my office wall) of a boy and girl walking hand-in-hand, anxious, self-assured, excited, curious, and vulnerable into a forest, I think of curriculum. To me the forest represents the life ahead of them. Curriculum is the attempt of educators to help their journey. What do they need to know, feel, and do? Why do they need it? What do they learn about living and from what sources? What should they learn about living and from what sources? What should be provided by those specialized agencies called schools that are set aside by advanced industrial societies to teach that which children need but do not receive from everyday living?

Nearly eighty years of effort to answer these and related questions is charted in more than 1100 books[8] by curriculum scholars and practitioners. It is incumbent upon current and future curriculum scholars and practitioners to know the heritage of their field. It is their responsibility to build upon, criticize, and renew that heritage.

[1]See Fadiman (1978) in dedication to Adler; cited in note 7 below.

[2]Fleury, Claude. The History of Choice and Method of Studies, 1695.

[3]There are those who debate whether the study of curriculum is a bonified field of study. [See I. Westbury and W. Steimer, Curriculum: A Discipline in Search of its Problems, School Review, February, 1971, 79 (2).] Technically, the argument is persuasive. Nevertheless, the term field is used throughout this book as synonymous with area of study. It is not intended to imply that curriculum study is more unified by a common conception of problems, methodology, or language than it is.

[4]In 1976 Ann Fraley polled the Professors of Curriculum at their meeting during the Annual Conference of the Association for Supervision and Curriculum Development in Miami, Florida, and generated a list of 28 curriculum classics. The fourteen classics listed from 1900 to 1940 were produced by nine authors: Dewey, Bagley, Bobbitt, Kilpatrick, Charters, Morrison, Counts, Caswell, and Campbell, and by two professional associations. It is rare to find substantial mention of the many other curriculum authors of this early period by writers in the Fifties and Sixties.

[5]Ponder, G.A. The Curriculum: Field Without a Past? Educational Leadership, February, 1974, 31, 461-464.

[6]See for example: L. Cremin, Curriculum-making in the United States, Teachers College Record, 1971, 73 (2), 207-220; A. Bellack, History of Curriculum and Practice, Review of Educational Research, June 1969, 39, 283-92; H. Kliebard, Persistent Curriculum Issues in Historical Perspective, in E.C. Short (Editor) A Search for Valid Content for Curriculum Development. Toledo, Ohio: College

of Education, University of Toledo, 1970; and D. Tanner and L.N. Tanner, Curriculum Development: Theory into Practice (historical sections), New York: Macmillan, 1980. These and other curriculum scholars called for serious inquiry into the curricular heritage.

[7]Should the student desire to pursue curriculum thought prior to the Twentieth Century, I suggest Robert Ulich's Three Thousand Years of Educational Wisdom (Cambridge: Harvard University Press, 1954) and Ronald Gross' The Teacher and the Taught (New York: Delta, 1963) for samples of original writings by eminent philosophers and other scholars on educational topics. Students are also advised to see one or more of the good histories of education that explicate both scholarly ideas about education (thus curriculum to an extent) and practices that prevailed in schools and other educational endeavors throughout history. Examples of such histories include: William Boyd's The History of Western Education (New York: Barnes and Noble, 1965), R. Freeman Butts' A Cultural History of Education (New York: McGraw-Hill, 1947), Lawrence Cremin's The Transformation of the School (New York: Alfred A. Knopf, 1961), A Short History of Educational Thought (London: University Tutorial Press, 1965) by S.J. Curtis and M.E.A. Boultwood, and Robert Ulich's History of Educational Thought (New York: American Book Company, 1950). These contain much that is relevant to curricular thought and descriptions of practice. Those who are interested in both literary and philosophical sources might start with Clifton Fadiman's The Lifetime Reading Plan (New York: Crowell, 1978), or Abraham Kaplan's In Pursuit of Wisdom (New York: Glencoe Press, 1977), for an excellent introduction to countless curricular ideas, overt and covert, nestled within the pages of literary classics, ancient to contemporary.

[8]Number of curriculum books produced (by year and decade):

10

1900 = 2	1910 = 0	1920 = 4
1901 = 1	1911 = 1	1921 = 3
1902 = 2	1912 = 0	1922 = 2
1903 = 0	1913 = 3	1923 = 8
1904 = 4	1914 = 0	1924 = 9
1905 = 2	1915 = 2	1925 = 8
1906 = 1	1916 = 1	1926 =10
1907 = 1	1917 = 2	1927 =20
1908 = 1	1918 = 3	1928 =10
1909 = 1	1919 = 1	1929 =13
15	13	87

1930 = 8	1940 = 12	1950 = 20
1931 =12	1941 = 8	1951 = 13
1932 =14	1942 = 11	1952 = 13
1933 = 3	1943 = 3	1953 = 18
1934 =11	1944 = 6	1954 = 9
1935 =12	1945 = 4	1955 = 10
1936 =13	1946 = 12	1956 = 9
1937 =17	1947 = 8	1957 = 12
1938 =12	1948 = 11	1958 = 12
1939 =11	1949 = 6	1959 = 5
113	81	121

1960 =26	1970 = 46
1961 =24	1971 = 51
1962 =16	1972 = 55
1963 =24	1973 = 41
1964 =32	1974 = 42
1965 =23	1975 = 49
1966 =40	1976 = 40
1967 =36	1977 = 38
1968 =35	1978 = 31
1969 =38	1979 = 21
294	414

Grand Total: 1,138

CHAPTER I

CURRICULUM LITERATURE AND CONTEXT:

1900-1909

Contextual Reminders[1]

The first decade of the Twentieth Century
found Britain still quite fully in the fore of
political events internationally. The Boer War
continued in South Africa, and the Boxer Rebellion
on the other side of the globe necessitated an
international expedition to bring a semblance of
relief. It was a time of colonial annexation in
Africa, and a time of independent British dominionhood for Australia. Queen Victoria died in 1901,
marking the end of an era, the same year that
President William McKinley was assassinated in the
United States six months after taking office.
Mid-decade saw the Russo-Japanese Wars rise and
wane over disputed interests in Manchuria. The
year 1905 brought Bloody Sunday, the workers'
revolution that caused the first council of
workers in Russia to be established. In France
in 1906, Alfred Dryfus was found innocent of trea-
son for which he had been held responsible for
twelve years. By the close of the decade Russia
and Britain formed an entente, and Italy, Austria,
and Germany renewed their Triple Alliance, setting
the stage for world war.

The decade, however, certainly cannot be
characterized by battles, annexations, trials,
murders, and revolutions alone; it was a time when
arts, sciences, and other scholarly activities
flourished with a special fervor. A young painter
named Pablo Picasso experimented with unusual
styles of painting that would bring Cubism to full
fruition, at least symbolizing the possibility of
multiple perspectives on the world. Paintings by
Derain, Rousseau, Matisse, Monet, Gauguin, and
Cezanne that today grace our galleries were created

13

during this period. It was a time of Puccini's
Tosca and Madame Butterfly, and the impressionistic compositions of Debussy. Both the
triumphant impressionism and the emergent abstract
experimentation depicted art's move into the human
psyche, with its portrayals of complexity in feelings and unpredictable responses to life's impossible dilemmas. Such inner mysteries of human
personality were given an impetus toward becoming
explainable in 1900 by Sigmund Freud in The
Interpretation of Dreams.

    Strides in the sciences brought discoveries
that pushed back the wall of mystery even further
and increased the probability of causal explanation:
Walter Reed's discovery of transmitting agents that
caused yellow fever, Takamine's isolation of
adrenalin, the discovery of secretin by Starling
and Bayliss, and Frederick Hopkins' discovery of
vitamins are among the most prominent. That
science wrought practical results was accentuated
in such technological inventions as Marconi's
wireless, the completion of the Aswan Dam, the
Wright Brothers' airplane, Einthoven's electro-
cardiograph, de Forest's vacuum tube, the building
of the Panama Canal, color photography via the
autochrome plate by the Lumiere brothers, the first
operation of the Trans-Siberian Railroad, the
Baekeland's invention of Bakelite.

    The immediate advantages of such technological
achievements may have influenced the patience
needed to realize the vast potential of such
artistic scientific imaginings as Max Plank's
development of the quantum theory of light in 1900
and Albert Einstein's publication of the special
theory of relativity in 1905. That explication of
fundamentals in any discipline had the power to
speed the evolution of that field is evident in
the publication of volume one of Principles of
Mathematics by Bertrand Russell. During this
decade the human spirit's desire to probe the
unknown is evidenced in quests to conquer the poles
by Nordenskjold in 1901 and Shakleton in 1909.
History was pushed back in the Mediterranean with

Arthur Evans' discovery of artifacts from the ancient Minoan culture in Crete. Frontier territories within the human brain opened for exploration as Harvey Cushing studied the pituitary gland. Yet unknown potential vistas of energy sources, possibilities for both reconstruction and destruction, were released with Rutherford's publication of Radio Activity in 1904.

Meanwhile, in the literary world, authors depicted the perils and ill-fated treatments of everyday strivings. Tragedies of those who strove for success were depicted in works by Joseph Conrad, Samuel Butler, Anton Chekhov, Henry James, Theodore Dreiser, Maxim Gorki, Auguste Strindberg, J.M. Synge. It was a time, also, of subtle sophisticated humor from O. Henry, pervasive scientific imagination from H.G. Wells, mystery and heroics from Arthur Conan Doyle, and the epitome of spots of glory in human evolution from G.B. Shaw's superman. The first decade of our present century brought a golden age in children's classics: Kipling's Just So Stories, Potter's Peter Rabbit, Barrier's Peter Pan, Grahame's The Wind and the Willows.

The long history of striving for equal rights on racial, sexual, and economic bases was nudged a bit further by the reluctant acceptance of the United States' Jack Johnson as the first black world heavyweight boxing champion, the founding of the Women's Social and Political Union by Emmeline Pankhurst in Britain, and the creation of Russian Land Laws to improve peasant conditions there.

Curriculum Thought and Literature

Although it is impossible to draw direct lines of cause and effect between the activities described above and educational developments in the same decade, it is certain that the latter were influenced by many combinations of the former.[2] Science, technology, and industrialization profoundly

15

affected education, as was true of all avenues
of life. With increased urbanization came changes
in home, work, recreation, and all social institutions. Pressures to provide universal schooling
coupled with the "rapid is better" ethic in the
factory model of production influenced the creation
of schools. Like factories, schools were sturdy,
large, cubical buildings with compartments for like
parts. One of the main parts was students who had
to be quickly removed from streets and work places
to satisfy a strange combination of legal, economic,
and humanitarian pressures. Students were grouped
by age and were given graded textbooks that cor-
responded to their ages. It was clear, in all this
rapidity, that somehow worthwhile substance needed
to be put into these books and, more importantly,
into experiences that students had in schools.

It became equally clear, to some at least,
that no one had a monopoly on the best knowledge
about how to determine this substance for school
learning. Surely, the problem had been dealt with
before, but not on such a massive scale. The need
for full time experts to engage in specialized
decision-making was a frequent occurrence in many
occupations. The emergence of an area of specialization within education, an area known as curriculum
development, was thus no surprise. Full-fledged
curriculum developers were not yet present, although,
they were on the horizon and would quite fully
present themselves in the next decade. Nevertheless, their ancestors were very much present.

These curricularists forged the rudiments of
distinct camps, each advocating its own special
brand of curricular philosophy. Each curricular
orientation, of course, was reputed to have certain
important benefits for the creation of learning
substance for students. As noted earlier, the labels
intellectual traditionalists, experientialists,
and social behaviorists will be used to discuss
general orientations. The labels are not sacrosanct
but are created to ease communication and to convey
a framework for discussion of curriculum as an
area of study. Evolving versions of each orienta-

16

tion or school of thought are discussed throughout the remainder of the book.

Intellectual traditionalists have been with us longest. Their position stems to ancient Greece and Rome and the classical tradition. They hold that certain subject areas, [namely, grammar, mathematics, music, speaking, exposure to great literature, and finally (if the student is able to master the prerequisites) philosophy, that paragon of all studies] cultivate the mind, harvest virtue, and reap the full person. In the Middle Ages the emphasis was on the classical trivium and quadrivium that made up the Seven Liberal Arts. The trivium consisted of grammar, rhetoric, and dialectic; the quadrivium was composed of arithmetic, geometry, astronomy, and music. Schools throughout the intervening centuries to 1900 catered to the economically well-to-do, and continued this tradition with a few exceptions. With the universal schooling movement in the Nineteenth and Twentieth Centuries, more social classes were served. Reading, writing, arithmetic, a bit of history or civics, and little else were primary constituents of early curriculum for children. In later schooling, reading became great literature (Latin, English classics, and sometimes Greek), writing evolved into essays and was often combined with the later stages of reading, and arithmetic evolved into algebra and geometry. These subjects were deemed basic to all living. It was assumed that they molded character, brought sharp logical thinking, and were generally applicable to any respectable domain of living.

An interestingly strange amalgam emerged in the early 1900's. It was the joining of this classical tradition with elements of a branch of psychology known as faculty psychology. Briefly, faculty psychologists likened the mind unto muscles that could be developed with practice in subjects of the classical curriculum. For example, it was held for some time that learning Greek, Latin, geometry, etc. built the faculty of reasoning or logical thinking. Similarly, particular kinds of "exercises" were thought to develop such

17

faculties as observation, perception, imagination, and memory, though the types of faculties differed relative to those who wrote about them. Nonetheless, it was clear that throughout most of the Nineteenth Century and much of the Twentieth, the predominant "curriculum theories," especially those practiced, were built around the notion of habits to be cultivated. These came to be known as mental disciplines. Concerned, thusly, with developing powers of the mind (intellectual powers) through exercises largely drawn from liberal arts that "stood the test of time" (tradition), proponents of this view may be fairly labeled intellectual traditionalists.

The influence of the intellectual traditionalists became altered, however, in the early Twentieth Century due to a combination of intellectual and social changes. Renowned scholars such as William James and Edward L. Thorndike, imbued with the methods of science, decided to test assumptions of faculty psychology. James, in the 1890's, concluded that the faculty of memory did not improve with practice. Later, while James turned to philosophic pursuits, Thorndike's inquiries caused him to decide that subjects such as Latin and mathematics did not improve the mind more than did less traditional subjects. These studies had an impact on the decline of classical subjects from the curriculum.

As great an impact may be attributed to increases in education for all, not merely for the elite. With universal education came heightened interest in the practical results of schooling, results that called for curriculum that did more than make the mind a touted instrument to be used in circles that valued high culture. Pressures demanded results of schooling that demonstrated upward mobility relative to socio-economic class, job acquisition, and capacity to handle the practical demands of everyday living. As represented in the literature and arts of the decade, the public was no longer content with the belief that intellectual life alone sufficiently guided the

18

complex process of living. The time was ripe for a revival of the broader perspective epitomized in the title of Herbert Spencer's book, Education: Intellectual, Moral, and Physical (1860).[3]

People looked at their everyday experience and the problems, feelings, and satisfactions obtained from it, concluding that worthwhile schooling could not ignore life as they knew it. Thus, the intellectual traditionalist position evolved to include a wider array of subject emphases. These emphases were, however, spearheaded by a commitment to a mental discipline style of thought. They are summarized in the work of the Committee of Ten and Committee of Fifteen in the late 1890's.[4] Composed primarily of college faculty members, the committees influentially promoted a subject oriented curriculum. Though the subjects differed somewhat from their classical ancestors, the idea that certain subjects are basic to proper human growth was clearly iterated. A procession of committee reports from government and professional associations echoed this sentiment throughout the first half of the century, giving the intellectual traditionalist position continuing visibility in the literature. Moreover, its preeminence in school curriculum seldom wavered. Even today it characterizes much public sentiment, exemplified in the "back to basics" movement.

The social behaviorists, or second school of curriculum thought, also began to emerge in the first decade. A faith in the method of science, based largely on evidence easily observed in an ever-increasing supply of technological products, contributed to widespread desire among scholars and the public alike to call for emulation of the natural sciences. In this vein, Alfred Binet and Theodore Simon developed the first test that claimed to determine intelligence in 1906, perhaps the single event of long-term impact that best epitomized the growing deification of science in education. A sentiment quickly emerged among many curricularists that curriculum for schools should be determined "scientifically," by carefully

19

analyzing the usual activities of ordinary adult life, and by inducting the young into society by teaching them tasks involved in such activities. This process of curriculum-making is frequently referred to as <u>activity analysis</u> or <u>scientific curriculum-making</u>. As an orientation to curriculum construction this process is sometimes placed within the <u>social efficiency movement</u>. Because it purports to mold or engineer behavior in certain socially acceptable ways, the label of <u>social behaviorists</u> is used. Social behaviorists brought a special appeal to both those who desired to emulate successes of natural sciences and technology, and to those who desired to prepare for the necessities of life in a business-like fashion. More is said about this group in the next chapter.

The third group of curricularists, the experientialists, put forth a set of beliefs that stemmed from the work of Johann Friedrich Herbart. Although Herbart died in 1841, American advocates of his line of thinking (e.g., Charles and Frank McMurry, Charles DeGarmo, and C.C. Van Liew) built a Herbartian conception of curriculum development at the turn of the century. Essentially, this position held, following the conviction of John Locke, that the mind is a <u>tabula rasa</u> to be given form and substance by experience. As experience and knowledge accumulate they form an <u>apperceptive mass</u> or stored repertoire via which the world is perceived and interpreted. Learning takes place only as outside knowledge and experience relate to the apperceptive mass.

A major curricular implication of this view was that method was of utmost import. Method was considered the necessary process of organizing the content or substance of learning to make it relevant to students' apperceptive masses. One of the foremost cues to such relevance was found in observable interests of children. Furthermore, the study of child development was deemed invaluable to constructing methods that brought desired curricula to students. Heretofore, few curriculum developers had given the study of child development a primary role

in their work. American psychologist G. Stanley
Hall turned to Herbartian emphasis for a portrayal
of child development as analagous to cultural epochs
in the evolution of the human race. A curricular
application of this notion was included in the
Second Yearbook of the National Herbart Society
in 1896.

Though puerile by today's standards in educational psychology, it reflected a desire among
some educators at the turn of the century to make
child study central to the process of curriculum
construction. Herbart's five stages of method
(preparation, presentation, comparison, generalization, and application) had paramount impact on
interpretations of instructional strategies for
many years to come. It is interesting to note
that these stages were not mere prescriptions about
the way that curriculum should be developed for
schooling. Instead, they were primarily interpretations of stages in the process of knowledge
acquisition by the apperceptive mass during
ordinary life experience. (The assumption here
is critical. Learning that occurs during ordinary
life experience provides great insight into the
way that learning should be developed for students
in schools). Implicit in Herbart's position was
that the end of learning should be ethically good.
That education must embrace the ethical is central
to the experientialist position.

The work of John Dewey continued, elaborated,
and reconstructed the experientialist position.
Noteworthy at this point is his "My Pedagogic
Creed," first published in the School Journal, LIV,
January 1897, 77-80. It is available in numerous
curriculum anthologies, and provides a good brief
introduction to Dewey's thought on education. The
student who wishes to acquire a broad understanding
of the curriculum field should consider the study
of several of Dewey's works indispensable. More
will be said about them throughout the discussions
of literature that follow. At this point it is
enough to note that Dewey and those who advocated
his ideas were a mainstay of experientialist

curriculum thought for several decades to come.

Let us now glance at the kind of books that appeared "before" curriculum study is usually thought to have begun. The fifteen books that appeared in the 1900-09 decade illustrate that the term curriculum at that time was sufficiently widespread to merit inclusion in book titles. Heretofore, it had been used in conjunction with books on education, and then sparingly. Bowsher's text of 1900 is the first book found to use curriculum in its title. Apparently, it had small distribution and little impact. Bowsher developed curricular prescriptions from a philosophical world view, an infrequent occurrence even today. American texts, presumably used to train teachers in normal schools and/or to influence curriculum developers and school administrators, mainly presented conceptions of what should be taught and guidelines for determining it. Books that appeared in Britain during this time, exemplified by Thompson (1905), treated curriculum as a matter of debate. Eight of the fifteen books emphasized curriculum at the elementary or primary levels. One, Meriwether (1907), was an historical treatment. The only curriculum books from this decade that had lasting impact as evidenced by their citation today were written by Dewey (1900, 1902), McMurry (1906), and Bagley (1905).

Both Dewey and McMurry could be categorized as experientialists. McMurry, a prominent neo-Herbartianist at the turn of the century, placed primary emphasis on method. As seen in his title, the term course of study is used instead of curriculum. This is, perhaps, a remnant of its etymology from Latin origins as a chariot course. The analogy is that of a neophyte who is guided by one who is experienced as they tour the land of accumulated wisdom of the human race. McMurry, therefore, outlines recommendations and discusses issues about essential human experience during the first eight grades. It is interesting to note that course of study was used frequently throughout much of the Twentieth Century as a near synonym for <u>curriculum</u>, especially in informal discourse.

With <u>The Child and the Curriclum</u> John Dewey etched his place in curriculum archives for time immemorium. In it he related both theory and practice as synthesized in the activity of the laboratory school at the University of Chicago. This work, together with his <u>The School and Society</u> (1900),[5] laid the groundwork for several interpretations of the experientialist line of thought that reached a stage that might be called its "golden age" in the Progressive Education era of the 1920's and 1930's. His treatment of a practical art/science of problem solving that attends to specific circumstances is portrayed in a lesser known work, <u>The Educational Situation</u> (1902). At the expense of over-simplification, the line of thought in these books saw humans as biological/social organisms who possess the potential for growth through utilizing the method of intelligence to adapt to and live in balance with the environment. Throughout history humans acquire experience in this process. Such experience must be passed on to subsequent generations. Experience that cannot be transmitted adequately outside of schools is passed on by schools. It is not, however, to be transmitted as it appears in adult-organized reservoirs of knowledge. Although it is desirable to obtain such knowledge, the best means to its acquisition is <u>psychological</u>, i.e., through study of the problematic situations that occupy genuine interests of students. Problem resolution can frequently be best obtained by the exercise of communication or group study through which trans-action of experience occurs among persons. This might more simply be called democratic living based on mutual regard. The labels "child-centered curriculum" and "education of the whole child" came to be attributed to Deweyan thought. So, too, evolved "problem solving" and "learning by doing." The latter was evident in descriptions in <u>The Child and the Curriculum</u> and <u>The School and Society</u> of children learning about past human problem-solving by reinacting activities such as tool making and

23

spinning thread.   The contributions of Dewey are far too pervasive to summarize here.

Those who are interested in arguments against the experientialists should consult writings of William C. Bagley, Charles H. Judd, and Henry C. Morrison as well as others throughout the next three decades. Bagley's (1905) treatment of educative process was not nominally a curriculum book, but was sufficiently comprehensive to have a major effect on curriculum and other educational thought of its day. Bagley's essentialist or intellectual traditionalist arguments epitomize a profound and perennial difference of assumptions with proponents of the experientialist and social behaviorist persuasions.

Hopefully, enough is said throughout this book to whet the appetite and build a context for the study of curriculum literature produced during the first decade of the Twentieth Century. Three lines of thought have been developed: the intellectual traditionalists, the social behaviorists, and the experientialists. Descendents of each are traced in subsequent decades. In concluding the discussion of the first decade, it is recalled that 1918 is often given as the birthdate of the curriculum field. If this developmental metaphor were elaborated, it could be fairly argued that the first decade was an advanced embryonic stage. As noted in the Introduction, the time from conception to birth was indeed extensive. It was conceived when humans first thought of teaching others and was born shortly after 1915. (This makes the gestation period of curriculum compared to that of even elephants seem analagous to that of elephants themselves compared to fruitflies.) The point is heartily emphasized that serious study of curriculum roots must probe into the thought, art, and action of the distant human past to the earliest attempts of humans to introduce their young to living.

Notes

[1]The Contextual Reminders sections of each
chapter are derived from a host of sources, often
too numerous to mention and too entwined in my
memory to list here. Some that were especially
appreciated reference works follow: H.G. Wells,
The Outline of History (Volumes I and II), Garden
City, New York: Garden City Books, 1961; T.
Walter Wallbank and Alastair M. Taylor, Civiliza-
tion: Past and Present (Volumes I and II), Chicago:
Scott Foresman, 1960; The Queensbury Group, The
Book of Key Facts, New York and London: Padding-
ton Press, Ltd., 1978; David Wallechinsky and
Irving Wallace, The People's Almanac, Garden
City, New York: Doubleday, 1975; David Wallechin-
sky and Irving Wallace, The People's Almanac #2,
New York: Bantam Books, 1978; George E. Delury,
The World Almanac and Book of Facts, New York:
Newspaper Enterprise Association, Inc., 1979.

Further, it should be re-emphasized that the highlights of events provided are decidedly oriented
toward American experience and that of the Western
world. The bias is intended to be only in amount
of emphasis not in interpretation of events. The
bias of emphasis is defended in that it sets the
tone of the predominantly American collection of
curriculum literature. It is an attempt to characterize the world that was in the experiential
foreground of the America in which curriculum
study evolved.

[2]This is the case with other chapters as well.
Direct assertions of causation will rarely be
advanced. The main purpose of presenting the
Contextual Reminders section is to set highlights
of the times before the reader. Hopefully,
readers will identify interesting possible
connections between curriculum thought and its
context. Hopefully, readers will further curriculum understanding by investigating such relationships.

[3]Spencer, Herbert. Education: Intellectual,

Moral, and Physical. New York: D. Appleton and Company, 1860.

[4]The National Education Association appointed the Committee of Ten on Secondary School Studies (chaired by Charles W. Eliot who was President of Harvard University) and the Committee of Fifteen in the 1890's. Their work cast much of the fate of school curriculum for decades to come toward the intellectual traditionalist orientation.

[5]The two are often considered companion texts as witnessed by their publication under the same cover by the University of Chicago Press (1956).

Bibliography of Curriculum Books, 1900-1909

1900

Bowsher, C.A. The absolute curriculum. Champaign, Ill., 1900.

Dewey, J. The school and society. Chicago: University of Chicago Press, 1900.

1901

Weet, H.S. The curriculum in elementary education. Rochester, N.Y.: University of Rochester Press, 1901.

1902

Dewey, J. The child and the curriculum. Chicago: University of Chicago Press, 1902a.

Dewey, J. The educational situation. Chicago: University of Chicago Press, 1902b.

1904

Columbia University Press. The curriculum of the elementary school. New York: Columbia University Press, 1904 (Also reports intermittently to 1915).

1905

Bagley, W.C. The educative process. New York: Macmillan, 1905.

Lodge, O.J. School teacher and school reform: A course of four lectures on school curriculum and methods. London: Williams and Norgate, 1905.

Payne, B.R. Public elementary school curricula.
    New York: Silver Burdett, 1905.

Thompson, H.M. Essays in revolt; being a
    discussion of what should be taught at
    school. London: J.M. Dent, 1905.

1906

Dodd, C. The child and the curriculum. London:
    S. Sonneschein, 1906.

McMurry, C.A. Course of study in the eight
    grades (Vol. I and II). New York: Mac-
    millan, 1906.

1907

Meriwether, C. Our colonial curriculum
    1607-1776. Washington: Capital, 1907.

1908

Horace Mann School. The curriculum of the
    elementary school of Horace Mann School.
    New York: Teachers College, Columbia
    University, 1908.

1909

Hayward, F.H. (Editor). Primary curriculum.
    London, 1909.

CHAPTER II

CURRICULUM LITERATURE AND CONTEXT:

1910-1919

Contextual Reminders

The second decade of the Twentieth Century,
that of World War I, is the decade most frequently
acknowledged as having given birth to the curriculum field. In Britain, Edward VII died and George
V succeeded him. The Union of South Africa became
an independent dominion under the British, and
Portugal experienced revolution resulting in the
declaration of a republic, both in 1910. The same
year brought Stravinsky's The Firebird, a ballet
that, together with his The Rite of Spring in 1913,
increased awareness of the value of dissonance in
musical composition. The next year provided visual
dissonance in painting as well, bringing even more
of a view of the inner workings of the human spirit
through the expressionist portrayals of Vassily
Kandinsky's colorful compositions, and Franz Marc's
Blue Rider group in Munich. Irving Berlin's
Alexander's Ragtime Band captured another spirit
of American musical sentiment, and Marcel Duchamp
solidified the ascent of artistic expressionism
in painting with his Nude Descending a Staircase.
In political arenas Theodore Roosevelt was wounded
in an assassination attempt, U.S. marines landed
in Cuba, and Woodrow Wilson became U.S. President.
Also in 1912 Balkan countries engaged in war and
tensions mounted throughout Europe, marked by
increased naval strength and strategic military
location on the part of Germany, France, and
England.

Meanwhile, discovery and scientific advancement
were far from a standstill. In 1910 Bertrand
Russell and Alfred North Whitehead produced the
initial volume of Principia Mathematica, continuing the previous decade's propensity to probe

and explicate fundamental principles in many areas.
In the same year Marie Curie isolated radium, an
event that might be said to have unleashed a chain
reaction of other events to issue in the era of
atomic power. In the next year, for example,
Rutherford continued his explication of atomic
theory, and in 1913 Soddy discovered isotopes in
the United Kingdom. Stature was achievable through
scientific discovery, and it did not always accrue
via laudable measures as evidenced by the finding
of hoax-riddled Piltdown Man's remains, also in
1912. The conquest of the poles continued with
Amundsen's reaching of the South Pole in 1911 and
Scott's similar feat in 1912 with its fatal
consequence on the return to Britain.

The grim head of prejudice arose again, this
time on an international scale in the field of
sports, when Olympian Jim Thorpe, an American
Indian, lost gold medals on what many considered
extreme technicalities accusing him of profes-
sionalism. Questions of equality arose on other
issues as well. Suffragettes demanded the right
to vote in Britain in 1913, the same year that
Mahatma Gandhi was arrested in India for exercising
civil disobedience. In 1918, a woman was elected
to Parliament and the vote was secured for a small
proportion of women in England.

Novels by Marcel Proust, D.H. Lawrence, and
James Joyce continued the previous decade's probe
into the human psyche with their existential
portrayals of absurdities and predicaments in the
human condition. Shaw, however, extended his
praise of superman in Pygmalion and Androcles and
the Lion. The popularity of Tarzan of the Apes by
Edgar Rice Burroughs in 1914 further attested to
hope in the ideal of a superior goodness and
strength in humankind.

The 1914 assassination of Austria's Archduke
Franz-Ferdinand unleashed other mounting tensions
that produced World War I. Although the U.S.
remained temporarily neutral, it entered the
conflagration via a declaration of war on Germany

in 1917, supported by new financial strength derived from the 1913 constitutional amendment to introduce income tax. A succession of Allied victories deflated German and Austrian powers bringing an end to the war in 1918.

Meanwhile, developments in science and technology augmented public faith in this mode of human creation. In 1913 Hans Geiger invented his now well-known radiation detector. The Panama Canal was opened for shipping. In 1914, medical science was advanced by Kendall's discovery of thyroxine. The trans-Atlantic Canadian railway was completed. In 1915 Alexander Graham Bell, while in New York, asked Mr. Watson to come to him. His reply from San Francisco was distinct, demonstrating the potential of telephone communication. The same year saw publication of Einstein's general theory of relativity. The next year brought the addition of electron valency to the growing atomic theory of matter and energy. New explanations for unconscious functioning were published by personality theorist Carl Jung, bringing marked departures from Freudian thought with a theory of archetypes in the collective unconscious.

Somerset Maugham portrayed the plights and delights of human interchange in Of Human Bondage (1915) and The Moon and Sixpence (1919). Matisse, Renoir, and Picasso continued to provide impressionistic and expressionistic insights on canvas, while the art of architecture embarked on a revolutionary thrust spearheaded by Frank Lloyd Wright's Imperial Hotel in Tokyo (1916) and Walter Gropius' Bauhaus school at Weimer (Germany) starting in 1919, emphasizing functional design appearing true to the construction medium. Another literary medium continued to ascend to popularity and sophistication during this decade. The best among films, exemplified by D.W. Griffith's Intolerance (1916) and Charlie Chaplin's Shoulder Arms (1918), became an art appreciated across social class barriers.

Curriculum Thought and Literature

The social behaviorist school of curriculum thought, taking its cue from further successes in natural sciences, advanced to a level of prominence under the influence of publications by Franklin Bobbitt. Not only did the tenor of the times demand·a scientific and technological approach to determining what was taught in schools, it demanded observable practical consequences from public education offered in schools. A 1913 conference in Cleveland gave social behaviorists both power and promise. Under the leadership of E. L. Thorndike, C.H. Judd, and W.S. Gray, The Cleveland Conference became an annual event that promoted the scientific study of curriculum.[1] Bobbitt assumed that what was necessary to teach was virtually identical with what adults did. Therefore, he introduced activity analysis, a procedure by which life's activities were analyzed in minute detail. Activities, particularly those most frequently needed in productive and efficient living, were carefully cataloged and translated into learning experiences for students in schools. Therefore, assumptions had to be made about what constituted efficient and productive living. This fact constituted a major seedbed of subjectivity in what was offered as a process of objectively oriented curriculum development procedures. In What the Schools Teach and Might Teach (1915) Bobbitt addressed the question of is versus ought, though this book was deemed less important than his The Curriculum (1918), a work often considered the first major modern book on curriculum.

Bobbitt's 1915 book, however, illustrated a development in curriculum thought that began to bud in the second decade of the Twentieth Century. This was the propensity of prescribing or forecasting that which should be, often contrasting it with that which is. Both the prescriptive and descriptive presumed the existence of schooling on a large scale. Gray (1911) was concerned with revisions at the secondary level. Gilbert (1913) overtly probed into reasons behind values implicit

in decisions to teach selected subject matter
at the elementary level. Weeks (1913) projected
into the future, attempting to advocate curricula that were consistent with economic democracy.
The pre-1900 trend of linking method with curriculum prevailed in Heckert's 1917 emphasis on
explicating relationships between the organization
of instructional materials and elementary school
curriculum. Later, organization became a permanent
curricular concern; similarly, the relation between
curriculum and instruction became a perennial
debate.

The experientialist school of curriculum
thought was given steadfast roots by Dewey's
educational magnum opus, Democracy and Education
(1916). Though not exclusively a curriculum book,
this work set curriculum issues in a political,
scientific, philosophical, psychological, and
educational context. Its direct and indirect
impact on curriculum thought and action was monumental. By relating the ordinary life functioning
of individuals with the social quest for problem
resolution, Dewey weaved a democratic conception
of education from which aims emerged as a continuous flow of consequences of intelligent action.
Growth and direction, he argued, were achieved
through a kind of situational scientific inquiry.
By arguing for a transacting mutuality of seeming
opposites--e.g., interest and discipline, independence and dependence, work and play, experience
and reflection, labor and leisure, the intellectual and practical, and interest and need--Dewey
provided the basis for a conception of curriculum
that united school with life and preparation
with living.

In 1918, W.H. Kilpatrick began his ardent
crusade to perpetuate Dewey's work by interpreting
its implications for method and curriculum. His
"project method" became widely known among curriculum scholars and practitioners. In the brief
1918 reprint of his eighteen page article, Kilpatrick promoted the idea that learning activities
should be built around the hub of shared student

33

interest, and that all subject areas could be related to and integrated with that central interest. Some scholars accepted this method as a consistent extension of Deweyan thought; others heatedly disputed it. The latter may have favored the interpretive records of the Horace Mann School (1913 and 1917) as more genuine expressions of experientialist thought since this renowned laboratory school at Columbia's Teachers College was thoroughly rooted in experience and reflection upon it.

Study of prevailing curriculum in schools provides ample evidence that the intellectual traditionalist line of thought was far from dormant during this decade. It served an instigating role in calls for revision by social behaviorists and experientialists alike. Though not purely intellectual traditionalist, the Cardinal Principles of Secondary Education (1918) has strong tendencies in that direction. As a political statement, it served to promote the cause of compromise by providing a broad conception of goals to which it would be difficult to deny allegiance, regardless of one's school of thought. Who, for example, would want to go on record as having opposed any of the following: (1) health, (2) command of fundamental processes, (3) worthy home membership, (4) vocational preparation, (5) citizenship, (6) worthy use of leisure time, and (7) development of ethical character? Such principles or general goals were not without precedent. They can be traced to the National Education Association Committee of Ten pronouncements of 1893, led by Charles Eliot's indefatigable admonition for an education that embraced both pure and applied sciences, modern languages, and mathematics, i.e., practical studies having practical results. This was followed by the report of the Committee of Fifteen that focused on elementary education. Both were highly subject oriented.[2] The Seven Cardinal Principles can be traced with even greater ease to Herbert Spencer's (1860)[3] five educational categories that lead to full living: (1) direct self-preservation, (2) necessities of life, (3) rearing offspring, (4) proper social and political relations, and (5) gratification of tastes and feelings. It requires no great intellectual contortions to see direct connections between these two highly influential documents. Further, it is quite evident that such statements are open to extraordinarily wide interpretations, thus, making them quite similarly acceptable and unacceptable to any of the major persuasions of curriculum thought. Their formation was at least as political as it was rational.

The conclusion of the second decade of the Twentieth Century brought solidarity to curriculum as a viable area of study. It was an area of study frought with controversy. It was, perhaps, curricularists' overarching concern for the substance of learning in schools that contributed to the longevity that this area of study has thus far attained. Playing no small role in sustaining that longevity was the Cardinal Principles of Secondary Education, a document that found more than a modicum of acceptance in worlds of both scholarship and practice, a kind of unifying power without which the separate schools of curricular thought may have splintered, atrophied, and faded away.

Notes

[1]Thanks are extended to Ralph Tyler for information concerning this, given to me during a May 18, 1979 interview with him.

[2]The National Education Association appointed the Committee of Ten on Secondary School Studies chaired by Charles W. Eliot who was President of Harvard University, and the Committee of Fifteen on Elementary Education in the 1890's. Their work cast much of the fate of school curriculum for decades to come toward the intellectual traditionalist orientation.

[3]See "note 3" of Chapter I.

Bibliography of Curriculum Books,
1911-1919

1911

   Gray, E.D. Mc Q. How the curriculum of the
        secondary school might be reconstructed.
        Albuquerque, New Mexico: University of
        New Mexico Bulletin, 1911.

1913

   Gilbert, C.B. What children study and why:
        A discussion of educational values in
        elementary course of study. New York:
        Silver Burdett, 1913.

   Horace Mann School. The curriculum of the
        Horace Mann elementary school. New York:
        Teachers College, Columbia University,
        1913.

   Weeks, A.D. The education of tomorrow: The
        adaptation of school curricula to economic
        democracy. New York: Sturgis & Walton,
        1913.

1915

   Bobbitt, F. What the schools teach and might
        teach. Cleveland: The Survey Committee
        of the Cleveland Foundation, 1915.

   Dewey, J. The school and society (Revised
        Edition). Chicago: University of Chicago
        Press, 1915.

1916

   Dewey, J. Democracy and education. New York:
        Macmillan, 1916.

36

1917

Heckert, J.W. Organization of instruction
materials, with special relation to the
elementary school curriculum. New York:
Teachers College, Columbia University,
1917 (AMS Reprint Available).

Horace Mann School. The curriculum of the
Horace Mann elementary school. New
York: Teachers College, Columbia Uni-
versity, 1917.

1918

Bobbitt, F. The curriculum. Boston: Houghton
Mifflin, 1918 (Reprint 1972 by Arno Press
and Norwood Editions).

Commission of the Reorganization of Secondary
Education. Cardinal principles of secon-
dary education. Washington: Government
Printing Office, 1918.

Kilpatrick, W.H. The project method. New
York: Teachers College, Columbia University, 1918 (Reprinted from the Teachers
College Record, September, 1918, 19(4),
18pps.).

1919

Richmond, K. The curriculum. London: Con-
stable & Company, 1919.

CHAPTER III

CURRICULUM LITERATURE AND CONTEXT:

1920-1929

Contextual Reminders

It was the "Roaring Twenties," the great war was over, prosperity seemed to establish itself once again. This was at least the case in the United States where the detached perspective provided by the Atlantic's vastness enabled Americans to sense a finality to European conflict brought by the Treaty of Versailles. A need for a sort of internationalism evolved, conceived by Woodrow Wilson as a League of Nations. Though sentiment was shared throughout much of the world, the United States voted not to join. British dominionhood began a gradual process of disintegration with the 1922 independence of Egypt, the 1921 creation of the Irish Free State, and continued protest under Gandhi in India. The year 1922 also saw Mussolini march on Rome and take over the Italian government. Josef Stalin became secretary-general of the Communist Party in Russia in the same year, helping to change that nation's status to the Union of Soviet Socialist Republics in the succeeding year; thus, seemingly bringing closure to the creation of the first major Communist power. Vladimir Lenin, the initiator of this process, through the revolutions of 1905 and 1917, died in 1924. In the U.S. the same year brought the infamous Teapot Dome scandal leading to the resignations of several prominent governmental officials. Sun Yat-sen, president of China, died in 1925, an event that was followed by confusion and civil war, eventually leading to the 1928 election of Chiang Kai-shek. Revolutionary leader, Leon Trotsky was expelled from Russia and took refuge in Mexico, later to be defended by John Dewey, among others. In 1927, Stalin achieved political control in the U.S.S.R. Provision for peaceful settlement of international disputes was acknowledged in 1928 by the signing of the Kellogg-Briand Pact by 65 nations.

During the 1920's the arts continued their turn inward to a soul frought with confusion by the perceived absurdities of life, bureaucracy, and human suffering. Sinclair Lewis produced Main Street in 1920 followed by Babbitt in 1922; 1921 brought D.H Lawrence's Women in Love. John Galsworthy continued the Forsythe Saga. Though hope of a realized dream permeated Fitzgerald's The Great Gatsby, it was a hope of false illusion anchored in an innocence from a past that only existed in the over-idealistic imagination. That innocence seemed exorcised by the existential "realities" that mocked the acquisition of dreams built on dignity, honor, and enlightenment, as portrayed in James Joyce's Ulysses, Eugene O'Neill's The Emperor Jones, T.S. Eliot's The Wasteland, e.e. Cummings' Enormous Room, Thomas Mann's The Magic Mountain, Theodore Dreiser's An American Tragedy, culuminating in Frantz Kafka's The Trial in 1925. It was a time when literature simultaneously conveyed that luck could overpower despair and inner sensitivity could be dulled to submission by the eroding wheels of human power and the blights of unexpected tragedy in Shaw's Back to Methuselah, Andre Gide's The Counterfeiters, Upton Sinclair's Oil! and Boston, Willa Cather's Death Comes to the Archbishop, Virginia Wolfe's To a Lighthouse, Sinclair Lewis' Elmer Gantry, Aldous Huxley's Point Counter Point, and Erich Remarque's All Quiet on the Western Front.

Expressionism continued in painting with Picasso expanding his contributions in a variety of works including the famed Three Musicians. Klee, Miro, and Chagall explored new dimensions of abstraction offering strong contrast with the stark realism of Grant Wood. The free floating forms of the former evoked a sense of teleological absence. The varied musical compositions of Prokofiev, Copland, Weill's Three Penny Opera, Coward's Bitter Sweet operetta, and Gershwin's Rapsody in Blue portrayed the dream-seeking amid dissonance of the era.

This was a decade for acquiring equality in several spheres. The nineteenth amendment to the U.S. Constitution obtained the right of women to vote in 1920. Women were also awarded degrees at Oxford University in Britain. The International Court of Justice was established at The Hague in the Netherlands. After 500 years, Joan of Arc made the trek from witchdom to canonization; in 1923 G.B. Shaw helped immortalize that journey with Saint Joan. British women were accorded the vote at age 21 in 1928. The emergent equality was not without setbacks. The teaching of Darwinian evolution was banned in Tennessee in 1925. Hitler's Mein Kampf was begun. And the governor of Oklahoma was removed from office after he tried to use that office to fight the Ku Klux Klan in 1923.

The unpredictability of dire human predicaments depicted in the existential literature of this decade found precedent in major disaster and rapid decline. Over 140,000 persons died in a 1924 earthquake in Japan. The mark became worthless and the German economy fell in 1927. The next year Brazil's economy collapsed. Economic crisis plagued the globe with the U.S. stock market crash of 1929, three years after John Maynard Keynes wrote The End of Laissez-faire.

A decade begun in prosperity and hope ended in depression and despair.

Curriculum Thought and Literature

The air of prosperity that began the 1920's was also present in the curriculum domain. Eighty-seven books appeared in this decade, compared with a total of twenty-eight in the two previous decades combined. Although the intellectual traditionalists continued to occupy a sizable proportion of practical school activity, the experientialists and the social behaviorists continued to grow in number and influence.

Curriculum began to emerge as an area of study with an increasingly distinct identity. In 1920,

Frederick Bonser characterized curriculum as experiences that students are expected to have in school, and the sequential order of such experiences (1920, p. 1). This characterization set the stage for years of subsequent writing and activity by other curriculum scholars. Curriculum scholars studied experiences that students were expected to have in schools; moreover, the primary interpretation that dominated the literature was prescriptive rather than descriptive. Curriculum scholars prescribed or advocated that which they thought schools should provide, the nature and order of learning experiences, much more frequently than they attempted to describe what schools did provide. The portrayal of practice was not absent, however, from early curriculum writing, as evidenced by Dewey's description of the University of Chicago Laboratory School and the three book-length reports by the Horace Mann School during the first two decades. Joining these in 1920 was Studies in Education prepared by the Francis W. Parker School faculty in Chicago. It might be expected that these writings would be largely descriptive. This however, constituted only a portion of the works. They were prescriptive, too, in the sense that they emerged from an interactive process of actually doing a school. This was particularly the case for schools that utilized progressive education. Thus, the experientialist school of curriculum thought moved into what might be called its "golden age." The book by the Francis Parker faculty is exemplary in the sense that it directly addressed a major tenet of the progressive phase of the experientialist position, namely, the primacy of individual students and the need to tailor or adapt curricula to their needs and interests.

The life of the child became an imperative concern of the experientialist educator as evidenced by Meriam (1920), Hill (1923), and the Rugg and Shumaker classic of 1928, The Child-Centered School. In the late 1920's the activity curriculum became a rather full-blown feature of the progressive school. The first large scale description of

42

its curricular features was provided by Ferriere in 1928. A fascinating attempt to translate Deweyan philosophy of education into curriculum principles and procedures was provided by L. Thomas Hopkins in 1929. Particular note should be given to his table of contents which is organized according to major and supporting questions that pervaded curriculum concern of that era. It is interesting, moreover, to consider the relevance of those concerns to the kinds of questions being asked by today's curricularists. The same decade brought an elaborate rendition of method by Kilpatrick (1926). In this work he laid foundations of much progressive thought and action in years that followed.

The trend to designate particular school audiences as targets for curriculum writing was continued and expanded. In previous decades some books were geared to the secondary schools and others to elementary schools. In the twenties the junior high school emerged as a separate area of concern in books by Koos (1920), Glass (1924), Hines (1924), The American Association of School Administrators (1927), Koos' second edition (1927), the National Education Association Department of Superintendence (1927), the National Education Association (1928), and Cox (1929). One book appeared on the junior college curriculum, Gray (1929). Several books emphasized curriculum applicable to the kindergarten and early primary school years: the International Kindergarten Union (1922), Burke (1924), Salisbury (1924), Keelor (1925), Carmichael (1927), and Skinner and Chappell (1929). Books on the secondary curriculum continued to flourish; representatives include Stout (1921), Clement (1923), Cox (1925), Counts (1926), Morrison (1926), Davis (1927), Koos (1927), Uhl (1927), Monroe and Herriott (1928), and the National Education Association (1929). The collection of books on the elementary school curriculum was also augmented by Bonser (1920), Meriam (1920), Wells (1921), Phillips (1923 and 1926), National Education Association (1924), and Tippitt (1927), among others.

The social behaviorist school continued prominence in the 1920's. Treatments of curricular objectives continued to be produced, sometimes as book length concerns. In some ways this stemmed from the goal statements by such groups as the Committee of Ten and the Commission on Reorganization of Secondary Education, noted in previous chapters. They were given a new twist in the work of D.S. Snedden. Snedden (1921) advocated placing students in what he called "case groups" based on their particular biographical data. Other sociologically oriented educators prescribed a more rigorous pigeon-holing of students, labeling them by use of more limited data; thus, solidifying conceptions of their potential and limiting their future lines of endeavor in occupational and educational domains. Bobbitt continued his methods of activity analysis, this time by application described in Curriculum Making in Los Angeles (1922). W.W. Charters set his name in curriculum fame with Curriculum Construction (1923), setting forth perhaps the most defensible theoretical framework in early social behaviorist writing. In 1924, Bobbitt continued by producing a more practice oriented text than that in 1918. This text, How to Make a Curriculum, focused more on prescription of means for actualizing the orientations advocated in the 1918 work. Bobbitt elaborated even more on applications of his social efficiency approach to curriculum-making in Curriculum Investigations (1926). In 1927 Snedden provided a more thorough interpretation of the sociological underpinnings of curriculum.

New areas emerged, perhaps appearing as trends during the 1920's, but accumulating to bolster the domain that falls under the rubric of curriculum. As mentioned above, Snedden's analyses brought sociological lenses into the curriculum arena. Hartman (1923) treated curriculum in the context of home and community life, moving a bit beyond the frequent propensity to focus on curriculum within schools as segmented from the rest of student life. C.A. McMurry (1923) emphasized the organization of learning experiences as a major element of

44

curricular concern. The scientistic reverence for facts gave impetus to an early fact-finding mission on curriculum by the National Education Association (1923).

Although curriculum studies at least partially grew out of the Herbartian emphasis on method, curricularists often maintained a rather sharp line of demarcation between the two domains, curriculum theory and practice, artificial though the separation may be. Phillips (1923), however, symbolized a reunion of curriculum and method that appears frequently throughout subsequent literature and is simultaneously no small cause for the perennial debate about the relation between curriculum and instruction. Burke (1924) symbolized the time-honored concerns about student behavior and the role of schools in moral development. When consumerism was at high tide, a few years before the stock market crash, Harap (1924 and again in 1927) became known by his emphasis on consumer education through curriculum materials development. A number of books, exemplified by Bower (1925), Betts (1924), and Acheson (1929), focused on the topic of curriculum in religious education. That any kind of advocacy, curriculum books being one, invariably involves legal issues is substantiated by Flanders (1925) and Hamilton (1927). Similarly, it is patent whenever generally stated ideas are offered to practitioners in books, they must be tailored to fit situations.

Thus, in this first decade that witnessed a flourishing of curriculum books, problems in application were noted (e.g., Sharp, 1925; and Briggs, 1926) and the need for adjustment to unique needs was perceived (e.g., Cox, 1925). The 1926 Yearbook of the National Education Association Department of Superintendence emphasized public roles in the development of public school curriculum. Stratemeyer and Bruner (1926) provided a book length realization that if objectives are made, and if curriculum is created and implemented based on those objectives, then the courses of study need to be evaluated. Though slow to start, this means-ends

45

technology of accountability is powerfully with us today. The whispers of moral development, much too early to be anticipatory of Kohlberg, took a novel turn with Carmichael (1927). He proposed that morals be used as the basis, not merely as desired outcomes, of curriculum construction. It comes as no surprise that special emphasis on curriculum study would issue in a plethora of curriculum materials. Knox (1927) was convinced that practitioners needed to be aware of such materials and the various activities that they facilitate, as evidenced in his sizable compendium on that topic.

Throughout the 1920's rural schools were far from on the wane. The new emphasis on curriculum presented the special problem of knowing how thoroughly curriculum was developed and implemented in each of the thousands of little red schoolhouses that dotted the American countryside. Holloway (1928) addressed this issue and advocated the need for inclusion of supervision within the curriculum arena, or at least as a very close relative. The idea of supervision was developed further in the work of Burton and Barnes (1929). The importance of adolescence, stressed for some time by psychologists, appeared in the curriculum literature of this decade (e.g., the National Education Association, 1928; and Owen, 1929). By the end of the decade, Snedden's (1921) emphasis on objectives was joined by Cox and Peters (1929) to produce a major statement that gave increased perspective to the role of objectives in education generally, and in curriculum particularly. The above developments may evidence early stitches in what is now referred to as the "patchwork" curriculum. A 1978 issue of Educational Leadership is devoted to that theme (November 1978, 36(2)).

Perhaps the best treatment of the diversity of orientations to curriculum thought was presented by Boyd H. Bode in Modern Educational Theories (1927). The first half of this work is devoted to an analysis of assumptions that undergird the several orientations to curriculum thought. Although his categorization of schools of thought that pertain

46

to curriculum differs somewhat from the one used
in this book, it is unmistakably among the sound-
est and most defensible statements on the matter.

Two other thrusts in the curriculum literature
of the Twenties are worth special note. The first
deals with the study of practice; the second with
attempts to provide literature for practitioners.
Frequently, curriculum writers of the 1970's can
be heard to criticize early curriculum writers
for ivory tower perspectives, for not being aware
of curriculum practices of their time. A number
of books indicate the contrary. Examples include:
a look at themselves by the Francis Parker faculty
through a treatment of their mechanisms of adaptation (1920); Stout's (1921) survey of curriculum
development in the North Central states; Bobbitt's
(1922) Los Angeles study; Collings' (1923) experiment with project oriented curricula; Glass's study
of intermediate and junior high curriculum practice
(1924); Keelor's (1925) study of curriculum in
the second grade; a California curriculum study by
Bagley and Kyte (1926); Bobbitt's (1926) investigations noted before; Lincoln School staff's
elaborate self-study (1927); a review of practical
curriculum applications by the Sisters of the
Order of Saint Dominic (1929); and of great import,
the excellent survey of innovative curricula presented in Part I of the Twenty-sixth Yearbook of
the National Society for the Study of Education
(1927).

The second thrust, that of writing to practitioners in ways that speak to their needs presented
a special problem. Perceived needs had to be
addressed. Practitioners did not have time to
traverse detailed intellectual journeys. They needed
to make curricula and implement it to students who
sat in schoolrooms, products of the technology of
mass schooling, students who sat there right now.
One response to this need, a tendency that remains
today, was to simplify and distill. Lists of what
came to be known as "principles" for curriculum
development appeared in the Twenties and flourished
in later decades. This approach, a "recipifying"

of curriculum knowledge, has roots in the following:
Clement (1923), Bobbitt (1924), Herriott (1925-26),
Monroe (1925), Craig (1927), Harap (1928), Acheson
(1929), and Wisehart (1929). Among these, special
note should be given to Harap who was acknowledged
by L. Thomas Hopkins as one who made great strides
to explicate curriculum for practitioners. Hopkins
considered this an important, certainly not a pejorative, development in curriculum literature. Hopkins writes:

> All books written up to 1928 were
> too long on theory and too short
> on its application in practice.
> Harap made the first real attempt
> to bridge this gap. He combines
> theory and practice into a series
> of steps to be followed by the
> curriculum maker in relating educa-
> tional aims to the construction of
> units of instruction.
> (Review of Educational Research,
> 1931, p. 5).

Surely problems can flow from the brevity of such
recipe-like orientations; the implications can indeed be pejorative. Nevertheless, it met the
increased practitioner demand for recipes. The
value, however, of such works to practice should
not be overlooked.

As mentioned earlier, the 1920's saw the formidable emergence of progressive education in both
literature and school practice. Thus, a dominant
brand of experientialist thought as characterized
here, flourished in a variety of shapes and sizes.
One can see literature built quite directly out of
practical experience in schools, such as that produced by faculties of Francis Parker School in
Chicago, and Lincoln and Horace Mann Schools at
Teachers College at Columbia University in New York.

One can also see the emergence of the project
method, heralded by Kilpatrick (1918), in the work
of Wells (1921) and Collings (1923 and 1926).

McMurry's (1923) emphasis on organizing the curriculum evolved from his sturdy Herbartian roots. Salisbury's (1924) and Ferriere's (1928) treatments of the activity curriculum represent a topic long associated with Deweyan thought and the experientialist traditions. George S. Counts, later to be quite thoroughly associated with the left side of progressive education, should be mentioned here for his early work on the high school curriculum (1926). The Child-Centered School (1928) by Rugg and Shumaker provided incentives as well as background to many a scholar and practitioner who possessed even an inkling of the progressive ilk. Continuing the experientialist line of thinking, with his own unique style, L. Thomas Hopkins attempted to fuse a Deweyan interpretation of curriculum with the requests for principles and procedures in his 1929 publication of Curriculum Principles and Practices.

Also appearing in 1929 was Alfred North Whitehead's The Aims of Education and Other Essays, a work destined to become a classic in education literature in general. Though Whitehead did not intend this work specifically for audiences in the curriculum realm, it is often cited in curriculum literature. Many of the ideas advanced by him are decidedly of the experientialist flavor, e.g., an emphasis on the interdependence of knowledge, a belief that education is the art of using knowledge, a disdain for inert ideas, and a concern for interest and development implicit in his idea of rhythms of education.

It is somewhat ironic that as the stockpile of literature authored by both experientialists and social behaviorists grew, [and as descriptors such as modern (Phillips, 1923), keeping pace (the National Education Association, 1925), and evolving (Davis, 1927) invoked an air of rapid innovation] most schools predominantly reflected a character that was intellectual traditionalist. It seems clear, however, that many schools felt pressures to provide the appearance of the projects and activities of progressivism or the scientific analysis of social efficiency. This is not to say that some

49

schools made no strides toward the ideal of either persuasion. Progressive education had a large number of followers. Though not large by comparison with those who perpetuated the traditionalist position, it was large enough to persuade scholars that they had some influence on practice. At least temporarily the conclusion seemed to be reached in the late 1920's that influence could be augmented if consensus were achieved among scholars.

Thus, under the leadership of Harold Rugg, an unabashed experientialist himself, Part II of the Twenty-sixth Yearbook of the National Society for the Study of Education was created to make visible a composite statement by curriculum scholars from differing persuasions. The book began with the posing of eighteen questions deemed central to foundations of curriculum-making. These were followed by a seventeen page composite statement that is signed by: Bagley, Bobbitt, Bonser, Charters, Counts, Courtis, Horn, Judd, F.J. Kelly, Kilpatrick, Rugg, and Works. In his 1975 critical appraisal of this work, Decker Walker referred to it as "a unique record of the thinking and of the hopes and fears of the founders of the curriculum field" (p. 264).[1] It represented the product of two and one-half years of deliberation by these founding scholars of the curriculum field. Their general statement is followed by minority opinions of the scholars individually.

The Twenty-sixth Yearbook, thus, exemplifies tendencies toward each of the three schools of curriculum thought set forth in this book: the experientialists, the social behaviorists, and the intellectual traditionalists. Moreover, the perennial nature of the questions discussed by these founding scholars of curriculum is attested to by a personal note. I frequently present excerpts from the composite statement to curriculum students who are almost invariably surprised that the publication date is 1927 rather than today.

Readers should not infer from the above praise that I believe that this early statement is beyond

50

reproach. The desire to achieve a semblance of consensus is always accompanied by certain portions of diluted ideas that are more productive when taken separately. Walker's criticism (also note 1) of the composite statement is recommended to allay the propensity to deify this contribution to curriculum thought. Nevertheless, it is an important statement, a necessary one for understanding curriculum development just prior to the 1930's. Perhaps of even greater importance than the statement's content is the precedent that its creation sets for interdependent efforts by major curriculum scholars to work together, a precedent seldom utilized in the years that followed, certainly not with similar magnitude of effort.

Notes

[1]Walker, D.F. The curriculum field in formation. Curriculum Theory Network, 4 (4), 1975, 263-280.

Bibliography of Curriculum Books, 1920-1929

1920

Bonser, F.G. The elementary school curriculum. New York: Macmillan, 1920 (Also 1921, 1922, 1923, 1927, and a 1978 reprint by Telegraph).

Francis W. Parker School (Faculty). Studies in education: The individual and the curriculum: Experiments in adaptation. Chicago, 1920.

Koos, L.V. The junior high school. New York: Harcourt, Brace and Howe, Inc., 1920.

Meriam, J.L. Child life and the curriculum. Yonkers-on-the-Hudson, New York: World Book, 1920.

1921

Snedden, D.S. Sociological determination of objectives in education. Philadelphia: Lippincott, 1921.

Stout, J.E. The development of high school curricula in the North Central states from 1860-1918 (Monograph Number 15). Chicago: University of Chicago Press, 1921.

Wells, M.E. A project curriculum, dealing with the project as a means of organizing the curriculum of the elementary school. Phildelphia: Lippincott, 1921.

1922

Bobbitt, F. Curriculum making in Los Angeles. Chicago: University of Chicago Press, 1922.

International Kindergarten Union. Bureau of
Education Committee. A kindergarten-
first-grade curriculum. Washington:
Government Printing Office, 1922.

1923

Charters, W.W. Curriculum construction. New
York: The Macmillan Company, 1923 (Also
1924, 1925, 1929, 1938; and 1971 by Arno
Press, New York).

Clement, J.A. Curriculum making in secondary
schools. New York: Henry Holt & Company,
1923 (Also 1924, 1927).

Collings, E. An experiment with a project
curriculum. New York: Macmillan, 1923
(Also 1924, 1925, 1926, and 1927).

Hartman, C. Home and community life, curriculum studies for the elementary schools.
New York: E.P. Dutton, 1923.

Hill, P.S. A conduct curriculum for kindergarten and first grade. New York: Charles
Scribner's Sons, 1923. (See Burke, 1924)

McMurry, C.A. How to organize the curriculum.
New York: The Macmillan Company, 1923.

National Education Association. Facts on the
public school curriculum. Research Bulletin, November, 1923.

Phillips, C.A. Modern methods and the elementary curriculum. New York: Century, 1923
(Also 1926).

1924

Betts, G.H. The curriculum of religious education. New York: Abingdon, 1924.

53

Bobbitt, F. How to make a curriculum. Boston:
Houghton Mifflin, 1924 (Also Norwood
Editions).

Burke, A., et al. A conduct curriculum for
the kindergarten and first grade. New
York: Scribner's Sons, 1924. (See Hill, 1923)

Glass, J.M. Curriculum practice in the junior
high school and grades five and six.
Chicago: University of Chicago Department
of Education Supplementary Educational
Monographs, Number 25, 1924.

Harap, H. Education of the consumer: A study
in curriculum material. New York:
Macmillan, 1924.

Hines, H.C. Junior high school curricula.
New York: Macmillan, 1924.

National Education Association. The elementary
school curriculum: Department of Superintendence Second Yearbook. Washington,
D.C.: American Association of School
Administrators, 1924.

Salisbury, E. An activity curriculum for the
kindergarten and primary grades. San
Francisco: Harr Wagner Publishing Company, 1924.

Smith, E.E. The heart of the curriculum.
New York: Doubleday, Page, & Company,
1924.

1925

Bower, W.C. The curriculum of religious education. New York: Charles Scribner's Sons,
1925.

Cox, P.W.L. Curriculum adjustment in the
elementary school. Philadelphia: J.B.
Lippincott, 1925.

Flanders, J.K. Legislative control of the elementary curriculum. Contributions to Education Number 195. New York: Bureau of Publications, Teachers College, Columbia University, 1925.

Keelor, K.L. Curriculum studies in the second grade. New York: Teachers College, Columbia University, 1925.

Monroe, W.S. Making a course of study. Urbana: University of Illinois, 1925.

National Education Association. Research in constructing the elementary school curriculum: Department of Superintendence Third Yearbook. American Association of School Administrators. Washington, D.C., 1925.

National Education Association, Research Division. Keeping pace with the advancing curriculum. Research Bulletin Number 3, September and November, 1925.

Sharp, L.A. Problems in curriculum construction. Boulder, Colorado: University Extension Division, 1925.

1926

Bagley, W.C. and Kyte, G.C. The California curriculum study. Berkeley, California: University of California Printing Office, 1926.

Bobbitt, F., et al. Curriculum investigations. Chicago: University of Chicago Press, 1926 (Also 1927).

Briggs, T.H. Curriculum problems. New York: Macmillan, 1926.

Collings, E. An experiment with a project curriculum. New York: Macmillan, 1926.

Counts, G.S. The senior high school curriculum. Chicago: University of Chicago Press, 1926.

Herriott, M.E. How to make a course in . . . (Arithmetic, 1925; Reading, 1926; Social Studies, 1926). Urbana: University of Illinois, 1925-1926.

Kilpatrick, W.H. Foundations of Method. New York: Macmillan, 1926 (Reprinted by Arno Press, 1972).

Morrison, H.C. The practice of teaching in the secondary school. Chicago: University of Chicago Press, 1926.

National Education Association. The nation at work on the public school curriculum: Department of Superintendence Fourth Yearbook. Washington, D.C., 1926.

Stratemeyer, F.B. and Bruner, H.B. Rating elementary courses of study. New York: Teachers College, Columbia University, 1926.

1927

American Association of School Administrators. The junior high school curriculum. Washington, D.C.: The Department of Superintendence of the National Education Association of the United States, 1927.

Bode, B.H. Modern educational theories. New York: Macmillan, 1927.

Carmichael. A.M. Moral situations of six-year old children as a basis for curriculum construction. Studies in Education. University of Iowa, IV, 6, 1927.

Craig, G.S. Certain techniques used in developing a course of study in science for the

Horace Mann elementary school. New York:
Teachers College, Columbia University,
1927.

Davis, C.O. Our evolving high school curriculum. New York: World Book, 1927.

Denver Public Schools. The Denver program of
curriculum revision. Denver, Colorado:
Board of Education, 1927.

Freeland, G.E., Adams, R.M., and Hall, K.H.
Teaching in the intermediate grades; a
study of curricula and methods of teaching
in grades four, five and six. Boston:
Houghton-Mifflin, 1927.

Hamilton, O.T. The courts and the curriculum.
Contributions to Education Number 250.
New York: Bureau of Publications, Teachers College, Columbia University, 1927
(AMS Reprint Available).

Harap, H. Economic life and the curriculum.
New York: Mamcillan, 1927.

Knox, R.B. A guide to materials and equipment
for elementary schools. School Activities
and Equipment. Boston: Houghton Mifflin, 1927.

Koos, L.V. The American secondary school.
Boston: Ginn and Company, 1927a (Reprinted
by Norwood).

Koos, L.V. The junior high school (Second Edition). Boston: Ginn and Company, 1927b.

Lincoln School Staff of Teachers College at
Columbia. Curriculum making in an elementary school. New York: Ginn, 1927.

National Education Association. The junior
high school curriculum: Department of
Superintendence Fifth Yearbook. Washington, D.C., 1927a.

National Education Association, Research Division. <u>Creating a curriculum for adolescent youth</u>. <u>Research Bulletin Number 5</u>, 1927b.

National Society for the Study of Education. <u>Curriculum making: Past and present</u>. <u>Twenty-sixth Yearbook, Part I</u> (Harold O. Rugg, Chairman). Bloomington, Illinois: Public School Publishing Company, 1927a (Also published in 1969 by Arno Press, New York).

National Society for the Study of Education. The <u>foundation of curriculum making</u>. <u>Twenty-sixth Yearbook, Part II</u> (Harold O. Rugg, Chairman). Bloomington, Illinois: Public School Publishing Company, 1927b (Also published in 1969 by Arno Press, New York).

Snedden, D.S. <u>Foundations of curricula; sociological analysis</u>. New York: Columbia Teachers College, Columbia University, 1927.

Tippitt, J.S., et al. <u>Curriculum making in an elementary school</u>. Boston: Ginn, 1927.

Uhl, W.L. <u>Secondary school curricula</u>. New York: Macmillan, 1927.

1928

Cocking, W.D. <u>Administrative procedures in curriculum making for public schools</u>. New York: Teachers College, Columbia University, 1928 (Also published in 1972 by AMS Press, New York).

Ferriere, A. <u>The activity school</u>. New York: The John Day Company, 1928.

Harap, H. <u>The techniques of curriculum making</u>. New York: Macmillan, 1928.

Holloway, W.J. Participation in curriculum planning as a means of supervision in rural schools. New York: Teachers College, Columbia University, 1928.

Monroe, W.S. and Herriott, M.E. Reconstruction of the secondary school curriculum: Its meaning and trends. Bureau of Educational Research. Number 41. Urbana: University of Illinois, 1928.

National Education Association. The development of the high school curriculum: Department of Superintendence Sixth Yearbook. Washington, D.C., 1928a.

National Education Association, Research Division. Creating a curriculum for adolescent youth. Research Bulletin Number 6, January, 1928b.

Rugg, E. Curriculum studies in the social sciences and citizenship. Greeley, Colorado: Colorado State Teachers College, 1928.

Rugg, H.O. and Shumaker, A. The child-centered school. Yonkers, New York: World Book, 1928.

Williams, L.A. The making of high-school curricula. New York: Ginn, 1928.

1929

Acheson, E.L. Construction of junior church school curricula. New York: Teachers College, Columbia University, 1929.

Burton, W.H., Barnes, W, et al. (Editors). The supervision of elementary subjects. New York: Appleton, 1929.

Cox, P.W.L. The junior high school and its curriculum. New York: Charles Scribner's Sons, 1929.

Cox, P.W.L., Peters, C.C., and Snedden, D.
Objectives of education. New York:
Teachers College, Columbia University,
1929.

Gray, W.S. (Editor). Junior college curriculum.
Chicago: University of Chicago Press,
1929.

Hopkins, L.T. Curriculum principles and
practices. New York: Benjamin H. San-
born & Company, 1929.

Indiana Department of Public Instruction.
Guiding principles of elementary curriculum
revision for the state of Indiana. Indianapolis: Department of Public Instruction, 1929.

National Education Association, Research
Division. Vitalizing the high school
curriculum. Research Bulletin Number 7,
September, 1929.

Owen, R.A.D. Principles of adolescent education. New York: Ronald Press, 1929.

Sisters of the Order of Saint Dominic. Curricular studies: Practical application of
the principles of Catholic education.
New York: Macmillan, 1929.

Skinner, M.E. and Chappell, E.P. (Editors).
A curriculum study for teachers of begin-
ners: A manual for use in standard training courses. Nashville: Cokesbury Press,
1929.

Whitehead, A.N. The aims of education and other
essays. New York: Macmillan, 1929.

Wisehart, R.P. Guiding principles of elementary
curriculum revision for the state of
Indiana: Bulletin Number 107. Indianapolis:
Department of Public Instruction, 1929.

CHAPTER IV

CURRICULUM LITERATURE AND CONTEXT

1930-1939

Contextual Reminders

Contrary to the 1920's, the 1930's began in
caution, despair, and neediness, and grew to
increased plenty when many Americans turned with
glib evasiveness from the mounting turmoil that
brewed in Europe. The desire to conquer the depression and its haunting accouterments by avoidance
can be understood, if not condoned, in the face
of dilemma. Yet, this is only a part of the
decade that followed the roaring-ness of the
Twenties. The arts, sciences, and technologies
continued to press forward.

In 1930 the Great Depression steadily grew
worse. Unemployment soared. The Allied occupation of Germany since the end of World War I terminated. Albert Einstein and others seeking
political and intellectual freedom took up residence in the United States.

Internationally, 1930 brought increased civil
disobedience by Gandhi in India in attempts to
obtain independence from England, the beginning
of Haile Selassie's long reign as Emperor of
Ethiopia, a major naval disarmament treaty by
France, the U.S., Japan, and Britain, and an
increase of elected political stature by the
National Socialist or Nazi Party in Germany. By
1931, after abandoning the gold standard, the
British recognized dominions of the Empire as
sovereign states. Japan also abandoned the gold
standard, invaded Manchuria, and set up a state
in that section of China. Uprising and war
characterized Spain, Peru, Colombia, Bolivia,
and Paraguay, while the USA and USSR joined in
world disarmament talks in Geneva in 1932.
Meanwhile the Nazi Party became the largest
party in Germany.

As is the case in very hard times, protest and disenchantment were on the increase in many nations. The 1932 hit song, Brother, Can You Spare a Dime?, characterized the times. Protest marches by the unemployed amassed thousands in most U.S. cities, eventually leading to legislation that spawned the House Un-American Activities Committee. In such a context it was not difficult to perceive injustice as pervasive. To wit: a best seller implying President Harding's death was caused by poisoning at the hands of his wife; the expose of horrendous prison abuses via the 1931 film, I Am a Fugitive from a Chain Gang; the long imprisonment of the "Scottsboro Boys" prior to their vindication for rape; and the Lindberg kidnapping in 1932. Countless other expressions of frustrations of "having not" involved diverse avenues of society, e.g., anti-prohibitionists, labor unions, tar paper shack dwellers, veterans, communists, miners, and students--many of whose protests were met with violence. The news media of 1933 carried stories about homeless children wandering the New York streets in numbers upwards of the seventy-thousands. In the face of this and the continued unemployment, President Franklin D. Roosevelt promised a "New Deal." In 1933 he established the Tennessee Valley Authority and Public Works Administration to combat unemployment, aid farmers, and remedy the depression.

Midway in the decade, Adolf Hitler had become chancellor of Germany and was, after the death of President von Hindenburg, granted dictatorial powers. Both Germany and Japan withdrew from the League of Nations; the USSR joined. Prior to 1935 the Balkan countries of central and eastern Europe braced themselves for the brewing conflict that seemed all too imminent.

Let us step aside for a moment and remember developments in the arts and sciences during the first half of the Thirties. Sinclair Lewis became the first American to win the Nobel Prize in literature in 1930. In the same year Somerset Maugham published Cakes and Ale, and playwrights Bernard Shaw and Noel Coward produced The Apple Cart and

62

<u>Private Lives.</u> A year later Pearl Buck published
<u>The Good Earth.</u> In 1932 Erskine Caldwell portrayed
dilemmas of the times in <u>Tobacco Road</u>, while Aldous
Huxley projected future perils in <u>Brave New World</u>.
Those who were even mildly interested in art during
the early Thirties will recall being awe-struck by
the Empire State Building. They will remember
seeing at once the appearance of such stark realism
as Grant Wood's <u>American Gothic</u> and Edward Hopper's
<u>Route 6</u> emerge juxtaposed with the abstractions of
Picasso, Matisse, Kandinsky, and Klee. The dissonance of artistic styles might well be symbolized
in the musical compositions of Stravinsky, just as
the desire for calmness, stability, and contentment
was epitomized in Hilton's <u>Lost Horizon</u>, i.e., of a
Shangrila in the glimmering hope of everyone.

This far off and detached perspective of the
imagination was, in a sense, corroborated in the
real world of science through the discovery of yet
another planet, Pluto, by Clyde W. Tombaugh in
1930. Looking inward at the micro "solar systems"
of the atom, Ernest Lawrence invented the cyclotron
to enable further insight in high energy physics
in the same year. Two years later discoveries of
the neutron by Chadwick, the positron by Anderson,
and the element deuterium by Urey added to the
repertoire of understanding about the constitution
of matter and energy. At a middle sized level,
i.e., the human level, humans plunged into the
unknown vistas of distance, height, speed, and
depth. In 1930 Amy Johnson flew solo from London
to Australia. In 1931, August Piccard entered the
stratosphere by balloon. In 1933 Wiley Post made
the first solo flight that circumscribed the globe,
and in 1934 William Beebe descended 900 meters
below the sea's surface in his bathysphere. The
fuel that propels humans themselves was understood
a good bit more, as well, with the identification
of Vitamin A by Paul Karrer in 1931 and the synthesis of Vitamin C by Tadeus Reichstein in 1934, both
in Switzerland.

By mid-decade the corner around which war
lurked was quite unmistakably turned with the 1935

German refusal to adhere to disarmament clauses of
the Treaty of Versailles and the Italian invasion
of Ethiopia, prompting the exile of Haile Selassie.
In 1936, Hitler and Mussolini announced the Berlin-
Rome Axis. Meanwhile, Edward VIII abdicated the
English throne to marry Mrs. Wallis Simpson, concluding an issue that raised no small measure of
constitutional crisis in Britain. In the U.S.,
Frankin D. Roosevelt was elected to a second term
as President. In Spain, Germany and Italy overtly
assisted Franco's reactionary forces in a civil war
that, by 1939, ousted the Spanish Republic. The
horrors of that war, and wars in general, were pre-
served by Picasso in his Guernica. Under Hitler's
direction in 1938 and 1939 German forces converged
on Austria, Czechoslovakia, and Poland. Italy conquered Albania. In 1939, Britain and France
declared war on Germany. Likewise, Russia, seeking
its share of Poland, invaded that nation from the
east and Finland as well.

Although the mounting strife in central Europe
quelled artistic endeavor in some respects,
artistic acuity often stems from depths of tragic
perception. In 1935, T.S. Eliot created Murder in
the Cathedral in Britain, and John Steinbeck published Tortilla Flat in America. That film could
portray the literary masterpiece was demonstrated
in 1935 by Clarence Brown's Anna Karenina, in which
"haves" and "have nots" were vividly juxtaposed.
Margaret Mitchell's Gone with the Wind (1936) warned
of the tragedy that war can bring to all, a year
after a Sinclair Lewis title captured a pervasive
public hope among peoples who seemed beyond the
vibrations of escalating war, It Can't Happen Here.
In America, many wanted to believe the secrets to
success had unfolded before them, evidenced by the
demand for Dale Carnegie's best seller, How to Win
Friends and Influence People (1936). Hemingway
himself immersed in the Spanish Civil War, portrayed
the state of affairs that war accentuates with his
1937 title, To Have and Have Not. If this were not
vivid enough, French philosopher-novelist Jean Paul
Sartre captured the feeling of absurdity implicit
in war and suffering with Nausea (1937). Steinbeck

64

continued to portray the plight of accumulated circumstance among the less fortunate, war or not, in Of Mice and Men (1937) and The Grapes of Wrath (1939). Though not nominally existentialist, Thorton Wilder accented absurdities of small town anywhere in the flow of routine and facade, striving and provincialism, passivity and dream, and the seemingly invincible wall of death in Our Town in 1938. The next year James Joyce concretized the existential predicament still further in his modern literary classic, Finnegan's Wake.

The arts were not all of unrelinquished despair in the Thirties. Children were given hope in the victory of goodness. Peter was victorious against the wolf in the story of Prokofiev's composition. Young persons of every age experienced delight and empathic trepidation as they viewed Disney's Snow White and the Seven Dwarfs and Chaplin's Modern Times.

Music continued to vary during the latter half of the decade; Gershwin's Porgy and Bess, Rachmaninov's rhapsodies, Copland's Billy the Kid, Richard Strauss' Daphne, and Bartok's experimental dissonance symbolized the diversity. Sculpture took a new turn with Henry Moore and his topological use of space within pieces often displayed in natural settings.

In science and technology in the late Thirties R.W. Watt developed radar, Britain began public television service, Frank Whittle advanced jet engine research, and Howard Aiken began work on digital computers. Hahn and Strassmann produced nuclear fission in Germany, and DDT was developed by Paul Muller. Of widespread note in everyday life was Georg Biro's introduction of ball point pens.

The interests of ordinary citizens were seen clearly in increased demands for desired equalities. In 1935 the Wagner Act was passed to insure the right of U.S. workers to collective bargaining. In the same year John L. Lewis created pressures that resulted in the merger of eight labor unions in a unit called the Committee for Industrial Organization as a part of the American Federation of Labor. In his presidential acceptance speech, F.D. Roosevelt warned of a kind of "government" that might evolve as a result of increased corporate power. In 1936, U.S. black athlete Jesse Owens riled Hitler at the Olympics in Berlin by winning four gold medals from the highly publicized Nazi athletes there. Yet, in 1939, black contralto Marion Anderson, was barred from appearing in Constitution Hall by the Daughters of the American Revolution, instead to be welcomed by Eleanor Roosevelt and 75,000 citizens at the Lincoln Memorial. In 1938 the Committee for Industrial Organization changed its name to the Congress of Industrial Organizations and became an opponent of the American Federation of Labor.

So the Thirties, a decade that began in economic strife, conquered some of it through legislation, hope, and hard work, although by 1939 the unemployed still numbered ten million. With the spark of hope kindled, the U.S. and other non-European nations understandably did not want to see the impending flow of war that was to involve all major nations of the planet.

Curriculum Thought and Literature

The contributions of the Twenties to curriculum thought were not easy acts to follow. The social behaviorist line of thought was staked out by Bobbitt, Charters, Snedden, and others. Dewey, the McMurry brothers, Counts, Rugg, and others carved the experientialist school. Intellectual traditionalists continued, with remnants of faculty psychology and classical heritage, to dominate practice. What is more, curriculum thought of the Twenties was capped with a monumental attempt by curriculum scholars from many persuasions to produce a unified statement, i.e., Part II of the Twenty-sixth Yearbook of the National Society for the Study of Education. It is interesting to note that a central concern of the authors of that year-

66

book was curriculum development for schooling in contrast with that of other educative forces.

It should also be re-emphasized that curriculum thought of the Twenties, and subsequently of the Thirties, was markedly influenced by three publications that were not overtly curricular but had numerous curricular implications. The first was a 1918 reprint of an article by W.H. Kilpatrick, from Teachers College Record, entitled The Project Method. It had great impact on certain lines of experientialist thinking evidenced by titles bearing the term project in the Twenties. The next two appeared in 1926: H.C. Morrison's The Practice of Teaching in the Secondary School and Kilpatrick's Foundations of Method[1] The influence of these works is much alive in the curriculum books of the Thirties.

The Thirties provide a body of literature that joined method and teaching with curriculum. Some titles in 1930 began to utilize the term program in lieu of curriculum, e.g., Caswell (1930) and Harrington (1930). More books dealt with curriculum in reference to particular states or cities. The emphasis on both program and increased specification bypassed unresolved questions about assumptions that were illustrated by Hopkins (1929) and the Twenty-sixth Yearbook (1927). More emphasis was placed on the procedural as epitomized by Harap (1928). Other illustrations include Broady, et al. (1931), Lide (1933), North Carolina (1934), Woody (1934), Draper (1936), Stigler (1936), Shearer (1937).

Treatments of assumptions behind procedures were, however, not absent from the literature. McCall (1930) reviewed conceptual bases in curriculum literature from 1900 to 1930. F.G. Bonser (1932) described curriculum that fostered education based on a conception of life needs. Milligan (1937) probed the relation of professed philosophy to curricular content and proposed learning activities. Patty (1938) took an extended look at the mechanics of educational advocacy in theory and practice, a study that posed particular implications for curriculum even though it treated the topic of mechanism in relation to education generally. Purposes were also addressed as being prior to procedures in a 1938 statement of the Educational Policies Commission entitled The Purpose of Education in a Democracy. Although not a statement that probed democracy in relation to education in great depth, it represented at least three salient developments in curriculum writing. First, it at least covertly recognized the accumulating impact of experientialist thought, particularly of Dewey's Democracy and Education (1916) on curriculum thought. Second, it represented a growing tendency to consider purposes as being contingent on socio-political values. Third, it represented an attempt to integrate disparate lines of educational thought. In this manner it was reminiscent of the 1918 statement of the Commission of the Reorganization of Secondary Education and that of the National Society for the Study of Education Twenty-sixth Yearbook Committee.

Integration took on another quite different meaning, as well, in curriculum thought of the Thirties. A propensity to de-compartmentalize curriculum thinking and to view heretofore separate categories as interrelated wholes evolved in the literature in a variety of ways. The notion of integration stemmed from the work of Dewey and other experientialist educators. One interpretation emphasized statements about the need to relate one subject to another. It is interesting to note that Dewey's theme of integrating dualisms and his expressed desire to integrate school life with non-school experience was often interpreted as an admonition to join subjects together. This is illustrated by Tuttle (1935), the National Council of the Teachers of English (1936), Connole (1937), Oberholtzer (1937), and Weeks (1938).

Jones (1939) advocated the notion of correlation as a means to integration, while promoting unit construction as a mechanism for actualizing the process. The unit, very familiar today, is a not too distant relative of Kilpatrick's project

68

method, but it frequently appealed to traditional teachers and to those who desired the appearance of systematization associated with science and technology. Now, often regimented and distant from its Deweyan origins, the unit appeals more to the social behaviorist and intellectual traditionalist than to the more spontaneity-oriented experientialist. This interpretation of units has great kinship with a regimented, statisticized, positivist notion of science espoused by educational researchers who ironically justify their work by appeal to the free-flowing, situation-oriented, instrumentalist, and practical problem-solving advocated by Dewey in his The Sources of a Science of Education.[2]

The curriculum work of the Thirties that provides the most accurate interpretation of integration related to the ideas of Dewey was produced by Hopkins (1937) and stands toward the opposite end of the continuum from a hobbled joining or correlation of subject areas, perhaps under the rubric of unit construction. That there is no better source of interpretation of a line of thought than its creator cannot be denied. To wit, Dewey must have been offended at some of the trends that attempted to emulate his thought. In Experience and Education (1938) he attempted to clarify misinterpretation of his thought. After concentrating his efforts primarily in philosophy for over twenty years since the production of his magnum opus, Democracy and Education (1916), Dewey returned to educational writing in an effort to clarify his orientation. Since he accepted education as a kind of testing ground for philosophy, he clearly had not lost touch with educational endeavors through philosophic pursuits in the intervening years. Instead, he had strengthened his position. Many considered Experience and Education (1938) to be Dewey's most concise statement of his educational thought. In it he captured the essence of his response to the raging altercations of both traditional educators and zealous but sometimes superficial interpreters of his position in the following passage:

69

> It is the business of intelligent
> theory of education to ascertain
> the causes for the conflicts that
> exist and then, instead of taking
> one side or the other, to indicate
> a plan of operations proceeding from
> a level deeper and more inclusive
> than is represented by the practices
> and ideas of the contending parties.
> (p. 5)

In this book he proceeded to spell out the tenets of such a theory, carefully restating central threads from <u>Democracy and Education</u>. The reader should note the revelance of arguments advanced in <u>Experience and Education</u> on conflagrations between progressive and traditional education of the Thirties to similar debates that occurred later, e.g., open vs. traditional education in the late 1960's and humanistic vs. "back to basics" orientations of the 1970's.

Thus, concerns varied markedly from the philosophical to the procedural, interpretative, and action-oriented. This variety, coupled with such influences as Morrison's emphasis on teaching and Kilpatrick's emphasis on method, contributed to the growing parameters of that which was accepted as curricular. Thus, the purview of curriculum literature embraced additional categories: teaching, instruction, methods, guidance, materials, administration, organization, and extra-curricular activities. Examples included: Phillips (1931) on methods; Stratemeyer (1931) on materials; Brewer (1932) on guidance; Trillingham (1934) on organization and administration; Jones (1935) on extra-curricular activities; Staley (1935) on sports; Wynne (1937) on teachers; Hopkins (1938) on pupils and teachers; McKowan (1938) on extra-curricular activities; University of Michigan (1938) on pupils; Melvin (1939) on teachers and curriculum committees; and Stretch (1939) on the child. As the areas of inclusion in the curriculum literature were augmented, the pervasive nature of curriculum inquiry was clarified but the definition of curriculum as an area of study was clouded. Sometimes it seemed that curriculum study could not be extricated from conflation with educational studies in general. This matter of definition is far from resolved today.

Categorization of curriculum literature according to level of schooling continued from the previous decade and was extended to greater inclusiveness in the Thirties. Elementary schools continued to be treated separately by some authors, e.g., Caswell (1930), Northern Ireland (1931), Phillips (1931), Stevens (1931), Caswell (1932), Woody (1934). Secondary curriculum continued as a special focus of attention: examples include Lull (1932), Weersing and Ricciardi (1932), The North Central Association (1933), The Society for Curriculum Study (1938), and Prosser (1939). The junior high emphasis kindled in the previous decade was continued by Harrington (1930). Curriculum construction at the college and junior college levels began to be given attention in the 1930's. Prominent illustrations were: A conference at Rollins College chaired by John Dewey (1931), Deyoe (1934), Headmasters' Conference (1935), Rugg, et al. (1935) on teacher education, Heaton and Koopman (1936), Colvert (1937), Minnesota (1937), Colvert (1939). Another interesting category of schooling given considerable emphasis during the 1930's was small schools. Noteworthy sources in this area are: Caswell (1930), Broady, et al. (1931), Caswell (1932), National Education Association (1933), and Broady (1936).

A sizable number of curriculum books focused on curriculum development in particular locales. In a sense these might be forerunners of current case study approaches. Examples include: Houston (1930), South Dakota (1930), Rollins College (1931), Jacob (1932), National College of Education (1932), Newlon, Bruner, et al. (1932), Wright (1932), Adams (1934), Sanguinet (1934), North Carolina (1935), Heaton and Koopman (1936), Pennsylvania (1936), Henderson (1937), Glencoe (1938), and of special note is Spears (1937) who drew upon administrative experiences in curriculum development to delineate strategies for curriculum building.

Miscellaneous areas of emphasis appeared in curriculum literature in this decade and should be noted due to the fact that some later became more widespread. Ricciardi (1930) described a conference method for curriculum construction. In the same year the common school was emphasized by Reisner (1930). Noting the governance of curriculum materials, Stratemeyer (1931) advocated their study for effective use. Similarly, Andrus (1936) emphasized the study of curriculum guides. McKowan (1938), Jones (1935), and Staley (1935) argued in favor of curricular roles for extra-curricular activities. Broady, et al. (1931), The National Education Association (1934), and Broady (1936) focused on the need for enrichment provisions in the curriculum. The National Society for the Study of Education (1937) stressed international cooperation as a worthy end for curriculum. Marshall and Goetz (1936) treated curriculum-making relative to one subject area--social studies. The topic of curriculum laboratories was elaborated by Leary (1938) in a series of bulletins that extended from 1934 to 1938.

The increased numbers of approaches to curriculum thought and practice being reported reflected a desire to discover more wide-spread information. To this end special studies and surveys were instituted to make curriculum knowledge more readily available. Examples that focused on schools include: Caswell (1930), Conference on Curriculum-making and Revision (1931), Langvick (1931), Caswell (1932), Newlon, Bruner, et al. (1932), The California Elementary School Principal's Association (1937), Milligan (1937), and Shearer (1937).

Adding to the repertoire of emerging inclusions in the literature were: Leary (1938) on curriculum laboratories; The Thirty-third Yearbook of the National Society for the Study of Education on the activity movement (1934); and the 1935 University of Michigan surveys of curriculum relative to innovative practices, social trends, and state and

national trends. Surveys of curricular research
and thought are exemplified by: McCall (1930),
special issues of the Review of Educational
Research (1931 and 1934), Trillingham (1934), the
Caswell and Campbell (1937) collection of readings
on curriculum. The latter was the first of a kind
that many would later emulate in the long saga of
books that came to be known, both praisefully and
pejoratively depending on quality, as books of
curriculum readings.

In the midst of this multitude of new dimensions in curriculum literature, a bit more should
be said about the three schools of curriculum
thought discussed in earlier chapters. Although
a revision of Charter's Curriculum Construction
appeared in 1938, the social behaviorist line
diminished in overt amount of publications, at
least temporarily. It might be more accurate to
say that it became more fully integrated into the
fabric of the intellectual traditionalist line
that dominated practice; thus, its proponents no
longer needed to draw separate attention to themselves.

The experientialists, however, produced a
plethora of literature during the Thirties, and
much of it was quite different from Herbartian
and Deweyan origins. Those who wrote about the
activity curriculum promoted it in the name of
Progressivism as had many of those who promoted
correlated curricula, projects, and units. That
which fell in the category of activity curriculum
usually had something to do with Dewey's notion of
learning by doing, perhaps in a substantive way
or perhaps nominally only. Illustrative of the
range of interpretations are: Clement (1931),
Stevens (1931), Hissong (1932), Adams (1934),
National Society for the Study of Education
(1934), Sanguinet (1934), Melvin (1936), Mossman
(1938), and of course Dewey's Experience and Education (1938), discussed earlier. A similarly
careful, earlier, attempt by Dewey to clarify his
position was entitled The Way Out of Educational
Confusion (1931), but it received considerably

less attention. In 1932, G.S. Counts extrapolated
the Deweyan idea of reconstruction to ask his famed
question that served as his book title: Dare the
Schools Build a New Social Order? This paved the
way to a new, more radical interpretation of
experientialist curricular purpose, i.e., a stance
that became known as a social reconstructionist
position. It should be stressed, however, that it
is no mean task to mass educate vast numbers of
curriculum practitioners in a perspective as complex as Dewey's. Schwab, [3] for example, in 1959
wrote persuasively about the difficulty of being a
progressive teacher, not to mention educating
progressive teachers and curriculum developers.
The Thirty-third Yearbook of the National Society
for the Study of Education, Part II (1934) includes
pieces that are quite admirable attempts to explicate extensions of Deweyan philosophy.

The Caswell and Campbell text (1935) represents another, quite comprehensive, tendency toward
Deweyan perspectives; more, however, will be said
about it later. Kilpatrick (1936) produced a small
book advocating a remaking of curriculum in his
interpretation of Deweyan pedagogy. Kilpatrick's
interpretation of Dewey had great impact on many
who read his work and listened to him speak, but it
was also an interpretation that many criticize for
oversimplification and missing the mark. Others who
attempted to translate Deweyan philosophy of education into advice for experientialist curriculum
developers and teachers include: American Life and
the School Curriculum (1936) by Rugg, Axtelle, Caswell, and Counts; Hopkins' (1937) explanation of
the meaning and application of integration; the
Thirty-eighth Yearbook of the National Society for
the Study of Education (1939) which was devoted to
investigating relationships between child development and curriculum stemming from Herbartian roots;
and the Third Yearbook of the John Dewey Society
(1939), a publication that addressed the relationship between curriculum and democracy.

Having great impact as a statement of guiding
purposes was an Educational Policies Commission

74

(1938) publication which listed 43 objectives that the well-educated person in American democratic society should strive toward. These are categorized under four headings: self-realization, human relationships, economic efficiency, and civic responsibility. Emulation of Dewey's Democracy and Education (1916), running the gamut in terms of both topics and sophistication, is quite clearly evidenced in the above works. One can scarcely fault Dewey for perceiving a need to offer his well-meaning and often creatively perceptive followers Experience and Education in 1938. Yet, study of both contemporary and subsequent developments in curriculum thought and action reveals a state of affairs that falls far short of bringing, in Dewey's words, "the way out of educational confusion," the title of his 1931 book. This is not intended as a disparaging commentary on the field; rather, it is simply evidence that pointing the way, though difficult in itself, is often less difficult than actualizing it.

All this writing was quite serious, perhaps as it should be, but levity and satire can influence at times when serious argumentation falls short. It was Harold Benjamin under the pseudonym of J. Abner Peddiwell, who, in The Saber-Tooth Curriculum (1939), contributed markedly to the experientialist desire to rid the curriculum of the intellectual traditionalist propensity to emphasize once instrumental skills and concepts that have atrophied beyond the point of utility. Posing as a researcher of prehistoric curricula, he lectured on the continuance of such curricular inclusions as "saber-tooth tiger chasing with fire" and "fish grabbing with the bare hands," long after glaciers had frozen both fish and streams and had chased the tigers southward, because major prehistoric curricularists deemed them inherently beneficial to the fully educated caveman.

The influx of new topics in the curriculum domain coupled with the barage of experientialist literature contributed to an interesting new phenomenon in curriculum literature of the Thirties;

75

namely, the propensity of authors to emphasize the trends, modernity, revision, and rapid pace of curriculum thought and activity. Titles well portray an underlying assumption that curriculum was advancing with tremendous rapidity. One got the distinct impression that if he/she did not read voraciously, he/she would soon be stifled amid the dust of curricular progress. Example titles include: The Evolution of the Common School (1930) by Reisner; The Case for Curriculum Revision (1932) by Browne; The Selection and Organization of Personnel for Curriculum Revision (1932) by Flavius; High School Curriculum Reorganization (1933) by the North Central Association; three reports on innovations and trends by the University of Michigan (1935); Curriculum Trends (1935) by Zirbes; The Changing Curriculum (1937) by Harap; The Curriculum and Cultural Change (1937) by Harris; The Changing Curriculum (1937) by the National Education Association and The Society for Curriculum Study; Procedures in Curriculum Revision Programs of Selected States (1937) by Shearer; and A Challenge to Secondary Education: Plans for the Reconstruction of the American High School (1938) by the Society for Curriculum Study.

Finally, a new form of curriculum book emerged during the Thirties. It was, in no small measure, a response to proliferation of trends and the emphasis on the need to keep up with modernity. It must have been felt that a mechanism needed to be developed that could embrace all of the evolving components of the curriculum mosaic at once--the trends; the survey results; the array of experientialist literature; the descriptions of happenings in specific locales, the emphases on integration in its various modes; the inclusion of administration, instruction, organization, evaluation, methods, teaching, materials, guidance, pupils, etc., in the curriculum domain; and the miscellany of sub-topics of curricular concern. All of these needed to be communicated to anyone who wanted to know about the field of curriculum and to participate effectively in it. The response to this felt need was the creation of books that served as great compendia,

encyclopedic portrayals of the ever-increasing
stockpile of curricular knowledge. A major function of such books was to introduce new members
to the curriculum field. Monumental examples were
Foundations of Curriculum Building (1936) by Norton
and Norton, and Curriculum Development (1935) by
Caswell and Campbell. In their 1935 text, Caswell
and Campbell treated the following as major topics:
the school in contemporary life; the social
responsibility of the school; influences on
curriculum; principles for curriculum development;
curricular aims and scope; pupil purposes; activities to develop purposes; subject matter selection;
grade placement and time allotment; teaching procedures; evaluation; organization; instruction;
units; courses of study; administration. This was
all supplemented by a vast list of references for
further study. Two years later the text was further
supplemented by Readings in Curriculum Development
(1937) which provided convenient exposure to articles considered central to a variety of curriculum
concerns. It should be noted that the use of
curriculum development became highly prominent
during the next two decades, almost becoming
synonymous with curriculum study at large.

As the reader will discover, books that followed and dominated the field for the next three
decades took on the encyclopedic character exemplified by these works. They were the major kinds
of writings that socialized curriculum decision-
makers (be they professors, administrators, consultants, or teachers) to the work that they pursued.
In subsequent chapters these books are referred to
as synoptic texts.

Notes

[1]These three works are cited in the bibliographical sections of chapters for the decade in which
they were published.

[2]See John Dewey, Sources of a Science of Education. New York: Liveright Publishing Company, 1929.

[3]Schwab, J.J. The Impossible Role of the Teacher in Progressive Education. _School Review_, Summer, 1959, _67_, 139-160.

Bibliography of Curriculum Books,
1930-1939

1930

Caswell, H.L. Program making in small elemen-
    tary schools. Nashville: George Peabody
    College, 1930.

Garretson, O.K. Relationship between expressed
    preferences and curricular abilities of
    ninth grade boys. New York: Columbia
    University, Teachers College, 1930 (Re-
    printed by AMS).

Harrington, H.L. Program making for junior
    high schools. New York: The Macmillan
    Company, 1930.

Houston, Texas, Independent School District.
    Curriculum revision and development in
    Houston, Texas, 1924-1930, Part II.
    Houston: Board of Education, 1930.

McCall, W.M. A critical review of various
    conceptions underlying curriculum-making
    since 1900. Columbia, Missouri: Uni-
    versity of Missouri, 1930.

Reisner, E.H. The evolution of the common
    school. New York: Macmillan, 1930.

Ricciardi, N. The application of the conference
    method to curriculum making. Bulletin
    Number G-5. Sacramento, California:
    California Department of Education, 1930.

South Dakota. Preliminary reports of ap-
    proaches to and theories regarding
    curriculum construction, general aims
    and guiding principles of education for
    the state of South Dakota. Bulletin
    Number 1. Pierre, South Dakota: State
    Department of Education, 1930.

1931

American Educational Research Association.
The curriculum. Review of Educational
Research. Washington, D.C.: American
Educational Research Association, January,
1931.

Broady, K.O., Platt, E.T., and Bell, M.D.
Practical procedures for enriching the
curriculum of small schools. University
of Nebraska Publication Number 84. Educational Monographs Number 2. Lincoln,
Nebraska, 1931.

Clement, J.A. Progressive trends in the external organization and in the curriculum
content of our schools. Urbana: Univer-
of Illinois Bulletin Number 54, February
24, 1931.

Conference on Curriculum-making and Revision.
Curriculum-making in current practice.
Evanston, Illinois: Northwestern Univer-
sity, October 30-31, 1931.

Dewey, J. The way out of educational confu-
sion. Cambridge: Harvard University
Press, 1931 (Also printed by Greenwood
Press, New York, 1970).

Langvick, M.M. Current practices in the con-
struction of state courses of study.
Washington: U.S. Government Printing
Office, 1931.

Northern Ireland. Committee of Inquiry on the
program of instruction in public elementary schools. Belfast: Her Majesty's
Stationery Office, 1931.

Phillips, C.A. Modern methods and the elementary curriculum (Revised Edition). New
York: Century, 1931.

Rollins College, Winter Park, Florida. The
    curriculum for the liberal arts college,
    being the report of the curriculum con-
    ference held at Rollins College, January
    19-24, 1931, (John Dewey, Chairman,
    together with the reports of Rollins
    College committees on curriculum). Win-
    ter Park, Florida: Rollins College,
    1931.

Scottish Council for Research in Education.
    Curriculum for pupils of twelve to fif-
    teen years (Advanced Division). London:
    University of London Press, 1931.

Stevens, M.P. The activities curriculum in
    the primary grades. Boston: D.C. Heath,
    1931.

Stratemeyer, F.B. The effective use of curric-
    ulum materials. New York: Teachers Col-
    lege, Columbia University, 1931 (Reprint-
    ed in 1972 by AMS, New York).

1932

Bonser, F.G. Life needs and education. New
    York: Bureau of Publications, Teachers
    College, Columbia University, 1932.

Brewer, J.M. Education as guidance; an exa-
    mination of the possibilities of a curric-
    ulum in terms of life activities, in
    elementary and secondary school and col-
    lege. New York: Macmillan, 1932.

Browne, G.S. The case for curriculum revision.
    Melbourne University Press, 1932.

Caswell, H.L. Program making in small elemen-
    tary schools. Field Studies Number 1
    (Revised Edition), Division of Surveys
    and Field Studies. Nashville, Tennessee:
    George Peabody College for Teachers,
    1932.

Counts, G.S. Dare the school build a new social order? New York: John Day, 1932 (Reprinted by Arno Press, 1969).

Flavius, L.D. The selection and organization of personnel for curriculum revision. Cleveland: Western Reserve University, 1932.

Hissong, C. The activity movement. Baltimore: Warick & York, 1932.

Jacob, T.N. The reconstruction of the curriculum of the elementary schools of India. Calcutta: Association Press, Y.M.C.A., 1932.

Lide, E.S. Procedures in curriculum making. National Survey of Secondary Education, Bulletin Number 17, Monograph Number 18. Washington, D.C.: Government Printing Office, 1932.

Lull, H.G. Secondary education: Organization and program. New York: W.W. Norton, 1932.

National College of Education. Children's School Staff. Curriculum records of the Children's School, National College of Education. Evanston, Illinois: Bureau of Publications, National College of Education, 1932.

Newlon, J.H., Bruner, H.B.,et al. The curricula of the schools. Report of the Survey of the Schools of Chicago, Illinois, Volume III. New York: Bureau of Publications, Teachers College, Columbia University, 1932.

Weersing, F.J. and Ricciardi, N. Curriculum making in secondary schools. Syllabus for course in Education 254B, University of Southern California, Los Angeles, 1932.

82

Wright, L.E. Units of work. A first grade at work; a non-reading curriculum. New York: Bureau of Publications, Teachers College, Columbia University, for Lincoln School of Teachers College, 1932.

1933

Lide, E.S. Procedures in curriculum-making. Washington: U.S. Government Printing Office, 1933.

National Education Association of the United States. Department of Rural Education. Organization of curriculum for one-teacher schools. Washington: National Education Association, 1933.

North Central Association of College and Secondary Schools. High school curriculum reorganization. The North Central Association of Colleges and Secondary Schools, Ann Arbor, Michigan, 1933.

1934

Adams, F. The initiation of an activity program into a public school. Contributions to Education Number 598. New York: Bureau of Publications, Teachers College, Columbia University, 1934.

American Educational Research Association. Review of educational research, the curriculum. Washington, D.C.: National Education Association, April, 1934.

Deyoe, G.P. Certain trends in curriculum practices and policies in state and normal schools and teachers colleges. New York: Teachers College, Columbia University, 1934.

National Education Association of the United States. Department of Rural Education.

83

Economical enrichment of the small
secondary-school curriculum. Washington,
D.C.: Department of Rural Education,
National Education Association, 1934.

National Society for the Study of Education.
The activity movement. Thirty-third
Yearbook, Part II (Lois C. Mossman, Chair-
man). Bloomington, Illinois: Public
School Publishing Company, 1934.

North Carolina. Suggested procedures for
curriculum construction and course of
study building, 1934-1935. Publication
Number 179. Raleigh, North Carolina:
State Superintendent of Public Instruction, 1934.

Sanguinet, E.H. An approach to curriculum
construction based on a child activity
survey in the Philippine Islands. Manila,
Philippine Islands: Philippine Teacher's
Digest, 1934.

Stanford Education Conference. Curriculum and
instruction. Stanford, California, 1934.

Stewart, H.H. Comparative study of the concentration and regular plans of organization in the senior high school. New
York: Columbia University, Teachers
College, 1934 (Reprinted by AMS).

Trillingham, C.C. The organization and administration of curriculum programs. Los
Angeles: University of Southern California Press, 1934.

Woody, C. Syllabus for the construction of
the elementary school curriculum. Ann
Arbor: Brumfield & Brumfield, 1934.

1935

Caswell, H.L. and Campbell, D.S. Curriculum

development. New York: American Book
Company, 1935 (Reprint by R. West 1978).

Jones, G. Extra curricular activities in
relation to the curriculum. New York:
Teachers College, Columbia University,
1935 (AMS reprint available).

Michigan, University of. Innovative practices
in the curriculum. Ann Arbor: School of
Education, 1935 a.

Michigan, University of. Social trends and
curriculum revision. Ann Arbor: School
of Education, 1935b.

Michigan, University of. State and national
trends in education. Ann Arbor: School
of Education, 1935c.

New York (State) University. Secondary school
curriculum reorganization. Suggestions
relative to sequences. Albany: The University of the State of New York Press,
1935.

North Carolina Department of Public Instruction.
A study in curriculum problems of the North
Carolina public schools. Suggestions and
practices, 1935. Raleigh, North Carolina:
State Superintendent of Public Instruction,
1935.

Rugg, E.U., Peik, W.E., Foster, F.K., John,
W.C., and Raup, B.R. Teacher education
curricula. U.S. Department of the Inter-
ior, Harold L. Ickes, Secretary. Office
of Education, George F. Zook, Commissioner.
Washington: U.S. Government Printing
Office, 1935.

Staley, S.C. The curriculum in sports.
Philadelphia: W.B. Saunders, 1935 (Also
by Stipes Publishing Company, Champaign,
Illinois, 1940).

Standing Joint Committee of the Headmasters'
    Conference and Incorporated Association
    of Preparatory Schools. Curriculum for
    the preparatory schools; being the report
    of the Standing Joint Committee of the
    Headmasters' Conference and Incorporated
    Association of Preparatory Schools. Win-
    chester: Warren & Sons, Ltd., 1935.

Tuttle, F.P. Correlated curriculum activities.
    Mankato, Minnesota: Creative Educational
    Society, 1935.

Zirbes, L. Curriculum trends: A preliminary
    report and challenge. Washington: Asso-
    ciation for Childhood Education, 1935.

1936

Andrus, R., et al. Curriculum guides for
    teachers of children from two to six
    years of age. New York: Reynal and
    Hitchcock (A John Day Book), 1936.

Broady, K.O. Enriched curriculum for small
    schools. Lincoln: University of
    Nebraska, 1936.

Bruner, H.B. A tentative list of approaches
    to curriculum and course of study con-
    struction with selected bibliographies.
    New York: Teachers College, Columbia
    University, 1936.

Draper, E.M. Principles and techniques of
    curriculum making. New York: D. Apple-
    ton-Century, 1936.

Heaton, K.L. and Koopman, G.R. A college
    curriculum based on functional needs of
    students; an experiment with the general
    curriculum at Central State Teachers
    College, Mount Pleasant, Michigan.
    Chicago: The University of Chicago
    Press, 1936.

Kilpatrick, W.H. Remaking the curriculum. New York: Newson and Company, 1936.

Marshall, L.C. and Goetz, R.M. Curriculum-making in the social studies. New York: Charles Scribner's Sons, 1936.

Melvin, A.G. The activity program. New York: Reynal and Hitchcock, 1936.

National Council of the Teachers of English. A correlated curriculum. New York: D. Appleton-Century, 1936.

Norton, J.K. and Norton, M.A. Foundations of curriculum building. Boston: Ginn and Company, 1936.

Pennsylvania Department of Public Instruction. Suggestions for the development and use of curriculum materials in the elementary school. Harrisburg: Pennsylvania Department of Public Instruction, 1936.

Rugg, H.O., Axtelle, G., Caswell, H., and Counts, G. American life and the school curriculum: Next steps toward schools of living. New York: Ginn and Company, 1936.

Stigler, W.A. Handbook for curriculum development. Austin: Texas State Department of Education, 1936.

1937

California Elementary School Principals' Association. Current curricular practices in elementary education. Los Angeles, California: Elementary School Principals' Association, 1937.

Caswell, H.L. and Campbell, D.S. (Editors). Readings in curriculum development. New York: American Book Company, 1937.

Colvert, C.C. A critical analysis of the
    public junior college curriculum. Nash-
    ville, Tennessee: George Peabody College
    for Teachers, 1937.

Connole, R.J. A study of the concept of integra-
    tion in present day curriculum thinking.
    Washington: Catholic University of
    America, 1937.

Harap, H. (Editor). The changing curriculum.
    New York: D. Appleton-Century, 1937.

Harris, P.E. The curriculum and cultural change.
    New York: D. Appleton-Century, 1937.

Henderson, H.R. A curriculum study in a moun-
    tain district. New York: Teachers Col-
    lege, Columbia University, 1937.

Hoban, C.F., et al. Visualizing the curriculum.
    New York: Cordon, 1937 (Also reprint by
    R. West).

Hopkins, L.T. Integration, its meaning and
    application. New York: D. Appleton-
    Century, 1937.

Joint Committee on Curriculum of the Department
    of Supervisors and Directors of Instruc-
    tion of the National Education Association
    and the Society for Curriculum Study. The
    changing curriculum. New York: D. Apple-
    ton-Century, 1937.

Milligan, N.G. Relationship of the professed
    philosophy to the suggested educational
    experiences; a study in current elemen-
    tary school curriculum making. New York:
    Teachers College, Columbia University, 1937
    (Reprinted in 1972 by AMS, New York).

Minnesota--University Committee on Educational
    Research. The effective general college
    curriculum as revealed by examinations.
    Minneapolis: University of Minnesota
    Press, 1937.

National Society for the Study of Education.
_International understanding through public
school curriculum_ (I.L. Kandel and G.W.
Whipple, Editors), Thirty-sixth Yearbook.
Bloomington, Illinois: Public School
Publishing Company, 1937.

Oberholtzer, E.E. _Integrated curriculum in
practice. Contributions to Education
Number 694._ New York: Teachers College,
Columbia University, 1937 (AMS Reprint
Available).

Shearer, A.E. _Procedures in curriculum revision
programs of selected states._ Nashville,
Tennessee: George Peabody College for
Teachers, 1937.

Spears, H. _Experiences in building a curricu-
lum._ New York: Macmillan, 1937.

Wynne, J.P. _The teacher and the curriculum._
New York: Prentice-Hall, 1937.

1938

Charters, W.W. _Curriculum construction_ (Revised
Edition). New York: Macmillan, 1938.

Dewey, J. _Experience and education._ New York:
Macmillan, 1938.

Educational Policies Commission. _The purposes of
education in American democracy._ Washington, D.C.: The Educational Policies Commission of the NEA and the AASA, 1938.

Glencoe Public Schools. _A guide for curriculum
planning._ Glencoe, Illinois: Board of
Education, 1938.

Hopkins, L.T. _Pupil-teacher learning._ Wilming-
ton, Delaware: The Delaware Citizens
Association, 1938.

Leary, B.E. Curriculum laboratories and divi-
sions: Their organization and functions
in state departments of education, city
school systems, and institutions of higher
education. Surveys of courses of study and
other curriculum materials--A series (1934-
1938) of bulletins. Washington: Office of
Education, 1938.

McKowan, H.C. Extra-curricular activities. New
York: Macmillan, 1938.

Michigan, University of. Pupil development and
the curriculum. Ann Arbor: School of
Education, 1938.

Mossman, L.C. The activity concept. New York:
Macmillan, 1938.

Patty, W.L. A study of mechanism in education.
New York: Bureau of Publications,
Teachers College, Columbia University,
1938 (Reprint 1972, AMS, New York).

Society for Curriculum Study. A challenge to
secondary education: Plans for the reconstruction of the American high school
(Samuel Everett, Editor). New York: D.
Appleton-Century, 1938.

Weeks, R.M. A correlated curriculum. Report of
the National Council of Teachers of English.
New York: Appleton-Century-Crofts, 1938.

1939

Benjamin, H. (Peddiwell, J.A.). The saber-
tooth curriculum. New York: McGraw-Hill,
1939 (Also 1959 reprint).

Colvert, C.C. The public junior college
curriculum; an analysis. Louisiana:
Louisiana State University Press, 1939.

Department of Elementary School Principals. Enriching curriculum for the elementary school child. Eighteenth Yearbook. Washington: National Educational Association, 1939.

Dix, L. A charter for progressive education. New York: Teachers College, Columbia University, 1939.

John Dewey Society. Democracy and the curriculum. Third Yearbook. New York: D. Appleton-Century, 1939.

Jones, A.J. Principles of unit construction. New York: McGraw-Hill, 1939.

Melvin, A.G. Activated curriculum: A method and a model for class teachers and curriculum committees. New York: John Day Company, 1939.

National Society for the Study of Education. Child development and the curriculum (Guy Whipple, Editor). Thirty-Eighth Yearbook, Part I. Chicago: University of Chicago Press, 1939.

Prosser, C.A. Secondary education and life. Cambridge: Harvard University Press, 1939.

Rugg, H.O. (Editor). Democracy and the curriculum: The life and program of the American school. New York: D. Appleton-Century 1939.

Stretch, L.B. The curriculum and the child. Minneapolis, Minnesota: Educational Publishers, 1939.

CHAPTER V

CURRICULUM LITERATURE AND CONTEXT:

1940-1949

Contextual Reminders

The horrors of war continued to ravage Europe led by the continued expansion of German forces including the bombing of Britain and the Russian invasions of Finland and Rumania. The impending gloom of disaster, atrocity, and fearful anticipation swept forbodingly across the Atlantic to America. By 1941, German and Italian forces who controlled most of Europe were joined by the Japanese who launched a surprise bombing attack on the United States base at Pearl Harbor in Hawaii. Almost immediately, the United States declared war on Japan and on its allies, Germany and Italy. In 1942 German and Italian expansion continued in Africa and Europe and met heavy setbacks in a Russian trap while attempting to seize Stalingrad. Japan continued expansion in the Pacific by capturing the Philippines and Hong Kong. United States forces entered North Africa, repeatedly bombed Germany and occupied-France, and blocked Japanese offensives at Guadalcanal, Midway, and the Coral Sea. In 1943, the tide of Axis expansion was quelled. Allied troops brought Italian surrender, Axis defeat in North Africa, and Nazi surrender to Russians in Stalingrad. Tito of Yugoslavia initiated an offensive against a weakened Germany. British and United States landings in Normandy brought D-Day in 1944. DeGaulle set up a provincial government in Paris. Russia entered Bulgaria, Rumania, and Hungary. The squeeze on Germany caused retaliation with rocket attacks on Britain and other counter attacks, but Nazi power was broken, resulting in Victory in Europe Day (May 8, 1945) as proclaimed by President Harry S. Truman, recently inaugurated following the death of Franklin D. Roosevelt. In

93

Italy, Mussolini was executed, and in Germany, Hitler was reputed to have committed suicide. In the same year, Churchill, Atlee, Truman, and Stalin met at Potsdam to determine Germany's future. Property demarcations were established.

Meanwhile, the war in the Pacific was finalized by a United States victory at Okinawa and the controversial nuclear bombing of Nagasaki and Hiroshima. Victory in Japan Day was established on August 14, 1945. In the same year the United Nations was formally created, and New York City became its permanent residence in 1946 on a site donated by John D. Rockefeller. That year also saw decisions by the Nuremburg Tribunal that passed death sentences on twelve Nazi leaders for genocide and other war crimes, and decisions by Albania, Czechoslovakia, Bulgaria, and Yugoslovia to adopt communist governments. General Douglas MacArthur administered the rehabilitation of a vanquished Japan.

The world at war both inhibited and stimulated artistic and scientific contributions, but it seems safe to say that neither scientist, artist, nor technologist was immune to the impact of the war, its tragedy, horror, and inkling of glory. In literature Hemingway's For Whom the Bell Tolls, Graham Greene's The Power and the Glory, and even Chaplin's film The Great Dictator, all appearing in 1940, reflected the warning of the times. Desire to escape is understandably prevalent in such times, and opportunity to do so was provided through the music of Stravinsky, Britten, Bartok, and Shostakovich as well as the perennially popular film Fantasia by Disney, and the peaceful New England landscapes of Grandma Moses. Painter Paul Nash, depicted the war in Bombers Over Britain in 1941, the same year that Russian Ilya Ehrenburg wrote about The Fall of Paris. The power and portent of rugged individualism were brought to question in Fitzgerald's The Last Tycoon and in film by Orson Welles' Citizen Kane, both in 1941. The Forties saw a continuation of paintings by John Piper, Stuart Davis, Marc Chagall, and Graham Sutherland, and sculpture by Henry Moore. Frank Lloyd Wright's

94

design of the Guggenheim Museum in New York was
another indication of his architectural genius.

The literary scene, as in the Thirties, provided readers and audiences with works by Noel
Coward, T.S. Eliot, and C.S. Lewis. Amid the
disillusionment and alienation that accompanies
war, there evolved a kind of literature that portrayed the lack of purpose in the slice of life
accorded to ordinary living. Portrayals ranged
widely from the existentialism of Camus in The
Stranger in 1942 to operatic depiction of inherent
injustices in Britten's Peter Grimes in 1945; and
from Somerset Maugham's interpretation of the
inner and outer portions of human conflict in The
Razor's Edge to Tennessee Williams' picture of
accumulated inwardness and retreat in The Glass
Menagerie, both in 1944. Each of these art works,
in its special uniqueness, conveyed that the
plights of human existence on this planet seemed
to greatly outweigh the delights. Similarly, the
injustice of misplaced concentrations of political
power was made vivid by Robert Penn Warren's
based-on-fact novel of 1946, All the King's Men.
A more direct, yet satirical, warning of unre-
strained power coupled with unquestioned reverence
for equality, and the ethical vacuum of both, was
presented by Orwell in his unforgettable Animal
Farm (1945).

In quite a different manner the potential to
rise to the top via sexual exploitation shocked
readers as depicted in Forever Amber in 1945 by
Kathleen Winsor. The demand for this best seller
combined with material shortages resulted in the
inauguration of paperback books. As evidence that
the literary reflection of public sentiment and
action was not all aligned to portray the world as
absurd and that chance wins in the end, one can
recall the popularity of Oklahoma, the famed 1943
musical by Rodgers and Hammerstein. Providing counterpoint to the uplifting quality of tribute to the
heartland, was New Poems of 1943 by Dylan Thomas.

In the technological realm, in addition to war materials which were many indeed, the early Forties provided the beginning of the era of wonder drugs. Australian Howard Florey developed penicillin in 1940, and in 1943 Selman Waksman of the United States developed streptomycin. The world of apparel was introduced to dacron, the first of polyester fibers in 1941, and DuPont replaced silk stockings with nylon in 1940, the invention of Wallace Carothers. The micro-world was increased in both clarity and perceived complexity with the 1940 invention of the electron microscope by Ladislaus Morton. In 1946 the ENIAC computer of Presper and Mauchly at the University of Pennsylvania issued a revolution in the art of calculation. The Forties also brought the tubeless tire, the electric blanket, the heli-copter, the drive-in bank, seeding of clouds, supersonic flights, the 33 1/3 rpm record, solar heating, cortisone treatment for rheumatism, and the invention of the transitor by Bardeen, Brattain, and Shockley.

The human quest for equality and well-being was addressed in President Franklin Roosevelt's 1941 appeal to support four essential freedoms throughout the world: freedom from want and fear, and freedom of religion and speech. In the same year, Congress passed the Lend-Lease Bill to provide aid to American allies. The immense atrocities of World War II, including the extermination of over six million Jews and Poles, the horror of combat and bombing on all sides, the death marches, and the grief stricken separation of loved ones, augmented the necessity of developing a world that could more fully provide the four freedoms. The post-war creation of the United Nations was an attempt to move in the direction of that hope through inter-national deliberation. A certain degree of atone-ment for suffering incurred by United States veter-ans was provided by the GI Bill of Rights in 1944, enabling them to receive vocational and educational benefits more readily. In 1946, the Atomic Energy Commission was established to foster the peaceful development and application of atomic energy, and the Marshall Plan brought over a hundred billion dollars in foreign assistance in 1948.

Though wartime wrought desire for freedom and cooperation, it also brought distrust accompanied by sharpened security. The Smith Act of 1940 required all aliens to undergo a fingerprinting process and outlawed organizations that advocated the overthrow of the American government. Following the war, President Truman issued an Executive Order that all Federal employees be required to undergo a loyalty investigation. Part of this 1947 procedure involved the listing of "security risks." In the same year the House Committee on Un-American Activities began a file of persons suspected or verified as potentially or actually subversive. It is interesting that files were maintained on educators John Dewey, George S. Counts, and Harold Rugg, among many others.[1] Suspicion ran rampant. Indeed, in 1948, film evidence hidden in a pumpkin in Maryland was brought to the attention of the House Un-American Activities Committee by Whittaker Chambers, implying that Alger Hiss had communist affiliations. At the international level, the United States joined Canada and ten Western European countries in signing the North Atlantic Treaty Organization pact, agreeing to mutual defense in the event of armed attack in 1949.

The later years of the 1940's brought a surge of hope for prosperity, not wholly unlike that which occurred following the wane of World War I. In 1947, however, Bernard Baruch warned that the United States was in the midst of "cold war," a year following Churchill's noted remark that no "iron curtain" was present on the European continent. By 1948, the USSR withdrew from the Allied Control Commission and began a blockade of West Berlin. The Western nations responded with an airlift. In the same year both North and South Korea were established as rival republics. In China, Mao seized control and forced Chaing Kai-shek to move to Formosa with his Nationalist forces, thus, making China a Communist power by 1949. In the same year, on the other side of the globe, the blockade of Berlin by Soviets was ended and East and West Germany were separated into democratic and communistic nations. The predicted cold war was in full bloom.

Nevertheless, the public hope for prosperity was not wholly unwarranted. Economic conditions improved with the 1947 General Agreement of Tariffs and Trades, involving 23 nations. United States and other aid provided temporary respite for the war torn nations. Rations were able to be terminated in most of the destroyed areas of Europe and Britain, and much rebuilding was accomplished with great perseverence.

The arts experienced a renewal, though not one that forgot the war, as illustrated by the posthumously published The Diary of Anne Frank. The architecture of Le Corbusier grew in prominence as did that of Frank Lloyd Wright. The painting of Jackson Pollock, Fernard Leger, and Picasso accentuated the medium and let the message be implied by the viewer. The music of Richard Strauss, Cole Porter, and Rodgers and Hammerstein brought at least a modicum of peacefulness to war-eroded souls. Yet, slice of life literature carried frequent reminders that it is through the erosion of our spirit, mind, body, and expectations that we experience knowledge of our aliveness, as provided by: Eugene O'Neill's The Iceman Cometh (1946); Wyler's (1946) film classic The Best Years of Our Lives; Tennessee Williams' A Streetcar Named Desire (1947); Norman Mailer's The Naked and the Dead (1948): Alan Paton's Cry the Beloved Country (1948); T.S. Eliot's Cocktail Party (1949); and Arthur Miller's (1949) Death of a Salesman.

At the close of the Forties, parts of the world not directly affected by the cold war experienced much change. Indonesian fighting resumed in their quest for independence against the Dutch. Later, it was quelled by a UN call for cease fire in 1947. That year also brought the division of India and Pakistan to partially provide for Hindu and Moslem differences. With assistance from Britain and the UN, Jewish peoples were able to proclaim the State of Israel in 1948 as their homeland, amid much turmoil. Not far away, a year earlier, a Jordanian shepherd boy discovered the Dead Sea Scrolls, an event that produced emotional and intellectual

98

turmoil in religious circles of many lands. The
year 1948 brought the shock of Gandhi's assassination, a year after which India became a republic
within the British Commonwealth of Nations.

A decade that began with war ended with a much
reconstructed world. It was a world that was better
off economically in some respects, but one which had
an ever-present state of tension centered in cold
war and the threat of nuclear annihilation. Feelings of contentment were accompanied by those of
personal nihilism. It was a time that was ripe for
the warning wrought by George Orwell in 1984.

Curriculum Thought and Literature

The economy's servitude to World War II, not
dissimilar in many respects to that during World
War I, quelled growth in many areas,including education and its several subdivisions. Eighty curriculum
books appeared during the Forties, and only thirteen
of these were published during the middle years,
1943-45, i.e., those books being ones that would have
been prepared during the most crucial funding
periods for the war.

The year 1940 brought a return to consideration
of purposes as the American Council on Education
reassessed what it deemed ought to be taught by
secondary schools. Again drawing upon his administrative experience, Harold Spears pointed directions
for the high school. Later in the decade Hollis
Caswell (1946) influenced curriculum thought by
treating the responsibility and promise of the
American High School. Purposes of schooling for
children were addressed by the 1940 White House Conference. The progressive education emphasis on
democracy seemed to permeate this statement's
interest in democracy relative to child growth.

Experientialist thought was generally represented in many curriculum books, e.g.: Wood's
(1940) treatment of curriculum as an interplay with
community life; the Lee and Lee (1940) emphasis on

99

the child as a sort of owner of curriculum; and Goggans' (1940) stress on units and interest centers as curriculum organizing factors. However, it is emphasized that these sources and many that follow provided a synoptic style that did not characterize earlier experientialist writings. Instead, they provided an integration of the several extant positions available at the time. Caswell and Campbell (1935) and Norton and Norton (1936) were noted as forerunners of synoptic texts in the preceding chapter.

A newer variation on the experientialist theme was advanced by Lorenzen (1940) who advocated a core curriculum that integrated subject areas to serve the study of social problems. A central feature of the core curriculum, one heavily emphasized during the next decade, was the integration of social problems with child interest or perceived problems. A problem that could be defended for both social and student-oriented relevance would serve as the core or center of inquiry that enabled students to expand their interests and simultaneously consider problems from a combination of subject matter perspectives. The justification of a Deweyan theory of knowledge was often used in defense of this approach. Such experientialist thought became increasingly integrated with the universal education thrust often promoted as America's great educational contribution stemming from the legacy of Horace Mann and Thomas Jefferson. The study of curriculum as a phase in a broad Deweyan interpretation of education became relegated to the study of curriculum as bounded by the limits of schooling. This emphasis was to some degree perpetuated by the work of H.C. Morrison, whose social evolutionist orientation guided his treatment of the common school curriculum as an agency to promote study of fundamental cultural institutions (1940). This treatment dealt with the topic from the early primary years through junior college.

The next year, 1941, brought several interesting books. Franklin Bobbitt, father of the social behaviorists, produced The Curriculum of Modern Education (1941), a book that is lesser known and some think out

100

of character with his works of two or three decades
before. Epitomizing his apparent alteration of
viewpoint is a statement that appears on page 298:
"Curriculum 'making' belongs with the dodo and the
great auk." This carries a bit of irony when juxtaposed with his 1924 title, How to Make a Curriculum.
Nevertheless, the point becomes clearer when it is
realized the Bobbitt treats education as greater than
schooling, a turn of emphasis from most earlier
social behaviorist literature. This perspective,
coupled with a sentence on the same page ("Current
curriculum discovery, one for each child and youth,
takes its place."), brings Bobbitt close to experientialist sentiments. He seemed to assume that each
child is educated by many experiential forces, that
these produce individuals who are unique, that
generalized curriculum-making misses much of that
uniqueness, and that individualized curricula need
to be developed. The impact, if any, that Bobbitt
had on the individualization movement is not easy
to document; however, because of his general noto-
riety in the field it seems plausible to attribute
some.

In 1941, L. Thomas Hopkins was again quite
visible, this time publishing Interaction, a book
that treated the role of democratic processes in
education. Much was to be written for many years
that followed on the kind of group deliberation that
best contributed to sound curricular decisions.
Noteworthy in this regard is J. Galen Saylor's
appearance on the scene. He studied factors that
are associated with participation in cooperative
programs of curriculum development, and he continued
to stress democratic curriculum planning in his
contributions that were destined to span the next
three decades. Cooperative planning was treated in
published form also by the National Commission on
Cooperative Planning, their title noting the emphasis given to this idea in 1941. The work of this
group gave special consideration to the subject
fields; thus, it accented a separate subject orientation that experientialists went to great length to
fuse, correlate, integrate, and "core-ify." Thus,
cooperation and interaction pertained both to subject matter and to the process of determining it.

Analyses of actual curriculum in schools were not absent in the first years of the Forties. Bruner and Evans (1941) attempted to discover what schools were teaching through analyses of courses of study in social studies, science, and industrial arts. J.C. Morrison (1941) surveyed examples of activity curricula in New York City elementary schools. National College of Education (1940) provided another book that recorded developments of their Children's School.

By far the most massive curriculum-oriented study of the first half century, The Eight Year Study, was published in 1942. This study compared traditional and progressive schools, and was presented in a five volume set; volumes by Aikin and Giles are most germane to curriculum. Aikin (Volume I) is an overview of the Eight Year Study, Giles et al. (Volume II) looks at the thirty schools involved in the study from the stance of curriculum consultants, and Smith and Tyler (Volume III) treat evaluation. Interpretations of the data vary, but in general it was found that comparisons of college work of some three thousand high school students (paired for such factors as race, family background, age, sex, and test scores) showed that those from experimental schools (schools that did not have to utilize usual college entrance requirements such as grades, class rank, required courses, etc.) did as well or better in college (relative to grades, extra-curricular activities, judgment, critical thinking, and knowledge) than those who attended traditional schools. One major problem is that little programmatic similarity existed among the experimental schools; experiences had by experimental students were quite diverse, making it difficult to generalize about the best curriculum organization or pattern developed. What seemed quite clear, however, was that the more novel the curriculum, i.e., the further it was from traditional, the more successful were students in college. The most novel curricular orientations involved students in community settings, made extensive use of community volunteers in schools, provided large amounts of individual contact between teachers and students, and involved peer teaching, integration of subject areas, and problem solving. Moreover, a follow-up study, Were We Guinea Pigs? was reported by Willis (1961). She studied the 1938 graduates of the Ohio State University Laboratory School, a novel experimental school in the Eight Year Study. These graduates were judged as highly successful in life according to questionnaire results that revealed considerable self-satisfaction, stable family situations, and contributions to professional leadership. Further, they were compared with Terman's subjects in his renowned study of geniuses, and were rated higher on the above characteristics than Terman's subjects.

Other previously emphasized categories of curriculum literature were bolstered in 1942. Corey provided a treatment of general education relative to the secondary school. Parker, Menge, and Rice also dealt with secondary education. C.C. Peters developed the idea of democratic education relative to curriculum. The idea of developing curriculum, previously accented by Caswell and Campbell (1935), was perpetuated by Pierce in his book on the high school. J. Minor Gwynn, highly prominent in curriculum and supervision during subsequent decades, initiated his extensive contributions to curriculum and supervision literature with Curriculum Principles and Social Trends (1943). In doing so he capitalized on several of the burgeoning attributes of curriculum literature. His book was synoptic in the Caswell and Campbell vein, it espoused principles of Harap's "how-to" variety, and it perpetuated the notion of modernity with extensive treatment of curriculum revision and change.

Particular locales again produced statements that usually paralleled the standard trends and cloudy technical language of emerging synoptic texts. Examples include: Lawson (1940) on city schools as contrasted with the small school thrust of the previous decade; National College of Education's (1940) Children's School Staff report; the California Elementary School Principals' Association statement on school environment in reference to curriculum

(1941); the Santa Barbara Schools' discussion of developmental curriculum (1941); the Universities of
Florida and Oregon report on cooperative school
projects (1942); and a guiding principles statement
by the New York City Department of Education (1943).
This emphasis on curriculum in specified locales was
given international attention as well; statements
about standards by the Ministry of Education in China
(1942, 1944, and 1946), and a treatment by the British Secondary School Examinations Council (1943) on
curriculum and examinations serve as examples.

Two contributions from the first half of the
1940's that moved curriculum thought in new directions were provided by Doane (1942) and Burton
(1944). Doane's work was an early example of needs
assessment of youth to enable more effective setting
of purposes. Burton dealt with the role of teacher
interaction or intervention in tailoring curriculum
or learning experiences to the needs and interests
of children. He included examples that point to the
necessity of continuous monitoring of student interaction with their school work in an effort to determine the extent to which they comprehend material
rather than merely learn to produce requested results.

A major extrapolation of Horace Mann's notion
of the common school took place in the mid-Forties
under the rubric of "general education." The central
concern was that if the ideal of the common school
exists in the United States, if almost all children
and youth attend school, what is the common core of
knowledge, skills, and attitudes that they should
acquire for intelligent citizenry? Stemming from
their The Purposes of Education in American Democracy
of 1938, the Educational Policies Commission of the
National Education Association devised a post-war
core of common learnings and stated them as imperative
needs of youth (1944). The statement was heavily
endorsed by the National Association of Secondary
School Principals. The ten imperative needs dealt
with: salable skills, health, competent citizenship, good family membership, defensible consumerism,
scientific methodology, aesthetic appreciations,
wise use of leisure time, democratic values, and
rational thought.

104

Even a cursory look at this statement of imperative needs would enable the curriculum student to note the implicit synthesis of schools of curriculum thought. Examples that prevailed include: the social and democratic perspective of the experientialist, the practicality and categorization of the social behaviorist, and the time-honored virtues of the intellectual traditionalist. Such statements seemed to be developing a tendency to amalgamate schools of curriculum thought. It is not clear whether this attempt to synthesize diverse perspectives produced statements that were greater than each constituent school taken separately or whether they resulted in watered down versions of each. Perhaps, they were attempts to placate proponents of each school by granting inclusion of some of their views. In any event the quest for the meaning of general education continued.

In 1945, the Harvard Committee on the Objectives of Education in a Free Society published General Education in a Free Society, a report that acknowledged the fact that three-fourths of high school graduates did not attend college; therefore, they should be provided with a general background in humanities, social sciences, natural sciences, and mathematics, as are college bound students, but in ways that are tailored to methods of learning and abilities that fit less gifted and less academically oriented students. These areas, they argued, should be presented in such a manner that enables all students to think effectively, communicate well, make relevant judgments, and develop values. The 1946 re-publication of the 1938 Educational Policies Commission statement of purposes in a larger document called Policies for Education in American Democracy bolstered the thrust of the general education movement.

The mid-Forties also brought continuation of several interpretations of the emphasis on novelty in curriculum literature. In 1944, the Association for Supervision and Curriculum Development (ASCD) produced Toward a New Curriculum as their yearbook. In the same year, Offner treated the matter of change

relative to curriculum in teachers colleges. In
Britain, too, the Council for Curriculum Reform
(1945) pushed for change toward the novel, labeling it "reform." Similarly, the National Society
for the Study of Education's Forty-fourth Yearbook
(1945), Part I, called for curriculum reconstruction in American education of the post-war period.
A number of scholars contributed to this work who
were to be highly influential in curriculum literature during the next several decades. Notable in
this regard were Ralph Tyler, a key evaluator in
the Eight Year Study, and Hilda Taba who laid groundwork for her later work in a chapter entitled
"General Techniques of Curriculum Planning" (pp. 80-
115).

The above interest in novelty and change was
combined with another interest from the Thirties,
that of decision making. A synthesis of both foci
is evident in the 1946 treatment of curriculum
change by Alice Miel. She saw curriculum decision
making as more than the exercise of rationality; it
was a social process as well. Although her book
had considerable impact, much time elapsed before
curricularists again expressed the import of the
message she advanced. Storen, however, produced
an ASCD publication in the same year that called
for lay participation in curriculum planning, i.e.,
a contribution to curriculum planning as a social
process.

Among the miscellaneous, though not less
significant, contributions to curriculum literature of the mid-Forties are: Baker's (1945) report
on curriculum planning based upon questions asked
by children; Martens' (1946) call for curriculum
adjustments for gifted students; and a Pennsylvania
(1946) plan for local participation in curriculum
revision.

Several new treatments of   perennial curriculum topics were made in the mid-Forties: Fleming
(1946) contributed to the relation of research and
curriculum; Cole (1946) provided a text on
elementary school curriculum with primary emphasis

106

on subject areas; and Jersild (1946) drew upon his extensive background in child development, advancing curriculum implications.

The last years of the 1940's brought another in the line of synoptic or comprehensive curriculum books, i.e., books that presented several curriculum orientations in encyclopedic fashion, and from them derived guidelines for curriculum developers to follow. In 1947, a synoptic text produced by Florence B. Stratemeyer and others added new dimensions to the evolution of that kind of text. The notions of development and of modernity were stressed throughout. She discussed bases and sources of curriculum development, its purpose and strategies, and disclosed a greater array of persons who contribute to curriculum development processes than were usually treated in the literature. She interpenetrated most of the book with continual emphasis on the role that childhood activity should be given in the curriculum development process. Namely, curriculum experiences should be drawn from analysis of persistent life situations faced by children and youth. She provided nearly two hundred pages of examples. Further, she argued that learners should have a primary role in developing curricula, and the actual teaching-learning situation should itself be considered curricular. In 1948, the Association for Childhood Education accented this kind of action-oriented dimension of curriculum construction.

Other variations on the synoptic text were introduced in the Forties and had considerable impact thereafter. One major type began with a comprehensive overview of the field and then moved toward specialization in either secondary or elementary curriculum. J.P. Leonard's Developing the Secondary School Curriculum (1946) is an example. It began with historical perspectives that set schooling and curriculum in historical context, and continued by providing discussions of trends, theoretical perspectives, and evaluation. Following these considerations, Leonard focused on secondary school curriculum by relating the core curriculum idea and units of work, and considering means for revision and modernization. In 1947, Harl R. Douglass edited a collection of articles on secondary curriculum which, by their organization, first established perspectives relative to society and schooling and moved into treatments of general curriculum development issues and specific subject areas at the secondary level. In the same year, Harold Alberty published Reorganizing the High School Curriculum, a book that was dedicated to and in many ways emulated the work of Boyd H. Bode. Alberty began with a discussion of foundations, moved to design and implementation which he called action, and treated planning and the process of deliberation extensively. Harold Spears added to the growing line of comprehensive texts, providing a distinctive practice-oriented flavor in his second edition of The Emerging High School Curriculum and its Direction (1948).

The late Forties also brought its share of miscellaneous topics, some of which would prove quite influential in subsequent curriculum literature. The topic of organization was given increased attention relative to elementary schools by the Association for Supervision and Curriculum Development in 1947. Noar's (1948) emphasis on units and the Bathurst (1949) treatment of the place of subject areas in the curriculum reflect this interest. A review of curriculum laboratories in the United States by Drag (1947) shows a concern for actual cases. So do reports on development in particular locales, e.g., California (1948), Loftus (1948), the N.E.A. (1948), Tasmania (1948), Wisconsin (1948), New York (1949), and Ohio State (1949). This desire to know what had occurred in certain spheres of curriculum development was responded to in 1949 by Harlan Shores, who critically reviewed research from 1890 to 1949 on elementary school organization. Post-war reflections brought realization that the armed services had, in fact, developed curricula to prepare members of the military for war and the concomitant conclusion that such curriculum development could be studied for its implications for schools. Goodman (1947) pursued such investigations.

Post-war sentiments also contributed to the decline of progressive education. It became apparent that reflection on the war, combined with evolving conservatism evidenced by quests for performers of un-American activities, provided escort service for a not-so-gradual exit from the curricular scene by progressive education. The influential status of progressive education prior to World War II established it as a convenient scapegoat for societal ills that surrounded the times. The growth of experientialist curriculum thought was temporarily halted. This was accompanied by an emerging attentiveness to the "nuts and bolts" of education, i.e., basic skills instead of progressive intangibles. This kind of reaction frequently accompanies the "let's get back to business" response that follows wars. Such was symbolized in Hildreth's (1947) Learning the Three R's. No small part of the return to basics was inherent in the problem of providing general education. The Educational Policies Commission spelled out the priority as revealed in the title of its 1948 publication, Education for All American Children.

The debate about purposes for American education was seriously pursued at length by Rugg (1947), and a sort of curricular consciousness raising about the purpose of knowledge itself was provided by Lynd in Knowledge for What? (1948)

Finally, and of immense impact not only in the Forties but in the whole of curriculum literature, was the 1949 appearance of Ralph Tyler's Basic Principles of Curriculum and Instruction. It was originally created as a course syllabus for Education 360 at the University of Chicago. Although this book raised issues considered by Dewey, Bobbitt, Harap, Hopkins, Charters, Caswell, Bode, Stratemeyer, and others who published earlier, it discussed them in ways that generated great impact. Essentially, Tyler raised four categories of consideration that he claimed were basic to curriculum development: purposes, experiences, organization, and evaluation. In raising these topics he provided the following: (1) sources and procedures which schools could use

109

to determine purposes; (2) principles and illustrations for studying and developing learning experiences that enable the attainment of the purposes; (3) considerations for organizing the learning experiences; and (4) procedures for evaluating the effectiveness of the learning experiences. It is more than coincidental that the format of curriculum guides, teachers' editions of school books, lesson plan books, evaluation instruments by accrediting agencies, course syllabi, and many curriculum books that appeared in the 1950's and 1960's are organized around Tyler's four topics.

Like others who have had impact, Tyler's work has not been immune to criticism. One type of criticism, however, erroneously assumes that Tyler intended that his questions be rigidly pursued in step-wise fashion. This kind of faulty interpretation was anticipated and countered by Tyler in the final chapter of his book. He clearly stated that the sequence of considerations is flexible and contingent upon a multiplicity of situational attributes. Other criticisms contend that he over-emphasized rationality as contrasted with political, social, and economic conditions. These often call for other categorical systems to map curricular phenomena. One point is clear, however: the curriculum student who looks carefully at the literature of the next three decades will not be able to deny the vast influence of Tyler's Basic Principles of Curriculum and Instruction. As a footnote in their study, such students would do well to keep in mind Tyler's advocacy of a unified view of curriculum and instruction. He apparently assumed that the same or similar principles apply to both. The relation of curriculum and instruction, as noted earlier, is a topic about which no small debate has raged in curriculum circles.

Thus, the curriculum literature of the Forties bolstered the character of the field by providing: (1) a strong precedent for curriculum research; (2) a tendency to centralize curriculum knowledge and priorities through the work of associations and commissions; (3) a continuation of synoptic curriculum texts; and (4) a concise formulation of categories that established boundaries of curriculum literature for at least two decades.

Notes

[1]Information on this is included in FBI Surveillance of Three Progressive Educators: Curricular Aspects, a paper presented to the Society for the Study of Curriculum History, Toronto, March 27, 1978, by M.R. Nelson and H.W. Singleton.

Bibliography of Curriculum Books,
1940-1949

1940

American Council on Education. American Youth
    Commission. What the high schools ought
    to teach; the report of a special commit-
    tee on the secondary school curriculum
    (Ben G. Graham, Chairman; Thomas H. Briggs,
    Will French, et al.). Washington, D.C.:
    American Council on Education, 1940.

Ch'en, T.H. Developing patterns of the college
    curriculum in the United States. Los
    Angeles, California: The University of
    Southern California Press, 1940.

Goggans, S. Units of work and centers of
    interest in the organization of the ele-
    mentary school curriculum. New York:
    Teachers College, Columbia University,
    1940 (Reprinted by AMS 1972, New York).

Lawson, D.E. Curriculum development in city
    school systems. Chicago: University of
    Chicago Press, 1940.

Lee, J.M. and Lee, D.M. The child and his
    curriculum. New York: Appleton-Century-
    Crofts, 1940.

Lorenzen, S. Planning a core curriculum.
    Bulletin Number 9. Connecticut Curricu-
    lum Center. Storrs, Connecticut: Con-
    necticut Curriculum Center, 1940.

Morrison, H.C. The curriculum of the common
    school, from the beginning of the primary
    school to the end of the junior college.
    Chicago: University of Chicago Press,
    1940 (Reprinted by Folcroft, 1977).

National College of Education. Children's

School Staff. <u>Curriculum records of the children's school, National College of Education</u>. Evanston, Illinois: Bureau of Publications, National College of Education, 1940.

Spears, H. <u>The emerging high school curriculum and its direction</u>. New York: American Book Company, 1940.

Umstattd, J.G. and Hammock, R. <u>Proceedings of the 1939 curriculum conference and study group</u>. Austin: University of Texas, 1940.

<u>White House Conference on Children in a Democracy: Final report</u>. United States Children's Bureau. Washington, D.C.: Government Printing Office, 1940.

Wood, H.B. <u>The school curriculum and community life</u>. Eugene, Oregon: University of Oregon, 1940.

1941

Bobbitt, F. <u>The curriculum of modern education</u>. New York: McGraw-Hill, 1941 (Also Norwood Editions).

Bruner, H.B., Evans, H.M., et al. <u>What our schools are teaching: An analysis of the content of selected courses of study with special reference to science, social studies, and industrial arts</u>. New York: Bureau of Publications, Teachers College, Columbia University, 1941.

California. Elementary School Principals' Association. <u>The elementary school environment and the modern curriculum</u>. Los Angeles, California: Elementary School Principals' Association, 1941.

Hopkins, L.T. <u>Interaction: The democratic process</u>. Boston: D.C. Heath, 1941.

Morrison, J.C., et al. The activity program: A survey of the curriculum experiment with the activity program in the elementary schools of the city of New York. Albany, New York: State Department of Education, 1941.

National Commission on Cooperative Curriculum Planning. The subject fields in general education. New York: D. Appleton-Century Company, Inc., 1941.

Santa Barbara (California) Schools. Developmental curriculum. Bulletin Number One, Revision Number One, November, 1941.

Saylor, J.G. Factors associated with participation in cooperative programs of curriculum development. New York: Bureau of Publications, Teachers College, Columbia University, 1941 (Reprinted by AMS, 1972, New York).

1942

Aikin, W.M. The story of the eight year study. New York: Harper and Brothers, 1942.

China. Ministry of Education. Curriculum standards for the elementary school. Shanghai: Cheng Chung Book Company, 1942.

Corey, S.M., et al. General education and the American high school. Chicago: Scott Foresman, 1942.

Doane, D.C. The needs of youth: An evaluation for curriculum purposes. New York: Teachers College, Columbia University, 1942 (Reprinted by AMS, 1972, New York).

Eight Year Study. Adventure in American education series, volumes I-V. New York: Harper Brothers, 1942. [Volume I, by W.M. Aikin, cited above; Volume II, by H.H.

Giles, S.P. McCutchen and A.N. Zechiel,
cited below; Volume III, by E.R. Smith
R.W. Tyler, and the Evaluation Staff,
cited below; Volume IV, by D. Chamberlin,
E.S. Chamberlin, N.F. Drought and W.E.
Scott, Did they succeed in college?; and
Volume V, by the thirty schools, Thirty
schools tell their story.]

Florida, University of; and Oregon, University
of. Cooperating school projects as a
technique of curriculum improvement.
Gainesville, Florida: University of
Florida, 1942.

Giles, H.H., et al. Exploring the curriculum:
The work of thirty schools from the viewpoint of curriculum consultants. Eight
Year Study, Volume II. New York: Harper
and Brothers, 1942.

Parker, J.C., Menge, W., and Rice, T.D. The
first five years of the secondary school
curriculum, 1937-1942. Lansing, Michigan: Michigan Study of the Secondary
School Curriculum. State Board of Education, 1942.

Peters, C.C. The curriculum of democratic
education. New York: McGraw-Hill, 1942.

Pierce, P.R. Developing a high school curriculum. New York: The American Book
Company, 1942.

Smith, E.R., Tyler, R.W., and the Evaluation
Staff. Appraising and recording student
progress. New York: Harper and Brothers,
1942.

<u>1943</u>

Britain: Secondary School Examinations Council.
Curriculum and examinations in secondary
schools. London: Her Majesty's Stationery
Office, 1943.

Gwynn, J.M. Curriculum principles and social trends. New York: Macmillan, 1943.

New York City Department of Education. Guiding principles in curriculum development. Brooklyn: Department of Education, 1943.

1944

Association for Supervision and Curriculum Development. Toward a new curriculum. 1944 Yearbook. Washington: Association for Supervision and Curriculum Development, 1944.

Burton, W.H. The guidance of learning activities. New York: D. Appleton-Century, 1944.

China. Ministry of Education. A plan for the six years' curriculum standard in secondary schools. Shanghai: Cheng Chung Book Company, 1944.

Educational Policies Commission. Education for all American youth. Washington: National Education Association, 1944.

Indiana. Department of Public Instruction. A good start in school; a curriculum handbook for primary teachers. Indianapolis: Department of Public Instruction, 1944.

Offner, H.L. Administrative procedures for changing curriculum patterns for selected state teachers colleges; with special reference to New Jersey, New York and Pennsylvania. New York: Bureau of Publications Teachers College, Columbia University, 1944.

1945

Baker, E.V. Children's questions and their

116

implications for planning the curriculum with special reference to the contribution of the natural and social sciences in the intermediate grade curriculum. New York: Teachers College, Columbia University, 1945.

Council for Curriculum Reform. The content of education; proposals for the school curriculum, being the interim report of the Council for Curriculum Reform. Bickley, Kent: University of London Press, Ltd., 1945.

Harvard Committee on the Objectives of Education in a Free Society. General education in a free society. Cambridge: Harvard University Press, 1945.

National Society for the Study of Education. American education in the postwar period: Curriculum reconstruction (N.B. Henry, Editor). Forty-Fourth Yearbook, Part I. Chicago: University of Chicago Press, 1945.

1946

Caswell, H.L. (Editor). The American high school: Its responsibility and opportunity (Eighth Yearbook of the John Dewey Society). New York: Harper and Brothers, 1946.

China. Ministry of Education. Curriculum standards for the normal school. Shanghai: Cheng Chung Book Company, 1946a.

China. Ministry of Education. Revised curriculum standards for junior and senior high schools. Shanghai: Cheng Chung Book Company, 1946b.

Cole, L. The elementary school subjects. New York: Rinehart and Company, Incorporated, 1946.

117

Educational Policies Commission. Policies for
    education in American democracy. Washing-
    ton, D.C.: The Educational Policies Com-
    mission of the NEA and the AASA, 1946.

Fleming, C.M. Research and the basic curriculum.
    London: University of London Press, 1946.

Jersild, A.T. Child development and the curric-
    ulum. New York: Teachers College, Colum-
    bia University, 1946.

Leonard, J.P. Developing the secondary school
    curriculum. New York: Rinehart and
    Company, 1946.

Martens, E.H. Curriculum adjustments for gifted
    children. Washington: U.S. Office of
    Education, 1946.

Miel, A. Changing the curriculum: A social
    process. New York: Appleton-Century,
    1946.

Pennsylvania Department of Public Instruction.
    Local participation in state-wide revision
    of the elementary school curriculum. Harris-
    burg, Pennsylvania: Pennsylvania Depart-
    ment of Public Instruction, 1946.

Storen, H.F. Laymen help plan for the curriculum.
    Washington: Association for Supervision
    and Curriculum Development, 1946.

1947

Alberty, H. Reorganizing the high school
    curriculum. New York: Macmillan, 1947.

Association for Supervision and Curriculum
    Development. Organizing the elementary
    school for living and learning. Washing-
    ton: National Education Association, 1947.

Douglass, H.R. (Editor). The high school curriculum. New York: Ronald Press, 1947.

Drag, F.L. Curriculum laboratories in the United States. San Diego, California: Office of the County Superintendent of Schools, 1947.

Goodman, S.M. Curriculum implications of armed services education programs. Washington: American Council on Education, 1947.

Hildreth, G.H. Learning the three R's (Second Edition). Minneapolis: Educational Publishers, 1947.

Rugg, H.O. Foundations for American education. Yonkers-on-the-Hudson, New York: World Book Company, 1947.

Stratemeyer, F.B., Forkner, H.L., and McKim, M.G. Developing a curriculum for modern living. New York: Bureau of Publications, Teachers College, Columbia University, 1947.

1948

Association for Childhood Education. Curriculum at work (F. Mayfarth, Editor). Washington: Association for Childhood Education, 1948.

California Elementary School Principals' Association. Principal and curriculum building. Twentieth Yearbook, 1948.

Chu, Chih-hsien. Curriculum for elementary schools. Shanghai: Commercial Press, 1948.

Educational Policies Commission. Education for all American children. Washington: National Education Association, 1948.

Loftus, J.J. The story of how a great school
system developed a new educational program. Chicago: F.E. Compton, 1948.

Lynd, R.S. Knowledge for what? Princeton:
Princeton University Press, 1948.

National Education Association of the United
States. Department of Secondary School
Principals. Curriculum trends in the
secondary school; a series of articles
that describe curriculum provision and
developments for youth in many sections
of the country. Washington, D.C.:
National Association of Secondary School
Principals, 1948.

Noar, G. Freedom to live and learn; techniques for selecting and developing units
of learning in the modern classroom.
Philadelphia: Franklin, 1948.

Spears, H. The emerging high school curriculum and its direction (Second Edition).
New York: American Book Company, 1948.

Tasmania, Education Department. Curriculum
for primary schools. Hobart: H.H. Pim-
blett, Government Printer, 1948.

Wisconsin Cooperative Educational Planning
Program. Underlying principles and
implementations. Madison: State Superintendent, J. Calahan, 1948.

1949

Bathurst, E.G., et al. The place of subjects
in the curriculum. Educational Bulletin
Number 12. Washington: Office of Education, 1949.

Central New York School Study Council Committee
on Flexibility. Toward a more flexible
elementary school curriculum: A second

report (Prepared by Arthur E. Smith).
Syracuse, New York: Central New York
School Study Council, 1949.

New York City Board of Education. Source
materials in curriculum development.
Brooklyn: New York City Board of
Education, 1949.

Ohio State University. How to develop a core
program in the high school. Columbus:
Ohio State University, College of Education (Directed by H. Alberty), 1949.

Shores, J.H. A critical review of the research
on elementary school curriculum organization 1890-1949. Urbana, Illinois:
College of Education, Bureau of Research
and Service, University of Illinois, 1949.

Tyler, R. Basic principles of curriculum and
instruction. Chicago: University of
Chicago Press, 1949 (Also 1969).

CHAPTER VI

CURRICULUM LITERATURE AND CONTEXT:

1950-1959

Contextual Reminders

The Second World War was over; rebuilding was
well underway. It seemed like a time of peace with
potential for prosperity, but simultaneously it
seemed that the entire world was on the brink of
destruction at any moment's unaware. It was the
Fifties; it was the Cold War. The world could never
forget the devastating power of atomic warfare that
closed the war with Japan. The world knew that
both Communistic and Democratic powers possessed
an ever-increasing stockpile of weapons that, by
comparison, dwarfed even those that destroyed
Nagasaki and Hiroshima. The fear that world war
meant world obliteration was real indeed and not
wholly unwarranted. This fear brought with it a
spirit of inquisition, and Joseph McCarthy led the
search for communists through the nooks and cran-
nies of the United States.

In 1950 the Korean War began. United Nations
forces aided South Korea under the leadership of
General Douglas MacArthur, and North Korea was
aided by China. For many who wavered on the issue
of the reality of the Cold War, Korea provided the
capstone to insure belief, warranted or not. In
1951, the fervor of the "beat the Communists" atti-
tude was reduced a bit from its headlongedness by
President Truman's removal of MacArthur in an
effort to quell the desire to attack China that he
prompted. Peace negotiations, imbued with Chinese
accusations that the United States used germ warfare in Korea, continued throughout 1952, and in
the same year the war ended with the signing of
the peace treaty at Panmunjon. South Korea and
the United States signed a mutual defense treaty
in the same year.

123

Meanwhile in Europe, economic cooperation was on the upswing. In 1950 Adenauer proposed cooperation between France and Germany, and in 1951-1953 a European Coal and Steel Company was planned, actualized, and implemented. In Britain, after a brief intermission as Prime Minister, Winston Churchill regained that role from Clement Attlee in 1951. In 1952 Britain's King George VI died and was succeeded by Queen Elizabeth II.

The rest of the world, as well, was not without its share of turmoil and change. Iran's nationalization of its oil industry led to altercation with Britain in 1951 and 1952. Egypt repealed treaties with Britain. India and Pakistan continued their dispute over Kashmir. Jordan's king was assassinated in Jerusalem. Nassar took control of Egypt in 1952. The same year saw Batista regain a cruel dictatorship in Cuba. In 1953, the president of the Kenya Africa Union was arrested for supporting Mau Mau terrorism. Egypt became a republic with dictatorial overtones. The dual forces of unrest that resisted and perpetuated colonialism began to pervade Africa, notably in Morocco in 1953, and in Egypt, Algeria, and the Gold Coast in 1954.

Changes in leadership of the two major world powers occurred in 1952 and 1953. Dwight D. Eisenhower became United States President with a sweeping victory over Adlai Stevenson. The death of Stalin brought a great power play for leadership in the USSR. In 1954, the USSR rejected Western suggestions that Germany be reunited; the occupation of West Germany terminated. Alliances evolved to prevent conflagration between major powers of the Free and Communist worlds. Under the leadership of Dag Hammarskjold, who succeeded Trygve Lie as Secretary-General, the United Nations made major strides. It also experienced impediments wrought by the major powers who increasingly controlled international decision and action, both economically and politically. In 1954, Japan and the United States established a mutual defense agreement, the same year that the Southeast Asian

124

Defense Treaty was actualized by Australia, Britain, France, New Zealand, Pakistan, the Philippines, Thailand, and the United States. The following year brought the Warsaw Pact, initiated by the USSR, to offset NATO in the continual press of major powers to achieve a slightly favorable imbalance in the balance of power. The effort was continued in 1955 by a Geneva conference, represented by seventy-two nations, to discuss peaceful uses of atomic energy.

While peaceful co-existence was actively sought through organized effort, internal conflict in the mid-Fifties provided seedbeds of international strife for many years hence. In 1954, Egypt and Britain agreed to the evacuation of British troops from the Suez Canal Zone. This was followed, in 1956, by Egypt's seizure of the canal which France and Britain primarily owned. French, British, and Israeli forces invaded the Canal Zone in Egyptian territory, at which point the USSR threatened to intervene. United Nations forces entered, and France and Britain withdrew. In 1957, Egypt re-opened the canal. Indo-Chinese forces established independence from the French for Vietnam, Cambodia, and Laos. Uprising continued in Greece and Turkey over the rightful place of Cyprus. Revolts in Argentina forced the exile of Juan Peron. In Hungary, Imre Nagy was ousted by the Communist Party, leading to the revolution of 1956 triggered by Communist shootings at a student protest of the installation of his successor. This was followed by the establishment of a coalition government coupled with Hungarian withdrawal from the Warsaw Pact, both under Nagy's leadership. Soviet invasion led to Nagy's death, much killing and injury, the escape of nearly 150,000 refugees, and the restoration of Communist rule. Tunisia, Morocco, and Sudan gained independence by 1956.

The arts and sciences continued to expand between the onset of the Fifties and mid-decade. Under the modern masters such as Picasso and Chagall abstract expressionism flourished. Picasso produced the timely Massacre in Korea in 1951, and

125

Salvador Dali unleashed his often morose brand of surrealism. Jackson Pollock mass-painted a sort of media unemcumbered by the human psyche, with his squeezing of tubes of paint from step ladders on canvas to be cut to size according to the consumer's wishes. The sculpture of Henry Moore was joined by abstractions of Barbara Hepworth, Reg Butler, and Lynn Chadwick, all from the United Kingdom. Although abstraction was the style of the day, there were exceptions; Sutherland's portrait of Churchill and Annigoni's portrait of Queen Elizabeth II are notable in this regard. The organic architecture of Eero Saarinen demonstrated the aesthetic quality of remaining true to the medium, perpetuating Wright's ideal that form follows function.

The early Fifties brought musicals, Guys and Dolls in 1950 and Wonderful Town in 1953. A number of operas appeared that were usually based on famous literary themes, e.g., Menotti's The Consul, Britten's Billy Budd, Williams' A Pilgrim's Progress, Stravinsky's Babel, Martinu's What Men Live By, Milhaud's David, and Shuman's Mighty Casey.

In literature as in art, authors continued to express inner dilemmas wrought by external circumstances; examples include: Ezra Pound's Seventy Cantos, Hemingway's portrayal of the relation of an old fisherman and young boy in pursuit of a great fish in The Old Man and the Sea, Herman Wouk's probe of the disturbed authoritarian psyche in The Caine Mutiny, J. D. Salinger's own version of the absurd in his social critique through the mind of an institutionalized teenager in The Catcher in the Rye, Steinbeck's gripping saga of a family in turmoil in East of Eden, Beckett's existential classic play, Waiting for Godot, and Arthur Miller's portrayal of interpersonal chemistry in The Crucible.

Science, technological invention, and discovery expanded in multiple directions in the early Fifties. New elements were added to the periodic table in chemistry. Thor Heyerdahl let the world know about his Kon Tiki expedition. The first jet airliner was produced in Britain, and atomic power was used to

126

produce electricity in the United States. The prehistoric was found to be living and doing well as
the coelacanth was discovered off the African coast
in 1952. This was the same year that an atomic
powered submarine was designed and a hydrogen bomb
was exploded, both under United States jurisdiction.
The next year brought a Soviet H-bomb explosion.
The famed "because it was there" conquering of Mount
Everest by Hillary, Norgay, and Hunt occurred in
1953. Meyrin, Switzerland, became an international
center for nuclear research, and Mount Wrangell in
Alaska became the residence of an observatory to
study cosmic rays. By 1955 radio waves were discovered to emanate from Jupiter. The year 1953 saw
the appearance of B.F. Skinner's Science and Human
Behavior, a key work in his behavioristic interpretation of human nature. Mid-decade brought Jonas
Salk's anti-polio vaccine, the ion microscope with
its 2.75 million x magnification, the discovery of
the neutrino, and a visual telephone. The last
three years of the Fifties ushered in a new technological age, the Space Age. The world, especially the United States, reacted in disbelief when
the Russians launched Sputnik I, the world's first
unmanned spacecraft in 1957, followed by Sputnik II,
known as "mutnick" because of its canine passenger,
later the same year.

Concern about the Space Age was, however, not
the primary concern everywhere. In Cuba, Fidel
Castro led a guerrilla rebellion against Batista's
dictatorship, taking control of sugar firms and
instituting a communist government by 1959. Soviet
leadership continued amid turmoil about who would
emerge as primary leader; by 1958 Nikita Krushchev
became the answer. In 1958, Egypt and Syria joined
to create the United Arab Republic. Martial law
was initiated in Jordan; United States troops were
called to maintain order in Lebanon while British
troops were requested to do the same in Jordan.
By 1959, Charles de Gaulle became President of the
Fifth Republic in France, after being requested to
return from retirement. He brought resolution to
the long-lasting French conflict in Algeria by
declaring that Algerians should be granted autonomy.

International alliances continued to mold the picture of economic and political conditions: the European Economic Community (an alliance of Belgium, France, West Germany, Italy, Luxembourg, and the Netherlands); the Bagdad Pact or Central Treaty Organization (an alliance of the United States, Turkey, Iraq, and Iran); and the European Free Trade Association (Austria, Britain, Denmark, Norway, Portugal, Sweden and Switzerland).

The quest for human rights and freedoms sounded clear in the 1950's in the already mentioned independence achieved by many Third World nations that were formerly colonies. Joining the list by the end of the Fifties were Cyprus and Mali, with the Belgium Congo moving in that direction. Colonial freedom was not the only kind of liberty pursued. Strides were made in freedom from racial discrimination, at no small price either. In the United States racial segregation in schools was declared unconstitutional by the Supreme Court in 1954, and in 1957 a Civil Rights Act brought a commission to investigate violation of civil rights. Riots, often necessitating the intervention of the military (e.g., in Little Rock, Arkansas in 1957) occurred in many parts of the world on the issue of racial equality. By 1959 the United Nations General Assembly issued a condemnation of both racial discrimination generally and apartheid in particular. The late Fifties saw a distinct rise in unemployment, but through the unification of the American Federation of Labor and the Congress of Industrial Organizations the power of laborers was considerably increased.

The arts continued to portray the times with the popularity of Bernstein's West Side Story showing non-urban America something of inner city life. Literature varied greatly from the penetrating insight into human feeling of Faulkner, to the sensible nonsense of Dr. Seuss, the philosophical stories of Iris Murdoch, the absurd realities of Saroyan's plays, and Jack Kerouac's characterization of the searching quests of the beat generation in such books as On the Road (1957).

128

The artistic films of Ingmar Bergman, and David Lean's The Bridge on the River Kwai illustrate the range of high quality work in that medium.

The new school of architecture, one characterized by functionalism, glass and steel, and cantilever construction, was furthered by LeCorbusier at the Tokyo Museum, Niemeyer's Presidential Palace in Brazilia, Mies van der Rohe's Seagram Building in New York, and Wright's Guggenheim Art Museum in New York. Henry Moore contributed sculpture and Jean Miro contributed murals to the UNESCO Building in Paris. The compositions of Stravinsky, Britten, Hindemith, Vaughn Williams, and Leonard Bernstein, among many others, brought enjoyment to what Rubinstein labeled a sixth sense. Variety in literature as exemplified by the appearance of Pasternak's Doctor Zhivago, Capote's Breakfast at Tiffany's, Huxley's further warnings in Brave New World Revisited, Pinter's The Birthday Party, and J. Edgar Hoover's Masters of Deceit all appeared in 1958. And in 1959 diversity continued with Faulkner's The Mansion, Mailer's Advertisement for Myself, Bellow's Henderson, the Rain King, Wesker's play, Roots, and Ionesco's theatre of the absurd depicted in The Rhinoceros.

Science and technological wizardry, always embracing art, were propelled by desire to embark on the conquest of space. The end of the Fifties brought keen competition for prowess in space between the United States and the USSR. In 1958 the United States launched Explorer I, among other satellites, and Russia launched Sputnik III. James Van Allen discovered a radiation belt around the Earth. The last year of the decade brought Russia's Lunik II and III to the moon; the latter returned with photographs of the moon's other side.

Thus, the Fifties brought new ages in several ways: the Space Age had begun; the Atomic Age swelled with both potential for progress and peril; an age of national recognition that international alliance was necessary for economic and social growth. It was also an age of emergence for the suppressed--

129

be it on racial, colonial, sexual, ethical, political, or economic grounds--to state with force that they too were human and needed more freedom where there was less. The journey of the maturing process for all of these "ages" was indeed arduous, yet the potential for human growth in each would be great enough to rekindle human imagination and productivity to new plateaus.

Curriculum Thought and Literature

The curriculum literature of the Fifties, 121 books, brought a continuance of the kind of curriculum writing that evolved in the previous decades, particularly the synoptic text. It might even be said that the Fifties was the heyday of this type of curriculum book, a contribution to the literature that, though sometimes faulted for both superficiality and hodgepodgity, implanted in the minds of many the idea that curriculum study was a viable subdivision of educational studies. The synoptic text portrayed a body of literature that aided the justification of curriculum as a field of inquiry. Although it is impossible to measure the impact of this type of book, it was an indisputable contributor to the solidification of curriculum's place in educational literature. The synoptic text was a major instrument used to prepare both practitioners and scholars in educational occupations; thus, it contributed markedly to the production, nature, and sustenance of curriculum roles in school systems. Such roles as the curriculum superintendent, director, and consultant were indeed prevalent in schools of the 1950's.

Among the best selling of the synoptic texts was Fundamentals of Curriculum Development by B. Othanel Smith, William O. Stanley, and J. Harlan Shores, which appeared in 1950 and was revised in 1957. Not only did this text provide encyclopedic background on the curriculum field, it added several dimensions which were to become mainstays of curriculum literature for some time to come. The authors set curriculum development in a socio-cultural con-

text by tying curriculum issues to the following:
an interpretation of the meaning and structure of
culture, community changes, economic considerations,
and social values. They augmented the ideas of
development and principle that were basic to curriculum literature of the 1930's by explicating criteria
for determining objectives, subject-matter or
experiences, content, sequence and grade placement,
and time allotment and distribution. Three dominant
orientations to curriculum organization (the subject,
activity, and core curricular patterns) were presented, and characteristics, problems, practices,
and criticisms of each were discussed. One can perceive similarity between categories of curriculum
discussion used by Smith, Stanley, and Shores with
those used by Tyler (1949); however, the kind and
degree of elaboration within each category sets them
apart. The Smith, Stanley, and Shores text devoted
considerable attention to the role of human relations and inter-personal politics in curriculum
change, revision, and decision-making. Finally, the
authors identified and discussed alternative viewpoints on theoretical curriculum issues. These
discussions, though somewhat general by comparison
with conceptual analysis prevalent in philosophy
today, were nevertheless more solidly grounded in
philosophy than the recipe-orientation to treatments of "principles" evident in many synoptic texts.
The authors referred to their discussion of issues as
theoretical (especially Part Five, 1957), doubtless
an attempt to inspire other curriculum writers to
probe assumptions when dealing with curriculum-
related problems. Authors of many subsequent texts
took this cue and devoted sections to what they
labeled curriculum theory.

The attempt to inspire theory development in
curriculum was pursued at a 1947 conference on
curriculum theory at the University of Chicago. The
conference convened under the leadership of Virgil
Herrick and Ralph Tyler, who subsequently published
the conference proceedings (Herrick and Tyler, 1950).
Actually, the conference participants (B. Othanel
Smith, Herman Frick, George E. Barton, Virgil Herrick, Gordon Mackenzie, Ralph Tyler, J. Paul

Leonard, Edgar Dale, G. Max Wingo, William M. Alexander, Hollis L. Caswell) hoped for a more ambitious outcome than inspiration. According to his thirty-years-later reflection, Ralph Tyler[1] indicated that the intent had been to develop tenets of theory that could more effectively explain and defensibly propose curriculum activity and research. Tyler expressed some satisfaction that the conference resulted in statements of conviction about what a sound curriculum theory should embrace, but he lamented that the desired theoretical formulations were beyond attainment at that conference.

Thus, 1950 brought both a synoptic text that was thought to be exemplary by many, and a set of admonitions designed to inspire if not exemplify the development of curriculum theory. In view of these two contributions alone the field was given momentum, although it must be acknowledged that considerable diversity exists among curriculum scholars about the worth of these and most other pieces of curriculum literature.

As great as their impact was on other authors these two contributions were not alone in 1950. Other formidable contributions in that year helped to initiate the work of the remainder of the decade. First among these were revisions of previously published texts. The demand for new editions indicates a fairly widespread assessment of usefulness of a text and its ideas. Jersild (1950) and Lee and Lee (1950) produced revisions of their texts that stressed relationships between understanding children and the development of curricular experiences. Both could be considered experientialist in their emphases on child study as a prime basis for curriculum development. Gwynn revised his Curriculum Principles and Social Trends, helping to perpetuate both the earlier notion of principles and the emphasis on modernity of curriculum thought. Another synoptic text, Curriculum Planning (1950) was produced by E.A. Krug, who tailored his treatment toward local situations by dealing with the relation of purposes to all-school

132

programs, curriculum guides, creation of specific
teaching-learning aids, relationships between
curriculum development and the teaching-learning
process, and specific suggestions for organizing
curriculum development in local school systems.

Despite the school-specific orientation mentioned above, overarching thrusts were also prevalent. National impetus to provide education
for all, not just the college bound, led to concern
for the utility of curriculum. Featherstone (1950)
provided an illustrative response with his functional curriculum. Similar accent was sponsored
by the U.S. Office of Education under the rubric
of life adjustment education. For a considerable
time they promoted efforts to offset the almost
exclusive college and vocational orientation to
high school curriculum that characterized the
Twenties and subsequent decades. An example of
this movement's continuance in the Fifties was
its support in a 1950 statement by the National
Association of Secondary School Principals.

The above statement is symbolic of emphasis on
cooperative endeavors in curriculum development that
emerged in the literature of the late Forties. It
was furthered by Taba (1950) and Evans (1950); the
former focused on intergroup relations in the
elementary school and the latter treated cooperation
in research and programs of improvement. Together,
the two illuminated a considerable range within the
purview of that which was considered curricular.
Together, they advocated reform through cooperative
organization.

Although much literature produced in 1950
advocated or prescribed more often than it described, the precedent for descriptive research on
school practice that prevailed in the Forties was
kept alive by Caswell and Associates (1950). Their
survey provided: (1) perspectives for evaluating
cases in curriculum improvement; (2) reports on a
wide range of curriculum programs; and (3) a report
on curriculum materials. Their descriptions and
accompanying discussions of actual curriculum

133

cases represent a major contribution to literature that analyzed extant curriculum practice.

The core curriculum, considered by many a more characteristically Deweyan interpretation than the activity or correlated curricula of years gone by, was given marked impetus by Smith, Stanley, and Shores (1950 and 1957) G.S. Wright (1950 and 1958), and Ovsiew (1951). Considerable elaboration was provided by Faunce and Bossing (1951 and 1958). It may be that the core represented an attempt to correct pervasive misinterpretations of Dewey in practitioner-oriented literature. It may be that a new label was needed to relieve the taint of post-war accusation associated with the activity curriculum. In any event advocates of the core emphasized a closer relation between student interest and interdisciplinary knowledge. This helped to correct for the preoccupation with caprice that was uncharacteristic of Dewey in many practiced activity curriculums.

In 1951, the Association for Supervision and Curriculum Development continued to emphasize curriculum revisions, calling them "improvements." Their yearbook and annual conference highlights of that year illustrated the thrust, and their publication on funds and time indicated practical considerations for getting the job done. Harold Hand added to the movement by advocating a program that could be applied to enhance improvement (1951). Toward the same end, but with greater thoroughness than any of the above, Benne and Muntyan wove the idea of improvement, christening it "change," with the idea of human relations implicit in the literature on cooperative endeavors in curriculum development. Their book of readings, Human Relations in Curriculum Change (1951), can be viewed as a forerunner of today's ideas associated with organizational development. It provided an important linking contribution to both change literature and curriculum literature.

Sometimes the curriculum literature on change, innovation, modernity, and related areas smacks

134

of bandwagonism, i.e., a desire to "keep up with the times" regardless of need. In response to this, Shane and McSwain provided <u>Evaluation and the Elementary School Curriculum</u> (1951), a text that stressed the need to carefully assess existing curriculum and the values embodied in it as a prerequisite to defensible change or revision. Their text provided two other contributions that should be noted: it represented a tailoring of the synoptic text idea to elementary curriculum and evaluation, and it provided separate sections on subject matter areas within an evaluation context. The latter seemed to perpetuate a new variety of intellectual traditionalist thought; namely, the separate subject areas were treated as "givens." This combined with the linear and systematic thought implicit in the "business" of social behaviorist evaluation technology. It also combined with a humanistically tempered experientialism that lingered from the progressive era. Taken together the three emphases represented a coming of age, a composite of curriculum knowledge that was assumed applicable to any educational level or subject area.

Little was said in this or the last chapter about the three schools of curriculum thought that emerged with characteristic distinctions in the first four decades of the Twentieth Century. The Forties represented a transition period during which a different style of curriculum book evolved. The synoptic text moved to predominance. During the Fifties these texts became the accepted preserver and conveyer of curriculum knowledge. Surely, one can see differences of orientation that roughly parallel the three schools of curriculum thought within the general category of synoptic curriculum texts. Nevertheless, an amalgamation of the intellectual traditionalist, social behaviorist, and experientialist schools was quite evident in most synoptic texts. Depending on one's personal orientation, one might tend to view this amalgamation as largely productive and refer to it as an eclectic synthesis, or conversely, as largely anti-productive and think of it as a watered-down oversimplification of each

135

of the positions. Such texts were no doubt offered to span across the diversity of school and classroom needs, i.e., to reach common goals.

Some authors, however, tried to speak to situational needs more fully; one example is Washburne's (1952) elaboration on the character of Progressive Education. The appearance of Sharp's Curriculum Development as Re-education of the Teacher (1951) and Spears' The Teacher and Curriculum Planning (1951) illustrated an increased emphasis on teacher roles in curriculum processes. The re-appearance of Burton's The Guidance of Learning Activities (1951), Stratemeyer's (1952) provision of guides to supplement and concretize her 1947 text, and Ragan's (1953) synoptic treatment at the elementary level, continued the acknowledgement of the importance of teachers in curriculum actualization. Ragan offered a significant departure. Not only was his work synoptic, not only did it offer subject matter perspectives, it also represented an attempt to help teachers realize that they, too, are curriculum creators. The risk of oversimplification in a single exposure of teachers to curriculum was indeed great, but so was the problem of no exposure at all.

Books began to appear that extended the subject orientation exemplified by Ragan, i.e., entire books that introduced teachers of secondary or elementary levels to mathematics curriculum, or language arts curriculum, or social studies curriculum, or science curriculum, and a host of other specialized areas. Such books usually dealt with methods and subject matter more than curriculum development; therefore, they are omitted from the present discussion unless they are considered by this author to represent a special advance in the way that curriculum can be viewed or studied. A noteworthy exception was Meier, Cleary, and Davis (1952) in their treatment of citizenship education, a topic that would seem to fall wholly within social studies. Their book, however, addressed citizenship as a basis, substance, and outcome, as well as a deliberative process in curriculum

136

development. The same kind of exception can be made for Harap's (1952) book that used social living as an organizing theme or core from which to derive, implement, and judge curricula, not merely as a certain body of knowledge to be amassed along with appropriate pedagogical techniques.

The emphasis on democratic deliberation that characterized the two books mentioned above was not only advocated by scholarly circles; it was sometimes practiced. Exemplary here was a faculty committee (representatives were from Andover, Exeter, Lawrenceville, Harvard, Princeton, and Yale) assembled to make recommendations about the issue of general education in schools and colleges. Not only was the value of cooperative decision-making given credence by their efforts, the cooperation was international as well, resulting in a publication entitled General Education in School and College (1952). In the same year the first volume of the Fifty-first Yearbook of the National Society for the Study of Education presented explorations into the meaning of general education in a context of the Fifties, a time of great post-war influx into educational institutions. Although no patented conclusion was accepted by all, questions about the nature of an education that would best produce an enlightened citizenry were given considerable scrutiny beyond dimensions that focused solely on vocational preparation and readiness for further education.

The theme of general education was firmly carried to many of the books on secondary curriculum in the first half of the Fifties, a time when the synoptic text came to fruition in secondary education. Briggs (1951), and Hand (1951) to a slighter extent, paved the way. In 1953, revised editions of Alberty's Reorganizing the High School Curriculum and J.P. Leonard's Developing the Secondary School Curriculum furthered the influence of such texts. Beck, Cook, and Kearney did the same at the elementary school

level with the publication of Curriculum in the
Modern Elementary School (1953), as did the aforementioned Modern Elementary Curriculum by Ragan
in the same year. That year also brought examples of synoptic books by McNerney and by the
American Association of School Administrators, both
of which provided encyclopedic backgrounds and
treatments of issues that were designed to apply
to curriculum development at all levels of schooling.

An area of study that received considerable
mention in synoptic texts dating to those by
Harap (1928), Hopkins (1929), Caswell and Campbell
(1935), Gwynn (1943), Tyler (1949), and Smith,
Stanley, and Shores (1950 and 1957) was organization. The issue of how to organize curricular
experiences for effective learning was addressed
at book length in the Fifties by Krug, Liddle, and
Schenk (1952) and Doll, Passow, and Corey (1953),
helping to solidify it as a problematic area for
curriculum inquiry.

Another area that received considerable note
in the mid-Fifties was democracy. It appeared in
several quite different interpretations. One of
these was the community school, a thoroughly
grounded integration of the school in community
functioning (Olsen, 1953 and NSSE, (1953). These
sources expressed democratic interpretations of
schooling that included deliberation and cooperative action as repeatedly emphasized in many
curriculum books. Action research, mentioned at
some length in synoptic texts of the Fifties, can
be seen as another extension of democracy into
curricular endeavors by giving teachers and other
school personnel skill and opportunity to provide
a necessary kind of educational research specific
to their own settings. Corey (1953) provided book
length discussion of action research as an important prerequisite to curricular revision. In 1955,
Corey joined efforts with Passow and Miles in a
call for a type of cooperative research that could
unite workers in different roles within curriculum
scholarship and practice. This focus on specific

138

educational settings had potential for providing
clearer visions of the characteristics and needs
of children and youth. It clearly related to the
first volume of the Fifty-second Yearbook of the
National Society for the Study of Education (1953)
which was devoted to the idea of adapting curricula to young people rather than molding them to a
desired end. The latter re-created images of the
experientialist persuasion.

The manifold list of developments in curriculum literature of the early Fifties led to
publications that discussed trends. Noting that
mid-century is a good time to reflect on progress,
Harap (1953) produced a book on this topic. Campbell (1953) reflected on trends in Canadian curriculum, and the Association for Student Teaching
(1953) discussed curriculum trends relative to
teacher education. Koos analyzed trends in the
development of junior high schools (1955), many
of which he was earlier instrumental in influenc-
ing. The same year brought an analysis of curriculum guides by Merritt and Harap. Finally,
Harold Shane's editorship of the Thirteenth Yearbook of the John Dewey Society (1953) provided
reflections on curriculum by several prominent
educators (e.g., John Childs, Arthur Foshay, Henry
Otto, Edgar Dale, Walter Moore, Celia Stendler)
on past developments and challenges that these
provided for the future.

In 1954, the reappearance of Adams' Educating America's Children illustrated the appeal of
the growing reunion of curriculum and methods that
was furthered by Ragan and other authors. The
same year brought two attempts to explain how to
develop curricula for adolescents, one by Romine
and the other by the Association for Supervision
and Curriculum Development. Of paramount impact
that year and for many years hence, in its
several revitalizations, was Curriculum Planning
for Better Teaching and Learning by Saylor and
Alexander. This text, both synoptic and oriented
to the preparation of curriculum-minded teachers
and administrators, was used widely in the educa-

tion of curriculum specialists. By the mid-
Fifties two books were on the market that dealt
primarily with characterizing the job of curriculum workers in schools: Kirk (1953) and
Columbia University (1955).

Curriculum books in the second half of the
Fifties began as a continuation of the curriculum
topics that emerged during or prior to the first
half. Otto (1955) treated curriculum enrichment
for gifted students within the regular elementary
school classroom. Relations between curriculum
and guidance were explored by Kelly (1955) and by
the 1955 ASCD Yearbook. Jackson (1956) and Lurry
and Alberty (1957) helped to sustain the idea of
core curriculum, the former focusing on staff
perceptions and the latter on the secondary
school. Hoppe (1957) treated the core at the
junior high school level. The revised edition
of Developing the Core Curriculm by Faunce and
Bossing and Wright's Core Curriculum Development,
both in 1958, continued this experientialist
emphasis throughout the 1950's.

The predominant kind of contribution to curriculum literature from 1955 through the remainder of the decade was the synoptic text in its
several variations. Examples include: Fitzgerald and Fitzgerald (1955), Beauchamp (1956),
Hurley (1957), and Shane and McSwain (1958) at
the elementary school level; Douglass' second edition of The High School Curriculum (1956) and
Venable (1958) at the secondary level; and Krug,
et al. (1956) at the level of administrative planning. Other authors continued the tradition of
dealing with curriculum development generally
instead of at a specific level. Examples include:
Anderson (1956); the revised edition of Smith,
Stanley, and Shores (1957); the revised edition of
Stratemeyer (1957); and Krug's 1957 revision of
Curriculum Planning.

Of perhaps greatest longevity, lasting through
the end of the 1970's and stemming historically to
the first speculations on curriculum, was the con-

sideration of purpose that appeared in new variations in the late 1950's. Foremost among such contributions was the 1956 taxonomical classification of cognitive objectives produced by Benjamin Bloom and others. This book's influence provided at least rival competition to the impact of Tyler (1949) in its appearance in both scholarly citation and the rhetoric of educational practice. Countless practitioners were exposed to Bloom's taxonomy and its six cognitive levels (memory, interpretation or comprehension, application, analysis, synthesis, and evaluation). Applications were indeed prodigious as applied to many areas: lesson planning, the writing of objectives, questioning techniques, and skills management systems. Clearly, not all of the uses were anticiapted or condoned by the authors. Nisbet (1957) produced one of the first major British curriculum books since the early years of the century. His book focused entirely on conceptions of purposes or ends of education conveyed by the curriculum. The 1956 ASCD Yearbook also addressed purpose relative to high school education by venturing responses to the question of what high schools should teach.

The quest for purpose was met not only with the rationality that one might expect from scholarly circles but with great reactivity as well when, in 1957, the world was shocked at the Russian launching of Sputnik. Many interpreters held that this technological achievement evidenced the educational superiority of the USSR to the United States and other nations. Thus, widespread criticism of American education coupled with anguished hopefulness gave hasty birth to programs, called curriculum projects, that would in their fruition become a mainstay of curriculum development in the 1960's. In their infancy many of these programs were presented in journals and at conferences. Others, mere unfunded eccentricities before Sputnik, were awarded massive funding by both governmental and private sources that catered to the expediency of "political necessity." Several forces, however, prevented major curriculum projects

141

from immediate emergence. The increasingly acknowledged perennial lag between social pressure and educational change is a prime example. Lag persisted and curriculum projects did not bloom full until the 1960's.

Other issues shared the spotlight in curriculum books for the remainder of the Fifties. Let us review some of these to round out the decade. Edwards (1956) evaluated a cooperative secondary curriculum development program. French (1957) provided one of the first book length treatments of behavioral goals in education since those of the social behaviorists early in the Twentieth Century, though it was an interpretation quite different from the notion of the behavioral objectives movement that swelled in the late Sixties and early Seventies. Spears (1957) noted the import of in-service programs in curriculum development, a phenomenon that characterized the widespread funding of new programs in the Sixties. The United Nations brought an international flavor to curriculum literature; examples, often appearing under the auspices of UNESCO include: Olson's (1957) emphasis on psychological foundations, Lourengo's (1957) treatment of primary curriculum in Latin America, a comparative study of primary curriculum by the Conference Internationale (1958), and UNESCO's book on research and revision of curriculum (1958).

The 1958 ASCD Yearbook treated the topic of continuity in school programs from level to level. An alternative solution to this organizational issue was offered by Goodlad and Anderson (1959). Their plan for nongradedness stirred much scholarly and practical thought and action; however, both were interpreted with great ambiguity. The relation between curriculum and the school plant itself constituted an organizational issue treated by Hefferman and Bursch (1958). In the same year, the National Society for the Study of Education rekindled the organizational pattern of integrating educational experiences, advanced by Hopkins and others in the Thirties. This was another

142

variation on the topic of organizational patterns for curriculum.

Curricularists themselves became the subjects of their books at times. It was not difficult to detect that many factors provided impediments to the work of the ever-increasing occupational role known as the curriculum consultancy. In her concern for this problem, Lawler (1958) addressed factors that contributed to successes of curriculum consultants.

The emergent issues and topics in curriculum were numerous indeed, a state of affairs that sparked Alcorn and Linley to edit a book of articles on curriculum issues in 1954 and again in 1959. Their books represent a thorough sampling of the thoughts of the times. This book provided an example for many collections that would follow.

The existence of curriculum as an area of study for half a century prompted historical portrayals as well as collections. Such was the response of the ASCD (though later historical analyses would be more thorough) in their discussion of improvements from 1857 through 1957 (1957).

A book that is difficult to classify, perhaps because it stemmed from a rare philosophic orientation, then uncommon to curriculum discourse, was Dynamics of Curriculum Improvement (1959) by P.T. Pritzkau. Pritzkau took a stance that might be labeled existentialist and provided a departure from the usual generalizations found in many of the synoptic texts, especially those that utilized the guideline or recipe notion of "principles." He did attempt to generalize about the decision-making process but acknowledged the essential uniqueness of situations, making his treatment complex and lacking the kind of quick answers that those in the field of action desire and often demand. This orientation to situational complexity was not without precedent; there was Dewey. Further, the interested reader should wait patiently, for there is more that is similar in

143

Phenix and Schwab in the 1960's and the "reconceptualists" and others in the 1970's. The
Emerging Self in School and Home (1954) by L.
Thomas Hopkins also provides great strides to
explicate a curriculum deep within the fabric
of human experience.

Finally, the Fifties ended with a book that
was instrumental in creating the curricular
character of the high school in subsequent years.
With considerable backing from the Carnegie
Foundation, enough to supply many school boards
with copies of his book, James Bryant Conant
produced The American High School Today (1959).
In it, he outlined a kind of high school curriculum, complete with college preparatory, vocational, and general dimensions, that today many
consider to be the perennial high school character.   The number of credit requirements or
Carnegie units of mathematics, English, languages,
science, social science, humanities, etc. which
seem so familiar were in no small measure perpetuated by the impact of Conant's work. He
recommended school consolidation and thereby
the reduction of numbers of small schools. He
advocated counseling systems, individualized
program scheduling, required courses and elec-
tives, ability grouping by subject, transcripts,
special emphasis on English composition, emphasis on marketable skills, special programs for
slow readers, special programs for academically talented and extra provision for highly
gifted students, prerequisites for advanced
courses, honors lists, six to eight period days,
increased emphasis on foreign language and science
preparation, courses that enhance the vocational
preparation and home skills needed by girls, and
study of American government in the twelfth
grade. In short, Conant promoted the development of the comprehensive high school designed
to facilitate general education, college preparation, and the gamut of vocational education
simultaneously.

In the Fifties we have seen a pinnacle in
production of synoptic texts, a call for theo-

retical soundness of purpose, a continuation of
the core curriculum, a call for curriculum evaluation, an expansion of the domain of curriculum
considerations, and a continuation of concern for
social adjustment. Many of these topics were
de-emphasized amid frustrations to equalize status with the Russians. But this was more of a
problem for the Sixties. The continuation of
the synoptic text as the dominant form of curriculum writing in the Fifties, coupled with the
uniquely American rise of the comprehensive
school further solidified the amalgamation of
schools of curriculum thought. Thus, while not
wanting to understate the existence and worth
of varied tendencies within both curriculum
literature and practice, it seems safe to assert that an assumption underlying both was
that most things necessary for the education of
most persons could be contained within one
source. In other words, that which curriculum
decision-makers needed could be presented in the
synoptic text, and that which students needed
could be presented in the comprehensive schools.
Benefits of this tendency to mass produce knowledge and disseminate it efficiently must be
weighed against the debits of uncritical synthesis, inordinant pigeonholing of ideas, simplification of guidance, the rhetoric of having
provided more substance where less is justifiable, and the tendency of such syntheses to
propagate values and activities of the most
powerful social groups in a society.

Notes

[1]Ralph W. Tyler, Toward Improved Curriculum
Theory: The Inside Story. Curriculum Inquiry.
6:4, 1977, pp. 251-256. It should be noted that
the remainder of the issue of Curriculum Inquiry
containing these reflections was devoted to
publication of proceedings of a 1976 curriculum
conference held at the State University College
of Arts and Science in Geneseo, New York, a
conference designed to discuss the curriculum
field's progress in the area of theory building.

Bibliography of Curriculum Books,
1950-1959

1950

Bathurst, E.G. Where children live affects
the children. Educational Bulletin
Number 7. Washington: Government
Printing Office, 1950.

Caswell, H.L., and Associates. Curriculum
improvement in public school systems.
New York: Teachers College, Columbia
University, 1950.

Columbia University, Teachers College.
Institute of Field Studies. Public
education and the future of Puerto
Rico, a curriculum survey 1948-1949
(Gordon N. Mackenzie, survey director).
New York: Bureau of Publications,
Teachers College, Columbia University,
1950.

Conference on Problems of Curriculum
Development. Problems of curriculum
development. Salem, Oregon, 1950.

Evans, H.M. (Editor). Cooperative research
and curriculum improvement. New York:
Bureau of Publications, Teachers College, Columbia University, 1950.

Featherstone, W.B. A functional curriculum
for youth. New York: American Book
Company, 1950.

Gwynn, J.M. Curriculum principles and
social trends (Second Edition). New
York: Macmillan, 1950.

Herrick, V.E. and Tyler, R.W. (Editors).
Toward improved curriculum theory.
Supplementary Educational Monographs.

146

Chicago: University of Chicago Press, 1950.

Illinois. Western Illinois University, Macomb. Curriculum revision for more effective living. Macomb, Illinois: Western Illinois University, 1950.

Jersild, A.T. Child development and the curriculum. New York: Teachers College, Columbia University, 1950.

Jobe, E.R. Curriculum development in Mississippi public white high schools, 1900-1945. Nashville: Bureau of Publications, George Peabody College for Teachers, 1950.

Kobayashi, T. Our curriculum. Japan: Niigata University, Department of Education, Elementary School, 1950.

Krug, E.A. Curriculum planning. New York: Harper and Brothers, 1950.

Lee, J.M. and Lee, D.M. The child and his curriculum (Second Edition). New York: Appleton-Century-Crofts, 1950.

National Association of Secondary School Principals. Life adjustment in the secondary school curriculum. Number 171. Washington: The Association, 1950.

Scottish Education Department. The primary school in Scotland: A memorandum on the curriculum. Edinburgh: Her Majesty's Stationery Office, 1950.

Smith, B.O., Stanley, W.O., and Shores, J.H. Fundamentals of curriculum development. Yonkers-on-the-Hudson, New York: World Book Company, 1950.

147

Taba, H. (Director). Elementary curriculum in intergroup relations. Washington: American Council on Education, 1950.

Tennessee. Department of Education, Division of Public Schools. Curriculum planning for our schools; a unified plan for curriculum improvement developed during the summer of 1949 by workshop groups at the University of Tennessee and the A and I State College. Nashville: Department of Education, 1950.

Wright, G.S. Core curriculum in public high schools: An Inquiry into practices, 1949. Washington, D.C.: Government Printing Office, 1950.

1951

Association for Supervision and Curriculum Development. Action for curriculum improvement. 1951 Yearbook. Washington: The Association, 1951a.

Association for Supervision and Curriculum Development. Curriculum improvement in the world crisis; highlights of the 1951 ASCD convention, sixth annual meeting, February 10-15, 1951, Detroit, Michigan. Washington: Association for Supervision and Curriculum, 1951b.

Association for Supervision and Curriculum Development. Time and funds for curriculum development. Washington: The Association, 1951c.

Benne, K.D. and Muntyan, B. Human relations in curriculum change: Selected readings with special emphasis on group development. New York: The Dryden Press, 1951.

Briggs, T.H. The secondary school curricu-
    lum: Yesterday, today, and tomorrow.
    New York: Teachers College, Columbia
    University, 1951.

Burton, W.H. The guidance of learning
    activities (Second Edition). New York:
    Appleton-Century, 1951.

Faunce, R.C. and Bossing, N.L. Developing
    the core curriculum. New York: Pren-
    tice-Hall, 1951.

Hand, H.C. How the Illinois secondary
    school curriculum program in basic stu-
    dies can help you improve your high
    school. Springfield, Illinois:
    Superintendent of Public Instruction,
    1951.

Harvard University. Graduate School of
    Education Center for Field Studies.
    Pittsfield junior high school; stages
    in curriculum design, 1951-1960.
    Pittsfield, Mass.: Harvard Univer-
    sity, 1951.

Ovsiew, L., et al. Making the core work.
    New York: Metropolitan School Study
    Council, 1951.

Shane, H.G. and McSwain, E.T. Evaluation
    and the elementary school. New York:
    Bureau of Publications, Teachers Col-
    lege, Columbia University, 1951.

Sharp, G. Curriculum development as the
    re-education of the teacher. New
    York: Teachers College Press, 1951.

Spears, H. The teacher and curriculum
    planning. Englewood Cliffs, New
    Jersey: Prentice-Hall, Inc., 1951.

1952

Association for Supervision and Curriculum
Development. Bibliography on supervision and curriculum development (prepared by Thelma Byars and others).
Washington: Association for Supervision and Curriculum Development, 1952a.

Association for Supervision and Curriculum
Development. Time and funds for cur-
riculum development. Washington:
Iowa Association Chapter, 1952b.

Blackmer, A.R. (Chairman). General education
in school and college. Cambridge:
Harvard University Press, 1952.

England, Ministry of Education. Welsh
Department. The curriculum and the
community in Wales. London: Her
Majesty's Stationery Office, 1952.

General education in school and college:
A committee report by members of the
faculty of Andover, Exeter, Lawrenceville, Harvard, Princeton, and Yale.
Cambridge: Harvard University Press,
1952.

Harap, H. Social living in the curriculum:
A critical study of the core in action
in grades one through twelve. Nashville: George Peabody College for
Teachers, 1952.

Jones, L. Curriculum aids in continuation
education. Sacramento: California
Department of Education. Bulletin V
21, Number 12, 1952.

Krug, E.A., Liddle, C.S., and Schenk, Q.
Multiple period curriculum organization in Wisconsin secondary schools.
Madison: University of Wisconsin,
1952.

Meier, A.R., Cleary, F.D., and Davis, A.M.
A curriculum for citizenship. Detroit:
Wayne State University Press, 1952
(Reprinted by Greenwood Press, New
York, 1969).

National Society for the Study of Education. General education. Fifty-First
Yearbook, Part I. Chicago: University of Chicago Press, 1952.

National Union of Teachers, London. The
curriculum of the secondary school;
report of a consultative committee
appointed by the Executive of the
National Union of Teachers. London:
Efans Brothers, 1952.

Stratemeyer, F.B., Forkner, H.L., McKim,
M.G., et al. Guides to a curriculum
for modern living. New York: Teachers College, Columbia University,
1952.

Washburne, C. What is progressive education? New York: John Day Company,
1952.

1953

Alberty, H. Reorganizing the high school
curriculum (Second Edition). New
York: Macmillan, 1953.

American Association of School Administrators. American school curriculum.
Washington: National Education Association Yearbook, 1953.

Association for Student Teaching. Curriculum trends and teacher education.
1953 Yearbook (J.A. Bond and J.A.
Hockett, Editors), 1953.

151

Beck, R.H., Cook, W.W., and Kearney, N.C.
Curriculum in the modern elementary
school. Englewood Cliffs, New Jersey:
Prentice-Hall, 1953.

Campbell, H.L. Curriculum trends in Canadian education. Toronto: W.J. Gage,
1953.

Corey, S.M. Action research to improve
school practices. New York: Bureau
of Publications. Teachers College,
Columbia University, 1953.

Doll, R., Passow, H., and Corey, S. Organization for curriculum improvement.
New York: Bureau of Printing, Teachers College University, 1953.

Harap, H. Curriculum trends at mid-century.
Cincinnati: Southwestern Publishing
Company, 1953.

Kearney, N.C. Elementary school objectives:
A report prepared for the mid-century
committee on outcomes in elementary
education. New York: Russell Sage
Foundation, 1953.

Kirk, D.L. The role of the curriculum director in the administration of American
public school programs. Austin, Texas:
School of Education, University of
Texas, 1953.

Leonard, J.P. Developing the secondary
school curriculum (Revised Edition).
New York: Rinehart and Company, 1953.

McNerney, C.T. The curriculum. New York:
McGraw-Hill, 1953.

National Society for the Study of Education.
Adapting the secondary school program
to the needs of youth. Fifty-Second
Yearbook, Part I. Chicago: University of Chicago Press, 1953a.

National Society for the Study of Education.
The Community School. Fifty-Second Year-
book, Part II. Chicago: University of
Chicago Press, 1953b.

Olsen, E.G. (Editor). The modern community
school. New York: Appleton-Century-
Crofts, 1953.

Ragan, W.B. Modern elementary curriculum.
New York: Holt, Rinehart and Winston,
1953.

Shane, H.G. (Editor). The American elementary school. Thirteenth Yearbook of
the John Dewey Society. New York:
Harper and Brothers, 1953.

Western Illinois State College. Curriculum
revision and development. Macomb,
Illinois: Western Illinois State College, 1953.

1954

Adams, F. (Greene). Educating America's
children; elementary school curriculum
and methods (Second Edition). New
York: Ronald Press Company, 1954.

Alcorn, M.D. and Linley, J.M. (Editors).
Issues in curriculum development. New
York: World Book Company, 1954.

Association for Supervision and Curriculum
Development. Developing programs for
young adolescents; a booklet prepared
for ASCD by the Department of Supervision and Curriculum Development of the
Florida Education Association. Washington, D.C.: Association for Supervision and Curriculum Development, 1954.

Cassidy, R.F. Curriculum development in
physical education. New York: Harper,
1954.

Hopkins, L.T. The emerging self in school

and home. New York: Harper and
Brothers, 1954. (also 1970).

New York (State) University, Bureau of
Elementary Curriculum Development.
The elementary school curriculum; an
overview. Albany: New York (State)
University, 1954.

Ohio State University, Columbia University
School. A description of curricular
experiences: the lower school . . .
kindergarten through grade six (Revised
Edition). Columbus: Ohio State University, 1954.

Romine, S. Building the high school curriculum. New York: Ronald Press,
1954.

Saylor, J.G. and Alexander, W. Curriculum
planning for better teaching and learning. New York: Holt, Rinehart and
Winston, 1954.

1955

Association for Supervision and Curriculum
Development. Guidance in the curricu-
lum. Yearbook. Washington, D.C.:
The Association, 1955.

Columbia University. Teachers College.
Seminar in Supervision and Curriculum
Improvement. The work of the curriculum coordinator in selected New Jersey
schools; a report to the New Jersey
curriculum coordinators. New York:
Bureau of Publications, Teachers College, Columbia University, 1955.

Fitzgerald, J.A. and Fitzgerald, P.G.
Methods and curricula in elementary
education. Milwaukee: Bruce Publishing Company, 1955.

154

Kelly, J.A. Guidance and the curriculum. Englewood Cliffs, New Jersey: Prentice-Hall, 1955.

Koos, L.V. Junior high school trends. New York: Harper and Brothers, 1955.

Lee, J.M. (Editor). Selected bibliography for curriculum workers. Washington: Association for Supervision and Curriculum Development. (Briefer versions were published in 1953 and 1954 under similar titles), 1955.

Merritt, E. and Harap, H. Trends in the production of curriculum guides. Nashville: George Peabody College for Teachers, 1955.

National Council of Churches. A guide for curriculum in Christian education. Chicago: Division of Christian Education, National Council of Churches, 1955.

Otto, H.J. (Editor). Curriculum enrichment for gifted elementary school children in regular classes. Austin: University of Texas, 1955.

Passow, A.H., Miles, M.B., and Corey, S.M. Training curriculum leaders for cooperative research. New York: Teachers College, Columbia University, 1955.

<u>1956</u>

Anderson, V.E. Principles and procedures of curriculum improvement. New York: Ronald Press, 1956.

Association for Supervision and Curriculum Development. What shall high schools teach? 1956 Yearbook. Washington: The Association, 1956.

Beauchamp, G.A. Planning the elementary
    school curriculum. New York: Allyn
    and Bacon, 1956.

Bloom, B.S. (Editor). Taxonomy of educa-
    tional objectives, handbook I: Cog-
    nitive domain. New York: David
    McKay and Company, 1956.

Douglass, H.R. (Editor). The high school
    curriculum (Second Edition). New York:
    Ronald Press, 1956.

Edwards, T.B. The regional project in
    secondary education; evaluation of a
    program of cooperative curriculum
    development. Berkeley: University
    of California Press, 1956.

Hoppe, A.A. Students help improve the
    curriculum in Indiana. Bloomington,
    Indiana: Division of Research and
    Field Services, Indiana University,
    1956.

Jackson, D.M. Staff perceptions of develop-
    ing core programs. Chicago: Univer-
    sity of Chicago, 1956.

Krug, E.A., et al. Administering curricu-
    lum planning. New York: Harper and
    Brothers, 1956.

1957

Association for Supervision and Curriculum
    Development. One hundred years of
    curriculum improvement, 1857-1957.
    Washington: The Association, 1957.

French, W., et al. Behavioral goals of
    general education in high school.
    New York; Russell Sage Foundation,
    1957.

Hoppe, A.A. The core in junior high school. Bloomington, Indiana: Division of Research and Field Services, Indiana University, 1957.

Hurley, B.J. Curriculum for elementary school children. New York: Ronald Press, 1957.

Krug, E.A. Curriculum planning. New York: Harper and Brothers, 1957.

Lourengo, M.B. Primary school curricula in Latin America. Paris: UNESCO, 1957.

Lurry, L. and Alberty, E.J. Developing a high school core program. New York: Macmillan, 1957.

Nisbet, S.D. Purpose in the curriculum. London: University of London Press, 1957.

Olson, W.C. Psychological foundations of the curriculum. Paris: UNESCO, 1957.

Smith, B.O., Stanley, W.O., and Shores, J.H. Fundamentals of curriculum development. (Revised Edition) New York: Harcourt, Brace and World, 1957.

Spears, H. Curriculum planning through in-service programs. Englewood Cliffs, New Jersey: Prentice-Hall, 1957.

Stratemeyer, F.B., Forkner, H.L., McKim, M.G., and Passow, A.H. Developing a curriculum for modern living. (Second Edition, Revised and Enlarged). New York: Bureau of Publications, Teachers College, Columbia University, 1957.

1958

Association for Supervision and Curriculum
Development. A look at continuity in
the school program. 1958 Yearbook.
Washington: The Association, 1958.

Bereday, G.Z.F. and Lauwerys, J.A. (Editors).
The secondary school curriculum: The
yearbook of education. New York:
Harcourt, Brace, Jovanovich, 1958.

Conference Internationale De L'Instruction
Publique. Preparation and issuing of
the primary school curriculum: A
comparative study. Paris: UNESCO,
1958.

Cummings, H.H. and Mackintosh, H.K. Curriculum responsibilities of state
departments of education. Washington:
U.S. Department of Health, Education,
and Welfare, Office of Education, 1958.

Faunce, R.C. and Bossing, N.L. Developing
the core curriculum (Second Edition).
Englewood Cliffs, New Jersey: Prentice-Hall, 1958.

Hefferman, H. and Bursch, C. Curriculum and
the elementary school plant. Washington: Association for Supervision and
Curriculum Development, 1958.

Lawler, M.R. Curriculum consultants at
work: Factors affecting their success.
New York: Teachers College, Columbia
University, 1958.

National Society for the Study of Education.
The integration of educational ex-
perience. Fifty-Seventh Yearbook, Part
III. Chicago: University of Chicago
Press, 1958.

Shane, H.G. and McSwain, E.T. Evaluation and the elementary curriculum (Revised Edition). New York: Henry Holt, 1958.

UNESCO. Curriculum revision and research. Paris, 1958.

Venable, T.C. Patterns in secondary school curriculum. New York: Harper, 1958.

Wright, G.S. Core curriculum development: Problems and practices. Bulletin Number 5, U.S. Office of Education, 1958.

1959

Alcorn, M.D. and Linley, J.M. (Editors). Issues in curriculum development. Yonkers-on-the-Hudson, New York: World Book Company, 1959.

Conant, J.B. The American high school today. New York: McGraw-Hill, 1959.

Frederick, R.W. The third curriculum: Student activities in American education. New York: Appleton-Century-Crofts, 1959.

Goodlad, J.I. and Anderson, R.H. The non-graded elementary school. New York: Harcourt, Brace and World, 1959.

Pritzkau, P.T. Dynamics of curriculum improvement. Englewood Cliffs, New Jersey: Prentice-Hall, 1959.

CHAPTER VII

CURRICULUM LITERATURE AND CONTEXT:

1960-1969

Contextual Reminders

The Sixties began with headlong concern among
leaders of major world powers to demonstrate technological superiority, particularly in the space
race. Simultaneously, the Sixties began with third
world peoples' demands to be allowed basic freedoms and a share of the pie, not only in third
world nations but in third world constituencies or
oppressed people everywhere. As the Sixties progressed, and as small scale but profound wars developed and lingered in many parts of the world,
inquisitions and suspicions developed that were re-
versed from the McCarthy-ism of the early Fifties.
Massive protestations were unleashed by political,
racial, ethnic, consumer, poverty-stricken, envi-
ronmental, and intellectual groups of citizens.
Demands were directed to authorities, both economic and governmental, calling for conceptions
of equity on multifarious grounds. The inquisitions came from the grassroots as well as from the
top down. Let us look more closely.

In 1960, fourteen African countries became independent. Violent demonstrations against apartheid occurred in South Africa, and the premier of
that nation barely survived an assassination attempt.
Turmoil and revolution plagued Zaire and Ethiopia.
Brezhnev's succession to the presidency of the USSR
took place in the same year. The U.S. was angered
by seizure of its private property in Cuba, and Cuba appealed to the United Nations for assistance in
dealing with U.S. "aggression" there. U.S.-USSR relations were further strained by the shooting down
of a U.S. U-2 plane, piloted by Gary Powers flying
over Soviet territory, making ineffectual the planned
Paris summit meeting between Khrushchev and Eisen-

hower. It was the year of presidential debates in
the U.S., and John F. Kennedy was elected president. The next year, 1961, brought the U.S.-sup-
ported "Bay of Pigs' invasion by Cuban exiles and
Kennedy's admission of responsibility. The Berlin
Wall was built. Albania was ousted from the Communist bloc countries due to relationships with China.
Dag Hammarskjold was killed in an air crash and was
succeeded by U Thant as UN Secretary-General. Memories of Nazi Germany were rekindled with the discovery, trial, and execution of Adolf Eichmann.
In 1962, Cuba and Russia signed a trade agreement
and a Russian fishing base was established in Cuba,
somehow evolving into a missile base which was eliminated after the U.S. blockade in 1962. Uganda and
Algeria became independent. With the dissolution of
the West Indies Federation, Jamaica and Trinidad and
Tobago became independent. The U.S. military established an advisory command in South Vietnam. By 1963,
relations between the free and communist worlds
seemed on the road to improvement with the establishment of a telephone "hot line" between Moscow and
Washington, D.C. This was accentuated by a nuclear
test ban treaty signed by the U.S., the USSR and 114
other nations. The same year brought the tragic
assassination of U.S. President John F. Kennedy, the
succession to presidency by Lyndon B. Johnson, and
continued controversy concerning causal factors in
the Kennedy assassination. In South Vietnam the
assassination of President Dinh Diem brought martial
law. African nations continued the quest for autonomy and several established republics. In Ethiopia,
also in 1963, The Organization of African Unity was
formed. The next year brought increased conflict in
two critical centers: Greeks battled Turks on Cyprus
with the United Nations attempting to maintain peace;
and U.S. and North Vietnamese forces attacked one
another. In Russia, Khrushchev was replaced by a
leadership headed by Kosygin and Brezhnev. By 1965,
the war in Vietnam escalated. U.S. Marines were
sent to quell an uprising in the Dominican Republic
and remained in charge to prevent a questionable
fear that communists would control in their absence.
Indian and Pakistani disputes raged over domination
of Kashmir.

162

Human rights were sought with vigorous dedication on many fronts in the early Sixties. In 1960, the first female prime minister took office in Ceylon. In the same year, the "sit-in," initiated as a black protest of standing-only rules at Southern U.S. lunch counters, swept the South. In less than a year, eating establishments were integrated in well over a hundred major U.S. cities. Contraceptive pills were approved for sale by the Federal Drug Administration. World-wide protest accompanied the execution of seemingly rehabilitated convict Caryl Chessman, including appeals for his life by Albert Schweitzer, Aldous Huxley, and Pablo Casals. President Kennedy had established the Peace Corps in 1961 to meet needs for skilled man-power in underdeveloped countries. The same year brought "Freedom Riders" who traveled in buses and trains throughout the southern U.S., testing desegregation laws and encountering great violence, finally being aided by the protection of federal marshals. In 1962 James Meredith became the first black student at the University of Mississippi after being aided on his fifth try for admission by federal marshals in an effort that caused riots, two deaths, and well over 100 injuries.

Another kind of freedom, freedom from unchecked side effects of technology, was vividly brought to public attention by Rachel Carson's Silent Spring, a book that did much to stir ecological awareness. This work exemplified a growing suspicion that human rights were indeed curbed by the use of excess power by major corporations. In 1961 nearly thirty electrical companies were found guilty and sentenced fines by the U.S. government for rigging bids and fixing prices in the sale of heavy electrical equipment. In 1962 President Kennedy encouraged the awarding of a five million dollar defense department contract to a small steel firm to prevent U.S. Steel and other major companies from actualizing a large proposed price hike. By 1963 civil rights advocates protested segregation, brutality, and job discrimination; soaring to high pitch with the killing of Medgar Evers, a black civil rights leader from Mississippi. August of the same year culminated in a march on Washington by more than 200,000 civil rights proponents, and a meeting of black leaders with President Kennedy during which Martin Luther King heatedly called for citizenship rights due blacks and all humans. Massive school boycotts protested de facto segregation in major U.S. cities in 1964. Half a year later President Johnson signed the most all-inclusive civil rights plan in U.S. history. It called for integration of public accommodations, forbade job discrimination by employers and labor unions on grounds of race, sex, or religion, and included provisions for education, elections, federal funding, and legal protection. The law was tested amid much turmoil, often resulting in major violence, looting and protestation throughout the U.S. In the same year, Martin Luther King received the Nobel Peace Prize for his leadership in the civil rights movement and for his promotion of nonviolence.

Meanwhile, attention was turned to the escalating war in Vietnam. Opposition to the war by Senators Gruening and Morse in 1964 marked the inclusion of high ranking governmental officials in the student-dominated protests of U.S. involvement in Vietnam. The Gulf of Tonkin Resolution, used subsequently in lieu of a Declaration of War, enabled the U.S. President to order military action in the war in Vietnam. Students, frequently investigated for subversive activities, staged numerous protests of governmental interference in their lives and activities and those of others. In 1965, both the racial situation and the Vietnam protests continued to inflame; Malcolm X was murdered. Blacks who attempted to register to vote in Alabama were violently resisted, and were assisted by federal troops. The AFL-CIO pledged support of U.S. halting of communist aggression in Vietnam. The step-up of the military draft led to increased protest and a law forbidding draft card burning.

Literature in the first half of the Sixties signaled the need for human rights. In 1960 Lionel Bart's _Oliver_, a remake of Dickens' _Oliver Twist_,

164

brought musical reminders of the perennial dispari-
ties between rich and poor. William Shirer portrayed the relation of Nazi power to human freedoms
in The Rise and Fall of the Third Reich. Vance
Packard began his crusade against exploitation by
those who disseminate the rampant flow of technological products with his The Waste Makers. In his
play, A Man for All Seasons, Robert Bolt showed the
intolerance attributed to those who outspokenly go
beyond the ideological, cultural, and moral bounds
of their day. In much different settings and with
different media, the novel To Kill a Mockingbird by
Harper Lee and the film Exodus by Otto Preminger
portrayed the ugliness of prejudice, the physical
and emotional uprooting that it can engender, and the
strength that can overcome it. The futility of hopes
in everyday life, amid bureaucracy, power, accident,
and ignorance made the cry of injustice often wane
into detachment; such was depicted in the novels
and stories of Salinger, the plays of Albee, Joseph
Heller's Catch-22, and Tennessee Williams' The Night
of the Iguana. In 1962, Ken Kesey sensitized audiences to life among those often unwarrantedly labeled insane in his play One Flew Over the Cuckoo's
Nest. The same year brought Solzhenitsyn's One Day
in the Life of Ivan Denisovich and Pasternak's In
the Interlude. The Making of the President by T.H.
White appeared that year as well.

Literature of the next year reflected the
increased liberation in morals and living situations that moved into society at large as derivatives of the so-called new left; illustrations
include Mary McCarthy's novel, The Group; Ionesco's
play Exit the King; and the film interpretation of
Fielding's novel Tom Jones. Concern for the effects
of unleashed power was exemplified by artistic crea-
tions of 1964: Jerry Bock's musical play Fiddler on
the Roof; Stanley Kubrick's film Dr. Strangelove;
Peter Brook's film Lord of the Flies; C.P. Snow's
novel The Corridors of Power; and Gore Vidal's novel
Julian. The same time period was a coming of age
for television as a new form of public literature in
which the good were victorious and the admirable were
successful. This did much to confirm that sentimen-
tality lurked in the souls of a seemingly detached
and suspicious populace.

165

In an era of protest, some of the fine arts remained characteristic of former days,but even the avant-garde of the near past was not immune to association with the establishment. Thus, while opera by Britten, electronic music by Stockhausen, opera by Barber, symphonies by Stravinsky, symphonies by Bernstein, and electronic music by John Cage contributed to the musical advance of the times, it was an emergent popular group named the Beatles and the protest music of Bob Dylan that moved masses, issuing in the gradual acceptance of the messageless message and message-bearing protest of combinations of jazz, folk, primitive, electronic, croon, band, orchestral, and rock-n-roll to form a new species of musical expression. In art, too, architecture was furthered by Saarinen and Le Corbusier, and painting by Picasso, Miro, and Dali; yet, it was in a showing of pop art by such artists as Andy Warhol, Robert Rauschenberg, and Jasper Johns at a 1963 exhibition at New York's Guggenheim Museum that abstraction began to blend with realism, the bizarre with the ordinary, and the arts of painting, sculpture and architecture began to fuse. These musical and artistic amalgamations exemplified a more pervasive tendency to synthesize in many domains; curriculum was no exception as illustrated by the synoptic text.

The first half of the Sixties occasioned its share of developments in science, technology, and discovery. Most of these related to the space and armaments races. Americans developed the laser beam and the French tested a nuclear bomb in 1960. In the following year the USSR sent the first person into space, Yuri Gagarin in the spaceship Vostok, shortly before Alan Shepherd made similar history for the U.S. In 1962 the U.S. sent three astronauts into orbit, developed and actualized communications satellite Telstar, and produced an unmanned spacecraft named Ranger that successfully reached the Moon. In 1963, Valentina Tereshkova became the first woman to orbit the Earth as a Russian cosmonaut. The next year U.S. Ranger VII photographed the Moon and Mariner IV began its travel to do the same on Mars, succeeding in 1965. In the same year,

Soviet cosmonauts and American astronauts walked together in space. At the same time as the space race flourished, the U.S. Navy descended to an unprecedented 36,000 feet by bathysphere in the Pacific. In 1961, Crick and Watson discovered the structure of DNA, thereby unlocking more of the mystery of gene and brain and opening the way for future quantum jumps in the genetic sciences and related areas. Science pointed to negative developments as well. In 1962 scientists discovered that thalidomide caused deformities in babies, and in 1964 the official Surgeon General's report was issued that linked smoking and cancer. In 1965 President Johnson signed into law that health warning must be printed on cigarette packages, thus contributing to the right to knowledge that influences health.

By mid-decade international developments were many, varied, and often heated. U.S. involvement in Vietnam was greatly augmented. Indonesia withdrew from the United Nations. West Germany began diplomatic relations with Israel. Major African nations achieved independence. France withdrew from NATO. Disputes between India and Pakistan were temporarily quelled by the Tashkent Declaration. Leadership underwent marked changes too: L.B. Johnson was elected to his first full term as U.S. President; Charles DeGaulle was re-elected President of France; Podgorny replaced Mikoyan as President of the USSR; South African prime minister H.F. Verowerd was assassinated and succeeded by B.J. Vorster; and Indira Gandhi became prime minister of India. Communist China, under Mao, denounced Russian relations with the West on numerous counts, and the Chinese Red Guard was begun in 1966 to activate the cultural revolution. This was followed by Brezhnev's assertion that Mao's policies posed a threat to the Communist movement throughout the world. In 1967 Greek army officers seized power, necessitating King Constantine's exile from that country and bringing the emergence of George Papadopolous as leader of the military government. Rhodesian declaration of independence was met with British animosity, U.S. trade bans, and United

Nations' sanctions. In 1967, tension mounted and
fighting erupted between Israel and the Arabs over
the Gulf of Aqaba, the Gaza Strip, the Golan
Heights, and Jordan territories. Upon United
Nations order, ceasefire was achieved. The next
year brought the seizing of the Pueblo by North
Korean forces, later to be returned amid strange
diplomatic circumstances. The same year brought
Russian and other Warsaw Pact troops into Czechoslovakia to depose Alexander Dubcek and to quell
freedoms initiated by him as newly named Communist
Party leader there. The Nigerian civil war continued, resulting in the secession of Biafra and,
concomitantly, great suffering to this group. In
Northern Ireland, eruptions mounted over rights of
Roman Catholic minorities, which involved British
troops by the end of the decade. Conflict between
Arabs and Israelis resumed with the 1968 hijacking
of an Israeli airplane by Arabs in 1968. In 1969,
Golda Meir became Israel's prime minister and called
upon the U.S. for aid. By the decade's conclusion,
DeGaulle resigned to be succeeded by Pompidou in
France, and in Spain, Franco designated Juan
Carlos as his successor.

     Meanwhile in the United States, the last half
of the Sixties was frought with increased protest
and dissention on issues of race and Vietnam involvement. The Supreme Court ruled that the Georgia
legislature must seat black legislator Julian Bond.
Robert Weaver was the first black appointed to the
U.S. Presidential Cabinet, Bill Russell became the
first black professional basketball coach, and
Edward Brooke became the first Negro U.S. Senator.
As chairman of SNCC, Stokely Carmichael brought a
shift of emphasis from civil rights to black power.
This stance was accepted by CORE but not wholly
endorsed by the NAACP and Martin Luther King. Riots
in 1967 struck well over 100 cities, most notably
Newark and Detroit. By 1968, FBI Director J. Edgar
Hoover called for a counter intelligence program
to prevent both the rise of a coalition of militant
black nationalist groups and that of a "messiah" to
lead them. In the same year Martin Luther King was
assassinated in Memphis, an act that led to violent

rioting in most major U.S. cities and the use of
Federal troops and National Guard forces to control
outbreaks. The next year Chicago Black Panther
leader Fred Hampton was killed by police acting
under orders from the FBI.

Protests of the Vietnam War continued to mark
the times. By 1967, a women's peace group, several
thousand scientists, Martin Luther King, and huge
numbers of students demonstrated for an end to the
war. Protests often focused on the draft, several
persons ignited themselves as suicide protests, and
Muhammad Ali was stripped of his title of World
Heavyweight Boxing Champion for refusing induction
on grounds of being a conscientious objector. Massive demonstrations occurred frequently in protest
of governmental over-involvement in foreign and
private matters, accusing the government of coalition
with bastions of economic power. Persons of fame
and from many walks of life joined in sympathy for
many elements of the protest arguments. In the
meantime the involvement in Vietnam continued to
increase, as did the daily reports of casualties.
By 1968, both Senators Eugene McCarthy and Robert F.
Kennedy who challenged President Johnson for re-
election from within the Democratic Party took anti-
war stances. Johnson withdrew from the race as the
desire for the war's end swept the country. In the
same year Robert Kennedy was assassinated after
winning the California primary election. At the
riot-plagued Democratic convention in Chicago in
1968, Hubert Humphrey became the Democratic candidate, to be closely defeated later in the year by
Richard Nixon. The end of the decade saw publications about the My Lai massacre, countless demonstrations in small towns and cities, and a culminating march of 150,000 to Washington in 1969.

The late Sixties also brought the emergence of
Nader's "raiders" who alleged economic and consumer
injustices. Jimmy Hoffa was re-elected as Teamsters
President despite his conviction for using union
funds as bail money. Reports appeared that the
National Student Association received several million dollars worth of support from the CIA through

169

fictitious foundations. Widespread air hijackings, Woodstock, the Paris Peace Talks, the Pope's ban on all forms of birth control but rhythm, the continuation of President Johnson's "War on Poverty," and Medicare to provide health care for the elderly all contributed to the tenor of the times.

Simultaneous with the Vietnam War and the movement for racial equality was the continuation of the space race. Luna 9 and 13 made soft unmanned landings on the Moon's surface in 1966. In the same year two U.S. spacecrafts joined together while orbiting Earth. In 1967 tragedy struck the U.S. space program when Apollo 3 exploded on the launch pad, killing three astronauts. A year later, Apollo 8 took three astronauts in orbit around the Moon. Finally, the great culmination of the first phase of space explorations took place in 1969. While the world watched on television, Neil Armstrong became the first man to walk on the Moon, followed by Edwin Aldrin, while Michael Collins piloted their orbiting craft, Apollo 11. Soon afterwards, Apollo 12 successfully transported astronauts to obtain lunar samples.

Scientific and technological advance was by no means detered by the concentration on space exploration. Offshoots occurred in many domains, some of which were highly unexpected. Still other developments occurred alongside those of space exploration, sometimes with great and lasting impact. Notable in this regard were: use of plastic hearts in surgery by U.S. physicians in 1966; South African Dr. Christian Barnard's first heart transplant in 1967; the 1968 discovery of pulsars by astronomer Martin Ryle; the discovery of the molecular structure of hemoglobin by Max Pertutz, also in 1968; the 1969 discovery of oil in Alaska; and the flight of the French supersonic Concorde airliner in 1969. By the end of the Sixties both China and France had exploded hydrogen bombs. In 1967, Francis Chichester entered the annals of both exploration and knighthood by circumnavigating the globe in his yacht, while an era of lavish sea travel was closed and another opened with Britain's replacement of the Queen Mary with the Queen Elizabeth II.

The aesthetics of space technology provided
widespread evidence of the too often unrealized
union of art and science. Great scientists and
artists of any era join together in sophisticated
image-making and intuitive empiricism as is apparent in their work from da Vinci to Chagall, and
from Archimedes to Einstein. In the late Sixties,
the art of technology may have overshadowed the
formal arts but there is a large sense in which
both illustrated the growth of human imagination
pulled by an aesthetic drive to produce the functional. Marc Chagall's mural, The Triumph of
Music, for the New York Metropolitan Opera House,
the operatic composition of Benjamin Britten, and
Schuman's contribution to ballet combined with
literary pieces by Graham Greene (The Comedians),
Truman Capote (In Cold Blood), and William Manchester (The Death of a President), to illustrate
samples of artistic endeavors in the limelight by
1966. The same year saw major art masterpieces
destroyed in the floods of Florence, Italy. In
1967, pressures associated with racial integration were made vivid in film by Stanley Kramer's
Guess Who's Coming to Dinner; Desmond Morris tuned
the American public to anthropological perspectives with his The Naked Ape; and Ira Levin horri-
fied many with Rosemary's Baby. The arts of 1968
brought continued work by Mies van der Rohe, Marc
Chagall, Gian Carlo Menotti, Gore Vidal, Arthur
Miller, Iris Murdoch, and Alexander Solzhenitsyn.
In the same year John Updike's Couples portrayed
the continuing sexual revolution as it moved from
the communes of those who "went to San Francisco"
to beginnings of sensitivity and encounter movements
that brought sexual openness to life in suburbia and
other "established" spheres of society. Sculpture
by Calder and music by Stockhausen, Tippet, and
Berio characterized arts of 1969. Literary contributions included James Gould Cozzens' Morning, Noon
and Night, Philip Roth's insight into Jewish life
and feeling in Portnoy's Complaint, and Mario Puzo's
inside look at a fictitious powerful family of
Sicilian background in The Godfather. Finally,
capturing the space conquest and pointing to new
directions and possible perils as science fiction

writers have often done, Stanley Kubrick helped con-
clude the decade with his film, 2001: A Space
Odyssey.

As a major phase of space exploration was completed in 1969, some wondered about the future
allocations of funding and the most important areas
of inquiry to emphasize. The quest for equality of
race was pushed forward at great cost to many committed to it, and its future was in no way clear.
The media exposed no small level of public disenchantment with the power of business and government,
focusing on the war in Vietnam, the domination of
the consumer and the devastation of the environment.
Far from resolved, these issues, combined with
mushrooming technological achievement and budding
commitment to fight poverty in urban areas, set the
stage for the emergence of the Seventies.

Curriculum Thought and Literature

If the production of curriculum books in the
Fifties was prolific as compared to previous decades,
the proclivity to produce them was magnified in the
Sixties. During this decade one-hundred seventy-three
more books were published than in the Fifties. This,
in no small measure, can be attributed to vast
increases in educational funding. As a response to
Sputnik, the National Defense Education Act of 1958
reached fruition in the early Sixties. In 1965, the
Elementary and Secondary Education Act continued the
funding augmentation. On another front, collective
bargaining for teachers greatly increased.

The above developments, the attention given
education by the press, the widespread granting of
funds for educational research and development from
both private and public sources, and a faith in
schools retained from the milder Fifties, all combined to issue in an era of unprecedented financial
support for education. If the Twenties and Thirties
were golden ages for Progressive curriculum and if
the Fifties brought a golden age for synoptic texts
and curriculum specialists in schools, the Sixties

172

was literally the age of "gold" for curriculum projects.

Curriculum projects, as most often conceived, consisted of highly structured sets of procedures and materials, usually designed by specialists in the academic disciplines dominated by the sciences, mathematics, and languages. Funding for curriculum projects usually was derived from the aforementioned federal programs, derivative programs that stemmed from them, numerous sources within the Department of Health, Education, and Welfare, and/or sources such as The National Science Foundation, The National Endowment for the Humanities, as well as private foundations such as Carnegie and Ford, etc. A covert if not overt hope of many project authors was to provide "teacher proof" materials, i.e., materials that would achieve goals without distortion by teacher implementation.

Psychologically oriented educators were often drawn upon to design the organizational properties of such projects. Chief among them were Jean Piaget and Jerome Bruner. Piaget was cited for his theories of a developmental structure implicit in the growing mind of the child. Many advised that his stages of cognitive development should be followed when designing curriculum materials and learning experiences. Bruner advocated a related conception, a structuralist position, known as the "structure of the discipline" approach. In his highly influential book, The Process of Education (1960, published with a new preface in 1977), Bruner argued that each discipline possessed an inherent structure that, when understood, opened the door to provide the learner with an essential ability to piece together elements of that discipline with relative ease.

In similarity to the interactionist epistemology of Dewey, both Piaget and Bruner stem from idealist epistemologies tracing to experientialist roots in the child study of Herbart and further to the idealist tradition created by Plato. Both Piaget and Bruner, along with Dewey and Herbart,

173

assumed the primacy of child interest and activity
in interacting with an environment to experience
constructions of knowledge that eventually lead to
the fund of knowledge organized in the growing
disciplines of academe.

The complexity of this argument and the necessity to mass-disseminate educational insight often
worked at odds with one another. It seemed impossible to convey such complicated ideas in meaningful ways to hundreds of thousands of practitioners
in brief periods of time. There is little wonder
why authors of curriculum projects of the Sixties
provided rigorously structured materials that were
not to be altered relative to teacher and student
needs and interests. While the design of some
projects was admirable, and while the assumption
that instructional materials are a prime source of
content for the curriculum was surely warranted,
later studies[1] point to marked discrepancies between
design and implementation. Work by Schaffarzick,
especially, points out that comparisons of the new
curriculum project results with those of traditional curricula are dependent upon the tendencies
of evaluation instruments themselves toward the
newer or the traditional curricula. One can find
descriptions of the curriculum projects in numerous
sources, including the synoptic texts of the 1960's
and 1970's. For more detailed treatment one may
refer to original project documents, journal articles, research reports, and books such as Heath
(1964).

A central point drawn from the above bears
heavily on the state of schools of curriculum
thought that were developed during preceding
chapters. In the Fifties the popularity of presenting curriculum literature in the synoptic text
tended to fuse experientialist, social behaviorist,
and intellectual traditionalist thought together.
One effect of this was that it promoted a unified
appearance to curriculum literature and helped
curriculum scholarship assert a tighter grip as
a recognized domain of inquiry. At the same time,
it tended to dilute each of the three positions.

It could be argued that unification had a positive influence, i.e., it reduced the pejorative tendency to myopically cling to one school of thought or another. Alternatively, it could be argued that unification brought undue simplification; an attempt to provide eclecticism where the pieces could not defensibly be fit together.

During the early Fifties, curriculum implementation in schools took a swing toward the intellectual traditionalist position. Although progressivism was manifest in the literature from 1920 to the mid-1940's, it always embodied an experientialist curriculum that took a back seat to the intellectual traditionalists in practice. Granted, during the Progressive era practice did sway in the experientialist direction. Despite the results of the Eight Year Study, the curriculum pendulum in the early Fifties swung away from the experientialists.

The social behaviorist flavor of precision, efficiency, and pre-packaging inched its way into practice in the Fifties. These characteristics became major features of the curriculum project movement. Propelled by the space race, proponents of this orientation leaped aboard the curriculum project bandwagon with considerable permanence in the Sixties. Oddly enough, they embodied quite different versions of structure as compared with the "structure of disciplines" approach that was a central feature at the movement's start. Drawn from Dewey, Piaget, and Bruner, and illustrated by Elam (1964) and Ford and Pugno (1964), structure was thought to be learned via interaction and discovery. It was earlier intended to connote structure developed through interaction between the person and the environment, more than outside imposition.

Despite this orientation, however, the spontaneity of discovery and the emergence of objectives or a sense of direction from activity gave way to another interpretation. It was replaced by a means-ends rationality with predetermined objectives that governed, or at least rationalized, systematically

designed learning activities. Such a turnabout
was promoted in many synoptic texts. If it was
not conveyed overtly, it was done covertly by the
brevity implicit in vast coverage. The result
embodied the technology of behaviorism and simplistic systems applications. It issued in a new
version of social behaviorism. With the growing
demands for government accountability in society
at large came increased demands for curricularists
to pre-specify what they planned to achieve, to
directly strive to obtain it, and to prove that
they did. Hence, behavioral objectives arrived
on the curricular scene.

    Robert Mager, a major popular promoter of
behavioral objectives, attacked the use of general
or global objectives that pervaded educational
literature. Global objectives were found to lurk
in many a curricular corner; exemplifications
include: vague pronouncements by zealots of Progressivism; writers of "principles" in synoptic
texts; and statements of goals by governmental
commissions and educational associations such as
the National Education Association. As an alternative, Mager and others called for increased
specification of objectives, stated in terms of
observable behavior, with time limits for actualization and criteria to evaluate accomplishment.

    It is interesting to note that Mager's humo-
rous and sensible but rather simplified books,
e.g., Preparing Instructional Objectives (1962),
were designed to move those who wrote objectives
away from the use of vague terms with multiple
interpretations. The immense popularity of the above
book, however, brought staunch proponents of this
new approach who rejected goal statements that had
even a tinge of vagueness, lacked time specifications, lacked definitive criteria for evaluation,
or failed to specify results in observable behaviors.

    Taken in moderation, the idea brought useful
clarification, not particularly novel to curriculum
literature, but in exaggerated interpretation it
became ludicrous. One could imagine teachers

176

agonizing about the observable behaviors that indicated appreciation of Beethoven's Sixth Symphony, or committees deliberating for years about all of the prerequisite specific behaviors needed to pursue matrix algebra. The "catch-22" here was that no one had time to thoroughly do these tasks but accountability pressures said that they had to be done. So, they were done superficially. Some publishers capitalized on this problem and provided stockpiles of behavioral objectives, sometimes known as performance objectives. Schools that had neither time nor desire nor ability to comply with demands to produce objectives could simply purchase the kind and number of objectives that met their requirements.

A variation within the movement included the specification of competencies assumed to equal proficiency in mastering course content. This, in turn, was coupled with mastery learning developed by Bloom, Carroll, Block and others. Sometimes competencies became substitutes for objectives. In some cases, thousands of compentencies were identified for certain aspects of curriculum, for example, in teacher education curriculum. Hence, effective teaching was equated with demonstration of a certain number of competencies. It does not take immense reflection to perceive the similarity between such approaches and those of the early social behaviorists, e.g., Bobbitt, Charters, Snedden, etc. whose work was discussed earlier.

Just as the latter sought to emulate the science and technology of their day, many proponents of behavioral objectives in the Sixties couched their pronouncements in the rhetoric of systems analysis and behavioristic psychology. Their justification of results with over-complex statistics is not an unfamiliar practice today. This, however, was apparently enough to satisfy many government agencies who were increasingly oriented to the language of business and technology.

Governmental mandates to justify programs

177

with quantitative portrayals of success often required work based on an epistemology that only admitted evidence of achievement or worth relative to pre-specified ends. Thus, the increased involvement in curriculum projects by behavioristic psychologists and other social scientists brought with it their methodology which fit, or created, the desire for quantitative assessment of means-ends productivity. From this time to the present, curriculum literature has been dominated by social science methodology. Subsequently, quantitative competence increased markedly; requirements in doctoral programs fostered it.

It is interesting to note that this movement was born in the social expediency of a space race which was permeated by a means-ends model of production and accountability. Both are clearly a part of the social behaviorist tradition. Both are quite different from the experientialist epistemology upon which the curriculum projects movement was initiated. Experientialist assumptions about an internal structure of knowledge, the importance of child study, student interest, experience, and genuine discovery faded into routinization and mass production. Proper form, behavioral objectives and their accouterments, became the emphasis rather than justifications for learning activities and curricular proposals. Focus on the problem of whether the means brought pre-specified ends became so central that it obscured deliberation about the worth of purposes and their assumptions.

The above background facilitates review of categories of curriculum books that appeared in the Sixties. Given this setting we will now consider the kinds of curriculum books that emerged.

A major category of curriculum text that appeared in the Sixties consisted of newer editions of earlier synoptic texts. Both those of the general variety and those that focused on elementary or secondary levels continued to appear in revised form. Examples include: Beck, Cook, and Kearney (1960); Gwynn (1960) and Gwynn and Chase (1969); Lee and Lee (1960); Ragan joined by Stendler (1960 and 1966); Alberty and Alberty (1962); Burton (1962); Douglass (1964): Saylor and Alexander (1966, with considerable changes from the 1954 version, including title changes); Van Til, Vars, and Lounsbury (1967); Sowards and Scobey (1968), and Tyler (1969, representing one of several reprintings). The appearance of reprints, new editions, and substantial revisions attests to the relevance attributed to certain texts. Sales provide evidence of demand for more of the same or similar; and sales are dependent upon the judgments of curriculum scholars who order books for courses that they teach. Thus, a sort of refereeing system is at work in producing the demand for subsequent editions of texts.

The refereeing process, no doubt, reminds readers of journals. Since this book directly treats only special journal issues as described in introductory sections, readers may wonder whether those extensive contributions are omitted here. To be sure, journals contain articles over the years that are major contributions to curriculum thought, often major initiators of lines of thought that later appear in texts. Although a systematic cataloging and discussion of articles has been described as beyond the scope of this book, such a project would certainly be useful to the curriculum student and scholar alike.

Indirectly, however, salient journal articles are included in this book due to the widespread emergence of another kind of curriculum book; namely, books of readings on curriculum topics. Such collections often provide seminal journal articles and sometimes original selections as well. Thus, the salient role of journal articles is not omitted from this exhibit of curriculum thought.

Although collections of readings can be traced in the curriculum literature to Caswell

179

and Campbell (1937), it was the Sixties that
brought full-fledged production of them. Examples of books that provided original pieces and/
or those selected from journals include: Passow
(1962), Sowards (1963), J.R. Wright (1963), Chasnoff (1964), Douglass (1964), Ether (1964), Huebner (1964), Passow (1964), Passow and Leeper
(1964), Rosenbloom (1964), Hass and Wiles (1965),
Leeper (1965a), Leeper (1965b), Unruh (1965),
Callaway (1966), Halverson (1966), Leeper (1966),
Macdonald and Leeper (1966), Martin and Pinck
(1966), Robison (1966), Alexander (1967), Alpren
(1967), Berman (1967), Leeper (1967), Heller and
Rosenthal (1968), Kerr (1968), Kopp (1968), Leeper (1968), Short and Marconnit (1968), Steeves
(1968), Unruh and Leeper (1968), Witt (1968),
Bar (1969), Dragositz (1969), Frazier (1969),
Guttchen and Bandman (1969), Hamilton and Saylor
(1969), Jones (1969), Rubin (1969), and Vars (1969).
The curriculum student can, of course, obtain
great value from surveying journals. Direct
study of journals can provide a context of
historical perspectives and a flavor of that
which was deemed important in a particular time
period.[2]

New variations on the synoptic text and new
types of curriculum contributions appeared in the
Sixties. Chief among the latter are books that
dealt with varieties of organizational patterns
and their curricular implications. The literature was by no means confined to these areas.
Philosophical analyses, practical proposals,
historical inquiries, and a motley array of other
variations appeared. So many were the varieties,
and so defiant of categorization were they, that
the remainder of contributions in the 1960's will
be discussed on a yearly basis.

New general synoptic treatments in 1960
included Brown's Curriculum Development and
Wood's Foundations of Curriculum Planning and
Development. Synoptic books that appeared at the
elementary level were Elementary School Curriculum by Jameson and Hicks and Curriculum Develop-

ment in the Elementary School by Rucker. Published at the secondary level were Krug's The
Secondary School Curriculum and Preparation of
Secondary School Curriculum by UNESCO's International Bureau of Education. McNally, Passow,
and Associates produced Improving the Quality of
Public School Programs (1960), a book which provided an overview of change, a process for
curriculum improvement, administrative considerations and procedures, as well as seven cases
about actual curriculum improvement programs.
Other case approaches in 1960 included: Butter-
wech and Spessart on the unified curriculum;
Ewing on primary curriculum in New Zealand; a
treatment of the junior high curriculum in London
by the National Union of Teachers; and a description of curriculum revision in Japan.

Several other authors of 1960 kept awareness
of ideas that dominated previous decades alive:
Carlin and Blackman on general education; Anderson on cooperative curriculum improvement; Rudy
on liberal arts curriculum; and Ward, et al., on
integration. Snyder provided arguments for the
self-contained classroom, the most prevalent
elementary school organizational pattern, yet a
pattern that was under continual fire from those
who proposed other grouping strategies. Thelen's
Education and the Human Quest (1960), while not
explicitly a curriculum book, presented an experientialist viewpoint that illuminated major questions that are curricular at root. By explicating
four educational models (personal inquiry, group
investigation, reflective action, and skill
development), Thelen illustrated dynamic connections among assumptions, curriculum, instruction,
learning environments, and the flow of action.
As did Dewey, Thelen argued for a synthesis of
inquiry and action in the human quest for growth.

In 1961, the National Education Association
contributed to the legacy of national statements
on educational purposes by government agencies and
professional associations. The kinds of statements
produced by these groups exemplified global objec-

tives par excellence. Such were later the brunt of
criticism by behavioral objectives advocates. Both
groups were usually guilty of lacking serious theoretical justifications. Many seconded the need for
serious curriculum theory hailed as necessary by
the 1947 Chicago conference on that topic discussed
earlier. Finally, a book appeared in 1961 that was
devoted entirely to curriculum theory. This book,
Curriculum Theory by George A. Beauchamp, was almost
entirely written in the vein of systems theory and
engineering models that stemmed from natural
sciences. Although it bore some criticism for oversimplification and lack of specific applicability
to educational problems, demand brought new editions in 1968 and 1975. Furthermore, Beauchamp's
orientation represented a mode of curriculum theory
that fit the social behaviorist style of curriculum
research in the Sixties. The emphasis on combining
theory with research could be seen in many curriculum
books of this period, e.g., Haan (1961). The
engineering emphasis raised questions about who
should be involved in curriculum decisions. Research and theory were frequently viewed as best
presented from the top down, relative to organizational charts of schools. Balancing this top-down
orientation were treatments of the teacher's roles
in curriculum making by Leese, Frasure, and Johnson
(1961) and Sowards and Scobey (1961). A different
interpretation of balance was expressed in the
Association for Supervision and Curriculum Development Yearbook of 1961, Balance in the Curriculum.
Its authors questioned the variety of emphases that
school experiences brought to students. Variety of
experiences was also the concern of Phenix (1961);
his approach probed deeply into the fabric of
assumptions undergirding curriculum, stressing that
any desire to educate implies moral advocacy about
conceptions of the common good. Taking a philosophical stance of a different orientation, that of
analytic philosophy, Smith and Ennis produced a book
that made clear the need to scrutinize educational
and curricular concepts. School organization and
curriculum were a major concern, as evidenced in
proposals by Stoddard (1961) and Trump and Baynham
(1961). History of education and curriculum, with

182

special emphasis on the development and decline
of progressive education, was brilliantly reviewed
by Lawrence Cremin in his The Transformation of
the School. Old textbooks were reviewed by Nietz
in the same year.

In 1962, the publication of Hilda Taba's
Curriculum Development: Theory and Practice
marked a high point among synoptic texts that
treated curriculum development generally rather
than relative to a particular level or subject
area. Her text drew from a variety of disciplines, described forces that influence curriculum, discussed the areas made perennial by Tyler,
and added special emphasis on diagnosis and unit
construction. The experientialist flavor of
John Dewey, one of her mentors, can be found
throughout the text which was widely used in
curriculum courses, prompting a 1971 reprint.
Parker, Edwards, and Stegeman (1962) provided an
elaborate treatment of the state of curriculum
in America. In the same year Fraser contributed
perspectives on curriculum studies in academic
subjects. Harry Passow advanced an array of
interpretations of curriculum at the juncture
of past and present that merged as proponents of
synoptic texts and curriculum projects faced one
another. The appearance of the collected papers
of Virgil Herrick centralized many of his writings and materials that contributed incisively
and insightfully to the development of curriculum thought for many years. Another collection
of perceptive essays was made available in 1962
by Northrop Frye and titled Design for Learning.
Other 1962 citations revealed the following:
considerations of sources of curriculum by the
ASCD, scholarly interpretations of schooling by
the NEA, multidisciplinary approaches by Waetjen,
undergraduate curricular flexibility by Cole,
and core curriculum by Durham. While much that
had to do with curriculum was highly social behaviorist in nature, another thrust in 1962 that
moved in quite another direction was gaining
power. The re-emergence of humanized or personalized education was signaled by the popular

183

1962 ASCD Yearbook entitled Perceiving, Behaving, and Becoming. This new version of the experientialist position was triggered with essays by prominent writers who added existentialist and phenomenological perspectives to the child-centered, whole person, and interest-based features of experientialist thought.

Developments in curriculum literature of 1963 illustrate the growing concern for alternative forms of curricular organization. A revised edition of the influential Goodlad and Anderson conception of the nongraded elementary schools appeared along with Brown's interpretation of the same topic at the secondary level. Unit teaching by Hanna, et al., research on core approaches by G. Wright, and an emphasis on humanized curriculum by Manning rounded out the newer ideas about curriculum organization. In the years that followed, much literature emerged that profoundly influenced curriculum organization.

Readers are encouraged to review literature on such topics as individualized instruction, open education, ability grouping, multigrades, team teaching, departmentalization, differentiated staffing, minicourses, peer teaching, open space schooling, schools without walls, schools within schools, and alternative schools. When this author felt that treatments of these and similar topics directly addressed curricular implications of organizational patterns, they were included. Some were highlighted in the 1963 ASCD Yearbook, New Insights and the Curriculum, edited by Frazier. Still another organizational feature was aired by the ASCD in its publication of The Unstudied Curriculum, a publication that presaged by several years the notion of hidden curriculum, i.e., that argued that any intended curriculum has side effects and that the side effects often produce profound but unintended learning.

Other publications during 1963 continued to

present guidelines for curriculum planning in the vein of the synoptic texts; examples are by Davis, Goodlad, Fleming, Fraser, Leese, Shuster and Ploghoft, Thorton and Wright, Wiles, and Wood. Among these, Goodlad gave special attention to teachers, and Leese emphasized the role of superintendents in curriculum change. A combined effort by the American Association of School Administrators and the Association for Supervision and Curriculum Development called for action, not just proposals to improve curricula. Kimball Wiles attempted to communicate the impact of changing curricula at the high school level in the same year.

This emphasis on curriculum change weighed heavily in the literature of 1964. Alexander dealt with changing content. Anderson noted the need to find new avenues through which changes could meaningfully emerge. Doll combined emphasis on change with the style of the synoptic text in Curriculum Improvement: Decision Making and Process, a book that brought more revisions. Goodlad reviewed the recent reform movement organized around curriculum projects as it had thus far developed in the United States. Specific contributions to organizational conceptions include Beggs, Blocker and McCabe, Bush and Allen, and Hanson. Elam, and Ford and Pugno exemplified epistemological organization that facilitated the structuralist orientations of the curriculum projects movement. Another kind of structuralist position that has vast implications for curriculum organization was made visible at a curriculum conference at Cornell University, namely, the implications of Piagetian research and theory. Krathwohl, et al., continued the analytic approach to cognitive levels initiated by Bloom and others (1956) by extending a taxonomical structure into the affective domain. Both this work and the earlier taxonomy by Bloom gave organizational structure to curriculum projects and to behavioral objectives. Collections by Rosenbloom and by de Grazia and Sohn surveyed recent curriculum viewpoints,

185

organizational patterns, and technologies for implementing them. Provocative critical appraisals of such movements are provided in collections by Huebner, Passow, and Passow and Leeper.

Synoptic texts continued to appear in 1964 as exemplified by Beauchamp and by Crosby at the elementary level, and by Broudy, Smith, and Burnett at the secondary level. The latter was similar to the Smith, Stanley, and Shores text (1950 and 1957) in that it went far beyond the encyclopedic treatments of usual synoptic texts to build theoretical perspectives from which further curriculum thought could be generated. Thus, Democracy and Excellence in American Secondary Education by Broudy, Smith, and Burnett contributed to theoretical awareness of both classical realist and pragmatic theory as it applies to curriculum.

Another philosophical excursion in curriculum was provided by Philip Phenix who departed markedly from the usual philosophic origins of curriculum writing. His Realms of Meaning (1964) explored alternative epistemological bases and their implications for curriculum that fostered general education. In the historical vein, Elson's Guardians of Tradition provides a provocative rendition of text materials and their role in preserving values considered American through the institution of schooling. This is one of the rare attempts to analyze functions of schooling by studying the materials that, in fact, are the curriculum in the absence of serious local planning and imagination.

In 1965, books by Vernon E. Anderson and A.I. Oliver each added to the continued emergence of synoptic texts that were designed to present general overviews and guidelines for curriculum makers. McNeil provided a similar approach into the realm of administration, while Clark and others made similar applications at

186

the secondary level. Two ASCD publications attempted to define roles for professionals involved in supervision and curriculum development. Unruh and the Ontario Curriculum Institute produced books that continued to emphasize the novel and the rapidity of change in curriculum. Leeper contributed to the curriculum change literature by compiling a fine set of essays in Strategy for Curriculum Change. Books by Tanner and by Brown contributed to the accumulating literature on curriculum organization. Daniel Tanner called for schools that met the needs of youth, and B.F. Brown called for "appropriate placement schools," a variation on the non-graded concept. Shack wrote of curriculum from inside teaching in Armed with a Primer. The curriculum contributions of Virgil Herrick, (mentor of James B. Macdonald, John Goodlad, and Dwayne Huebner, among others) were made even more visible through the editorial efforts of Anderson, Macdonald, and May in their production of Strategies of Curriculum Development. Their selection of writings focused on Herrick's conception of the role of organizing centers in curriculum development, interconnections among curriculum and instructional planning and teaching, and other theoretical perspectives on curriculum and teaching. The matter of assessment in curriculum was moved to the fore by Leeper in his edited work on that matter under the auspices of ASCD. An excellent collection of articles was provided by Hass and Wiles to give a solid overview of curriculum thinking, a publication that would spawn several new editions.

In 1966, Jerome Bruner, author of The Process of Education (1960) discussed earlier, expanded on the instructional implications of this earlier work in Toward a Theory of Instruction. In the same year the National Education Association, this time through the American Association of School Administrators, produced another statement of focus for educational purposes, again calling them imperatives. Another

187

organization, the College Entrance Examination
Board with its continually growing influence,
published a work on the challenges presented
by curricular change. Two works appeared on
the matter of curricular change for which John
Goodlad was responsible: The Changing School
Curriculum and the Sixty-fifth Yearbook of the
National Society for the Study of Education.
Other books on change were authored by Haney;
Inlow; Jarvis and Wootton; Leeper; Martin and
Pinck; The Ontario Curriculum Institute; the
Organization for Economic Cooperation and
Development; Sand and Wilson; and Unruh and
Leeper. Goodlad and Richter devised a conceptual system for dealing with curricular and
instructional problems, and in School, Curric-
ulum and the Individual Goodlad wrote of the
interwoven nature of these three threads in curriculum fabric: society, institutions, and
individuals. These three areas carried considerable influence in subsequent study of
curriculum problems.

Several other major issues were raised
that provided alternative perspectives on
aspects of curriculum thought in 1966. Aceland raised the perennial question about the
relation between curriculum and life. King
and Brownell exemplified the need to develop
curriculum from a structure of epistemological
tenets, thereby contributing a piece of the
literature of curriculum theory. Macdonald
and Leeper raised issues about language and
meaning in educational and curricular discourse and practice. Parker and Rubin argued,
in an experientialist vein, that process could
indeed be the content of curriculum; they challenged curricularists to consider a synthesis
of process and content during a time when battles raged between those who demanded strict
adherence to content and others who considered
process preeminent. Rosenbaum and Toepfer discussed the relationship between curriculum
development and school psychology. The need
for serious consideration of evaluation was

promoted in publications by Lindvall and by Scriven. Additional perspectives on organizational patterns were contributed by the following: the Ontario Association for Curriculum Devlopment on decentralization; Callaway on the core curriculum; and flexible scheduling by Swenson and Keys. In Britain, P.H. Taylor introduced a dual relationship between purpose and structure in curriculum.

Meanwhile, 1966, a year of over forty curriculum books, also found synoptic texts steadily emerging, e.g., those by Cay, Koopman, and Jarvis and Wootton, along with new varieties of texts by Saylor and Alexander and by Ragan. As approaches to curriculum continued to roll off the presses a tendency prevailed to unknowingly reinvent already discovered curricular "wheels." Thus, the time was ripe for retrospect on earlier curriculum thought and contribution. Toward this end Mary Louise Seguel provided a history of what she titled the "formative years" of the curriculum field, the time from just before 1900 to approximately 1940. She dealt with the McMurry brothers, Dewey, Bobbitt, Charters, Rugg, and Caswell among others.

Several new thrusts were added to the repertoire of curriculum literature in 1967. A monograph series was begun to stimulate serious consideration of curriculum evaluation under the auspices of the American Educational Research Association. In the first book of the series Ralph Tyler, Robert Gagne, and Michael Scriven set forth perspectives that continued to carry great influence for at least a decade to come. While this AERA thrust was geared primarily to broadening perspectives of scholars, Fred T. Wilhelms spoke to both practitioner and scholar on evaluation in the 1967 yearbook of the Association for Supervision and Curriculum Development, advocating a dual role of feedback and guide in evaluation. Beauchamp and Beauchamp added possibilities for evaluation by bringing aspects of comparative education into the curriculum domain through publication of an analysis of curriculum systems in selected nations.

In 1967, works by Burnham, Michaelis, and Gagne helped begin to solidify design language in curriculum writings. Glaser made his concern for adaptive curriculum more visible, thus providing a kind of amalgam of the social behaviorist concern for systematization and that of the experientialist for the person as unique. In The Conditions of Learning, Robert Gagne presented his influential ideas about the hierarchical structure of learning with its progression from the simple and specific to the complex and general as a basis for design. He asserted that learning is an additive series of capabilities that moves from multiple discriminations, to concept learning, to principle learning, to problem-solving. In his learning theory he attempted to take into account diverse extant positions on learning. This work was given much credence by curricularists who advocated concept analysis, behavioral objectives, systems theory, structuralist approaches, and research methodologies of empirically-oriented social scientists. Another major developmental scheme for curriculum organization, that of Piaget, was given critical appraisal by Sullivan.

Miscellaneous, yet often significant, contributions to curriculum literature also appeared in 1967. They moved in both novel and previously treated domains. Books by Conner and Ellena and Neagley and Evans served as synoptic guidebooks for administrators who developed curricula in schools. The budding renewal of humanistic perspectives in curriculum was furthered by Berman and by Leeper. Aceland contributed to the accumulation of works on curricular integration, and Tewksbury expanded notions of non-gradedness. New curricula in Britain were treated conceptually in a work by Kerr, and practical descriptions of projects were provided in a publication of the Great Britain School Council. Verduin continued the group process orientation of Miel,

190

Benne, Lawler, and others on cooperative curriculum improvement. Venable reinforced an idea advocated only superficially in many synoptic texts by providing a book length treatment of philosophic roots of curriculum. D.K. Wheeler contributed to curriculum literature by carving out a conception of situation analysis and adding it to traditional categories of curriculum concern in his Curriculum Process.

In 1968, Louise Berman continued to explicate her humanistic orientation in New Priorities in the Curriculum by showing how such character dimensions as loving, perceiving, and valuing could be integrated with the usual subject areas of language arts, mathematics, science, social studies, etc. Another realm of experientialist curriculum emerged in England and soon was deemed worthy of emulation in America, namely, the British primary school. R.F. Dearden synthesized philosophical tenets of ideals undergirding schools in The Philosophy of Primary Education. Works by H. Grobman and by D. Karplus augmented perspectives on curriculum evaluation. H. Johnson called for evaluation through consideration of disciplines that served as fundamental building blocks of curriculum ideas. Organizational patterns were elaborated in proposals by Trump and Miller and in Alexander and others' work on the middle school. The "novel" and its relatives, innovation and change, were emphasized in works by Beck, et al.; Cave; Frazier; Keith, et al.; Kerr; Leeper; Maclure; Sowards and Scobey; Thomas, et al.; and Unruh and Leeper. Books by Witt and by Bangs and Hillestad illustrated the impact of technology on curriculum development. Revision of a landmark in British curriculum writing, i.e., Nisbet's Purpose in the Curriculum, came at a time when monies made a multiplicity of alternatives possible in America. Nisbet's work served as a rational stabilizer for curricularists whose propensity was to produce innovation qua innovation. The analytic sophistication of this work served to demonstrate, by comparison, the paucity of philosophic scrutiny in behavioral

191

objectives and many superficial proposals for
change. Of considerable import, Philip Jackson's Life in Classrooms began to sensitize
curricularists to the powerful impact of side
effects of intended curriculum and the schooling process itself on the actual learning
experiences of students. His work did much to
stimulate interest in the hidden curriculum and
its multiple interpretations.

A barrage of books that offered advice and
caution for the future, reviewed past developments, and reemphasized prior thrusts appeared
in 1969. Anderson provided guidelines for times
of change on the horizon. Frost and Rowland
prepared a synoptic text that pointed toward the
need to ready ourselves for a new decade. Alter-
ations in the fourth edition of Curriculum Principles and Social Trends by Gwynn and Chase did
a similar job. Works by H.T. James, et al.,
H.L. Jones, W.G.A. Rudd, and S.S. Symmes accented
the need to prepare for the future. Three humanistic thrusts were forwarded by Crary, Frazier, and
Hamilton. Mager's idea of objectives was
developed, refined and extended by Popham,
launching him into a position of prominence with
respect to curricular systematization, behavioral
objectives, and the growing push for demonstrating accountability through sound evaluation. The
necessity of giving primary consideration to the
subtle pervasiveness of moral education in all
curricular domains was advocated by Wilson. Grobman contributed again to the curriculum evaluation literature, as did the ASCD in a monograph
on assessment that included major statements by
Stake, Stufflebeam, and others. A reprint of
Tyler's Basic Principles of Curriculum and Instruction attested to the longevity of interest
in that work. Another time-honored curriculum
style, core curriculum, was coupled with interdisciplinary and team approaches by Vars. The idea
of comparing curricula was furthered by Springer,
while Bent and Unruh added to the synoptic literature on secondary curriculum.

The final year of the decade also added some
novel explorations in curriculum thought. One
that is too little known is a fine analysis of
the roles of knowledge, experience, and action in
effective education by Cassidy. Another book,
edited by Guttchen and Bandman, provided a set
of philosophical perspectives on curriculum problems. Also influential in the philosophic vein
was Meeker's epistemological portrayal of the
structure of intellect. Stockmeyer contributed
to philosophical perspectives on curriculum by
interpreting Rudolf Steiner's curriculum for the
Waldorf school. Bruce Joyce presented curricular
implications of alternative models of elementary
education. Hass related the idea of continuous
progress to curriculum and instruction, an application that would be heard a great deal more in
the instructional literature of the next decade.
Schwab and Walton each responded to a major
societal problem of the Sixties by providing
curriculum perspectives relative to it; Schwab
to student protest and Walton to the civil rights
movement.

Two publications, each published under the
auspices of a major educational society, captured
central features of the state of curriculum
thought at the conclusion of the Sixties. The
first was another of the special reviews of curriculum research prepared by the Review of Educational Research. The second, prepared by Louis
Rubin under the auspices of the Association for
Supervision and Curriculum Development, focused
on the kinds of life skills that enable effective
living in both school and society.

In conclusion, the quantity of curriculum
contributions during the Sixties was massive
indeed. The amalgamation of the three schools
of curriculum thought, manifest in the synoptic
texts of the Fifties, was perpetuated in the
Sixties. The response to the space race contributed to the curriculum projects movement with
offshoots that took on the character and rhetoric
of business, industry, and technology. This,

too, was an amalgam, but tendencies toward the
social behaviorists were obvious. Still, as
research and observation pointed out, the
intellectual traditionalists dominated practice.
In the midst of curricular technology, a new
experientialist movement began to emerge under
several, often different, guises, i.e., revivals
of the core curriculum, open education, free
schools, humanism, and tendencies toward existentialist orientations.

Although many of these experientialist
variations were distinct from the main course
of curriculum literature in the Sixties, they
would become emphasized in new ways in the
Seventies, not wholly unlike the experientialist
tradition of the progressive era. Such persuasions would, however, be overpowered in practice
by the continued mobilization of the technological and systematic rhetoric and practice of
social behaviorists. The case was similar with
research. The mode of scholarship that dominated
curriculum literature and complemented the
emergence of curriculum projects, behavioral
objectives, and accountability involved methodologies of social science and behavioristic
psychology. Increasingly sophisticated quantitative methods began to replace lists of
guidelines that were, presumably, derived from
involvement with schools as the accepted language of curriculum literature. Although quantitative research did not penetrate curriculum
scholarship as boldly as it did certain other
areas of education, its theoretic propensity
to seek generalizations did quite thoroughly.
In the Seventies alternative languages, ones
more consonant with the burgeoning philosophy,
situationalism and humanism of the late Sixties, would be offered for the development of
curriculum scholarship with a new kind of
experientialist character.

Notes

[1]See: Goodlad (1964) in School Curriculum
Reform in the United States; Goodlad and others
(1966) in The Changing School Curriculum; Walker
and Schaffarzick in Review of Educational
Research, Comparing Curricula, Winter, 1974, 44,
83-111; and Schaffarzick and Hampson (1975).

[2]Another means of acquiring curriculum perspectives within the larger arena of educational
thought is to survey yearbooks and special publications of educational societies. Two societies that frequently provide direct contributions
to curriculum are the Association for Supervision
and Curriculum Development (ASCD) and the National Society for the Study of Education (NSSE). The
Yearbooks of each portray major topical concerns.
Each of these and other societies (e.g., the
American Educational Research Association, Phi
Delta Kappa, and the National Education Association) publish special booklets, monographs, and
paperback books. When such publications dealt
directly with curriculum they were included in
the chronological bibliography presented in this
book. Frequently, they are highlighted in the
chapter discussions as well.

Bibliography of Curriculum Books, 1960-1969

1960

American Educational Research Association. Curriculum planning and development. Review of Educational Research, (30), June, 1960.

Anderson, R.H. Cooperative action program for curriculum improvement. Washington: ASCD, 1960.

Beck, R.H., Cook, W.W., and Kearney, N.C. Curriculum in the modern elementary school (Second Edition). Englewood Cliffs, New Jersey: Prentice-Hall, 1960.

Brown, A.F. Curriculum development. Philadelphia: Saunders, 1960.

Bruner, J.S. The process of education. Cambridge: Harvard University Press, 1960.

Butterweek, J.S. and Spessart, K.H. The unified curriculum; a case study grades 7-8. New York: Rinehart, 1960.

Carlin, E.A. and Blackman, E.B. (Editors). Curriculum building in general education. Dubuque, Iowa: W.C. Brown, 1960.

Downey, L.W. The task of public education: The perceptions of people. Chicago: Midwest Advisory Center of the University of Chicago, 1960.

Ewing, J.L. Origins of the New Zealand primary school curriculum, 1840-1878.

Wellington, New Zealand: New Zealand
Council for Educational Research,
1960.

Gwynn, J.M. Curriculum principles and
social trends (Third Edition). New
York: Macmillan, 1960.

International Bureau of Education. Preparation of secondary school curriculum.
Paris: UNESCO, 1960.

Jameson, M.C. and Hicks, W.V. Elementary
school curriculum: From theory to
practice. New York: American Book
Company, 1960.

Japan. Department of Education. Research
and Publications Bureau. Revised
curriculum in Japan for elementary and
lower secondary schools. Tokyo:
Department of Education, 1960.

Krug, E.A. The secondary school curriculum.
New York: Harper and Row, 1960.

Lee, J.M. and Lee, D.W. The child and his
curriculum (Third Edition). New York:
Appleton-Century-Crofts, 1960.

McNally, H.J., Passow, A.H., and Associates.
Improving the quality of public school
programs: Approaches to curriculum
development. New York: Bureau of
Publications, Teachers College, Columbia University, 1960.

Meriam, J.L. The traditional and the modern
curriculum: An emerging philosophy.
Berkeley, California: Mechanics and
Design, 1960.

National Union of Teachers, London. The
curriculum of the junior school; a
report of a consultative committee.
London: Schoolmaster, 1960.

197

Ragan, W. and Stendler, C.B. Modern elementary curriculum (Second Edition). New York: Holt, Rinehart and Winston, 1960.

Rucker, W. Curriculum development in the elementary school. New York: Harper and Row, 1960.

Rudy, S.W. The evolving liberal arts curriculum; a historical review of basic themes. New York: Published for the Institute of Higher Education by the Bureau of Publications, Teachers College, Columbia University, 1960.

Snyder, E.R. (Editor). The self-contained classroom. Washington: Association for Supervision and Curriculum Development, 1960.

Thelen, H. Education and the human quest. New York: Harper and Brothers, 1960.

Traxler, A.E.(Editor). Curriculum planning to meet tomorrow's needs. New York City: American Council on Education, 1960.

Ward, J.M., Suttle, J.E. and Oho, H.J. The curriculum integration concept applied in the elementary school. Austin: University of Texas, 1960.

Wood, H.B. Foundations of curriculum planning and development. Seattle: Cascade-Pacific Books, 1960 (Also 1963).

1961

Association for Supervision and Curriculum Development. Balance in the curriculum. 1961 Yearbook. Washington, D.C.: The Association, 1961.

Baughman, M.D. (Editor). Junior high school curriculum. Danville, Illinois: Interstate Press, 1961.

Beauchamp, G.A. Curriculum theory. Wilmette, Illinois: The Kagg Press, 1961 (Also 1968 and 1975).

Cremin, L.A. The transformation of the school: Progressivism in American education 1876-1957. New York: Alfred A. Knopf, 1961.

Educational Leadership. Who should plan the curriculum? Washington: Association for Supervision and Curriculum Development, 1961.

Educational Policies Commission. The central purpose of American education. Washington: National Education Association, 1961.

Fliegler, L.A. Curriculum planning for the gifted. Englewood Cliffs, New Jersey: Prentice-Hall, 1961.

Haan, A.E. Elementary school curriculum: Theory and research. Boston: Allyn and Bacon, 1961.

Japan. National Commission for UNESCO. Development of school curricula in Japan (by Takeo Miyata). Tokyo: UNESCO, 1961.

Kitzhaber, A.R., Gorrell, R.M., and Roberts, P. Education for college; Improving the high school curriculum. New York: Ronald Press Company, 1961.

Lapati, A.D. A high school curriculum for leadership. New Haven, Connecticut: College and University Press, 1961.

Leese, J., Frasure, K., and Johnson, M. Jr.
The teacher in curriculum making. New
York: Harper and Row, 1961.

McGrath, E.J. Analysis of the curricular
offerings in several independent liberal
arts colleges; a report to the U.S.
Commissioner of Education on contract
number 8AE 8193, project number 647,
Public Law 531, Eighty-third Congress.
New York: Teachers College, Columbia
University, 1961.

Nietz, J.A. Old textbooks. Pittsburgh:
University of Pittsburgh Press, 1961.

Pennsylvania Department of Public Instruction. Pennsylvania curriculum improvement series, Number 1. Harrisburg,
1961.

Phenix, P.H. Education and the common good:
A moral philosophy of the curriculum.
New York: Harper and Brothers, 1961.

Smith, B.O. and Ennis, R.H. (Editors). Language and concepts in education.
Chicago: Rand McNally, 1961.

Sowards, G.W. and Scobey, M.M. The changing
curriculum and the elementary teacher.
Belmont, California: Wadsworth, 1961.

Stoddard, G.D. The dual progress plan: A
new philosophy and program in elementary education. New York: Harper and
Row, 1961.

Trump, J.L. and Baynham, D. Focus on change:
Guide to better schools. Chicago:
Rand McNally, 1961.

Van Til, W., Vars, G.F., and Lounsbury, J.H.
Modern education for the junior high
school years. Indianapolis: Bobbs-
Merrill, 1961.

Willis, M. _The guinea pigs after twenty years_. Columbus: Ohio State University, 1961.

Wright, G.S. _The core program: One hundred selected references, 1956-1960; with an addendum of some basic references predating 1956_. Washington: U.S. Department of Health, Education, and Welfare, Office of Education, 1961.

Wyckoff, D.C. _Theory and design in Christian education curriculum_. Philadelphia: Westminster Press, 1961.

1962

Alberty, H.B. and Alberty, E.J. _Reorganizing the high school curriculum_ (Third Edition). New York: Macmillan, 1962.

Association for Supervision and Curriculum Development. _Perceiving, behaving, becoming: A new focus in education_. 1962 Yearbook. Washington: The Association, 1962a.

Association for Supervision and Curriculum Development (R.R. Leeper, Editor). _What are the sources of curriculum? A symposium_. Washington: National Education Association, 1962b.

Burton, W.H. _The guidance of learning activities_ (Third Edition). New York: Appleton-Century-Crofts, 1962.

Cole, C.C. _Flexibility in the undergraduate curriculum_. Washington: U.S. Government Printing Office, 1962.

Dottrens, R. _The primary school curriculum_. Paris: UNESCO, 1962.

Durham, J.T. An analysis and critique of
     core policies and programs. New York:
     Teachers College, 1962.

Fraser, D.M. (Editor). Current curriculum
     studies in academic subjects. Washing-
     ton: National Education Association,
     1962.

Frye, N. (Editor). Design for learning.
     Toronto: University of Toronto Press,
     1962.

Herrick, V.E. Collected papers and source
     materials on curriculum operations
     and structure. Madison, Wisconsin:
     College Printing and Typing Company,
     1962.

Mager, R.F. Preparing instructional objec-
     tives. Palo Alto, California: Fearon,
     1962.

National Education Association. The schol-
     ars look at the schools: A report of
     the Disciplines Seminar. Washington,
     1962.

Parker, J.C., Edwards, T.B., and Stegeman,
     W.H. Curriculum in America. New
     York: Thomas Crowell Company, 1962.

Passow, A.H. (Editor). Curriculum cross-
     roads. New York: Teachers College,
     Columbia University, 1962.

Taba, H. Curriculum development: Theory and
     practice. New York: Harcourt, Brace
     and World, 1962 (Also British Reprint,
     1971).

Waetjen, W.B. (Editor). New dimensions in
     learning: A multidisciplinary approach.
     Washington: Association for Supervi-
     sion and Curriculum Development, 1962.

1963

American Association of School Administrators and the Association for Supervision and Curriculum Development.
Action for curriculum improvement.
Washington: The Associations, 1963.

American Educational Research Association.
Curriculum planning and development.
Review of Educational Research, (33),
June, 1963.

Association for Supervision and Curriculum
Development. Commission on Teacher
Education. Criteria for curriculum
decisions in teacher education; a
report (George W. Denemark, Chairman
and Editor). Washington: Association
for Supervision and Curriculum Development, 1963 a.

Association for Supervision and Curriculum
Development. The unstudied curriculum:
Its impact on children. Washington:
The Association, 1963 b.

Brooks, N., et al. Curricular change in the
foreign language. Princeton, New
Jersey: College Entrance Examination
Board, 1963.

Brown, B.F. The nongraded high school.
Englewood Cliffs, New Jersey: Prentice-Hall, 1963.

Davis, R.A. Planning learning programs in
secondary schools. Nashville: George
Peabody College for Teachers, 1963.

Fleming, R.S. (Editor). Curriculum for
today's boys and girls. Columbus,
Ohio: C.E. Merrill, 1963.

Fraser, D.M. Deciding what to teach. Washington: National Education Association, 1963.

Frazier, A. (Editor). New insights and the
   curriculum. 1963 Yearbook. Washington: The Association for Supervision
   and Curriculum Development, 1963.

Gilchrist, R.S. Using current curriculum
   developments: A report. Washington:
   Association for Supervision and Curriculum Development, 1963.

Goodlad, J.I. Planning and organizing for
   teaching. Washington: National
   Education Association, 1963.

Goodlad, J.I. and Anderson, R. The non-
   graded elementary school (Revised
   Edition). New York: Harcourt, Brace
   and World, 1963.

Hanna, L.A., Potter, G.L., and Hagaman, N.
   Unit teaching in the elementary
   school; social sciences and related
   sciences. New York: Holt, Rinehart
   and Winston, 1963.

Leese, J. The superintendent and curriculum
   changes. Albany: State University
   of New York, 1963.

Manning, D. The qualitative elementary
   school; characteristics of an excellent curriculum. New York: Harper
   and Row, 1963.

National Education Association. Schools for
   the sixties: A report of the Project
   on Instruction. New York: McGraw-
   Hill, 1963.

Shuster, A.H. and Ploghoft, M.E. The emerging elementary curriculum: Methods and

204

procedures. Columbus, Ohio: Charles E.
Merrill, 1963.

Sowards, G.W. (Editor). The social studies:
Curriculum proposals for the future.
Chicago: Scott Foresman, 1963.

Thorton, J.W., Jr. and Wright, J.R. Secondary school curriculum. Columbus,
Ohio: Charles E. Merrill, 1963.

Wiles, K. The changing curriculum of the
American high school. Englewood
Cliffs, New Jersey: Prentice-Hall,
1963.

Wood, H.B. Foundations of curriculum planning and development. Eugene, Oregon:
The American-Nepal Educational Foundation, 1963.

Wright, G. The core program: Unpublished
research 1956-1962. Washington:
U.S. Department of Health, Education
and Welfare, Office of Education,
1963.

Wright, J.R. (Editor). Secondary school
curriculum. Columbus: Merrill, 1963.

1964

Alexander, W.M. Changing curriculum content.
Washington: Association for Supervision and Curriculum Development, 1964.

Anderson, V.E. Man must find new cowpaths.
Portland, Oregon: Portland State College, 1964.

Association for Supervision and Curriculum
Development (R.C. Doll, Editor).
Individualizing instruction. 1964 Yearbook. Washington: The Association,
1964.

Beauchamp, G.A. The curriculum of the elementary school. Boston: Allyn and Bacon, 1964.

Beggs, D.W. Decatur-Lakeview high school: A practical application of the Trump plan. Englewood Cliffs, New Jersey: Prentice-Hall, 1964.

Blocker, C.E. and McCabe, R.H. Relationships between the informal organization and the curriculum in six junior colleges. Austin, Texas: College of Education, University of Texas, 1964.

Broudy, H.S., Smith, B.O., and Burnett, J. Democracy and excellence in American secondary education: A study in curriculum theory. Chicago, Illinois: Rand McNally, 1964 (Reprinted by Krieger, 1978).

Bush, R.N. and Allen, D.W. A new design for high school education. New York: McGraw-Hill, 1964.

Centre for Educational Research and Innovation. Handbook on curriculum development. Britain: OECD: Her Majesty's Stationery Office, 1964.

Chasnoff, R.E. (Editor). Elementary curriculum: A book of readings. New York: Pitman Publishing, 1964.

Cornell University and University of California. Piaget rediscovered. Conference on Cognitive Studies and Curriculum Development, 1964.

Crosby, M.E. Curriculum development for elementary schools in a changing society. Boston: D.C. Heath, 1964.

Curriculum Study Center Conference. Curriculum development and evaluation in English and social studies. Pittsburgh: Carnegie Institute of Technology, 1964.

de Grazia, A. and Sohn, D.A. (Editors). Revolution in teaching: New theory, technology, and curricula. New York: Bantam Books, 1964.

Doll, R.C. Curriculum improvement: Decision-making and process. Boston: Allyn and Bacon, 1964 (Also 1970 and 1974).

Douglass, H.R. (Editor). The high school curriculum (Third Edition). New York: Ronald Press, 1964.

Elam, S. (Editor). Education and the structure of knowledge. Chicago: Rand McNally, 1964.

Elson, R.M. Guardians of tradition. Lincoln: University of Nebraska Press, 1964.

Ether, J.A. (Editor). Current curricular issues: three dimensions: Technology, morality, aesthetic. Albany: Center for Curriculum Research and Service, State University of New York at Albany, 1964.

Evans, W.G.E. Class of '84. Tenth Winter Conference. Toronto: University of Toronto Press, 1964.

Ford, G.W. and Pugno, L. The structure of knowledge and the curriculum. Chicago: Rand McNally, 1964.

Fulbright, E.R. and Bolmeier, E.C. Courts and the curriculum. American School Law Series, Cincinnati: W.H. Anderson Company, 1964.

Goodlad, J.I. School curriculum reform in the United States. New York: Fund for the Advancement of Education, 1964.

Hanson, C.F. Four track curriculum for today's high schools. Englewood Cliffs, New Jersey: Prentice-Hall, 1964.

Heath, R.W. (Editor). New curricula. New York: Harper and Row, 1964.

Huebner, D.E. (Editor). A reassessment of the curriculum. New York: Teachers College, Columbia University, 1964.

Krathwohl, D.R., et al. Taxonomy of educational objectives, handbook II: Affective domain. New York: David McKay, 1964.

Passow, A.H. (Editor). Nurturing individual potential. Washington: Association for Supervision and Curriculum Development, 1964a.

Passow, A.H. and Leeper, R.R. (Editors). Intellectual development: Another look. Washington: Association for Supervision and Curriculum Development, 1964b.

Phenix, P.H. Realms of meaning: A philosophy of the curriculum for general education. New York: McGraw-Hill, 1964.

Rosenbloom, P.C. (Editor). Modern viewpoints in the curriculum. New York: McGraw - Hill, 1964.

Schill, W.J. Curricular content for technical education. Urbana, Illinois: College of Education, University of Illinois, 1964.

1965

Anderson, D.W., Macdonald, J.B., and May, F.B. (Editors). Strategies of curriculum development: The works of Virgil E. Herrick. Columbus: Charles E. Merrill, 1965.

Anderson, V.E. Principles and procedures of curriculum improvement (Second Edition). New York: Ronald Press, 1965.

Association for Supervision and Curriculum Development. The humanities and the curriculum. Washington: The Association, 1965a.

Association for Supervision and Curriculum Development (R.R. Leeper, Editor). Role of supervisor and curriculum director in a climate of change. 1965 Yearbook. Washington: The Association, 1965b.

Association for Supervision and Curriculum Development. Toward professional maturity of supervisors and curriculum workers. Washington: The Association, 1965c.

Brown, B.F. The appropriate placement school: A sophisticated non-graded curriculum. New York: Parker Publishing Company, 1965.

Clark, L.H., Klein, R.L. and Burks, J.B. American secondary school curriculum. New York: Macmillan, 1965.

Cooperative Curriculum Project. The church's educational ministry: A curriculum plan. St. Louis: The Bethany Press, 1965.

Hass, G. and Wiles, K. (Editors). Readings

209

in curriculum. Boston: Allyn and
Bacon, 1965.

Leeper, R.R. (Editor). Assessing and using
curriculum content. Washington:
Association for Supervision and Curriculum Development, National Education
Association, 1965a.

Leeper, R.R. (Editor). Strategy for curriculum change. Washington: Association
for Supervision and Curriculum Development, 1965b.

McNeil, J.D. Curriculum administration:
Principles and techniques of curriculum development. New York: Macmillan, 1965.

Maccia, E.S. Methodological considerations
in curriculum theory building. Columbus, Ohio: The Ohio State University,
1965.

Macon, R.E. and Haines, P.G. Cooperative
occupational education and work
experience in the curriculum. Danville, Illinois: Interstate Printers
and Publishers, 1965.

Oliver, A.I. Curriculum improvement: A
guide to problems, principles, and
procedures. New York: Dodd, Mead
and Company, 1965.

Ontario Curriculum Institute. New dynamics
in curriculum development. Toronto,
1965.

Patterns for the administration of curriculum
development and instructional improvement. Proceedings of a conference in
Sacramento, California, January 25-26.
Sacramento: California State Department
of Education, 1965.

Shack, S. Armed with a primer. Toronto/
Montreal: McClelland and Stewart,
Ltd., 1965.

Stearns, F.K. Knowledge and the school
curriculum. Eugene, Oregon: University of Oregon (Oregon School
Study Council), 1965.

Tanner, D. Schools for youth--Change and
challenge in secondary education.
New York: Macmillan, 1965.

Teachers College. Department of Curriculum
and Teaching. Papers from the semi-
nars on advanced study in curriculum
and teaching. New York: Teachers
College, Columbia University, 1965.

Unruh, G.G. (Editor). New curriculum
developments. Washington: Association for Supervision and Curriculum
Development, 1965.

Wooten, W. SMSG, the making of a curriculum. New Haven: Yale University
Press, 1965.

1966

Aceland, R. Curriculum or life! London:
Victor Gollancz, Ltd., 1966.

American Association of School Administra-
tors. Imperatives in education.
Washington: National Education
Association, 1966.

Bruner, J.S. Toward a theory of instruction. Cambridge: Harvard University
Press, 1966.

Callaway, R. (Editor). Core curriculum:
The why and the what. Milwaukee:
University of Wisconsin-Milwaukee,
School of Education, 1966.

Cay, D.F. Curriculum: Design for learning. Indianapolis: Bobbs-Merrill, 1966.

College Entrance Examination Board. The challenge of curricular change (Edited by S.K. Bailey, et al.). New York: College Entrance Examination Board, 1966.

Goodlad, J.I. and Richter, M.N. The development of a conceptual system for dealing with problems of curriculum and instruction. Los Angeles: Institute for Development of Educational Activities, University of California, 1966.

Goodlad, J.I., Von Stoephasius, R. and Klein, M.F. The changing school curriculum. New York: Fund for the Advancement of Education, 1966.

Goodlad, J.I. (Editor). The changing American school. Sixty-fifth Yearbook of National Society for the Study of Education, Part II. Chicago: University of Chicago Press, 1966a.

Goodlad, J.I. School, curriculum, and the individual. Waltham, Mass.: Blaisdell Publishing Company, 1966b.

Halverson, P.M. (Editor). Curriculum innovations in 1966: Trends and issues. Syracuse, New York: Syracuse University, 1966.

Haney, R.E. The changing curriculum: Science. Washington: Association for Supervision and Curriculum Development, 1966.

Inlow, G.M. The emergent in curriculum. New York: John Wiley and Sons, 1966.

International Curriculum Conference
(Second). New dimensions in curriculum development. Toronto, 1966.

Jarvis, O.T. and Wootton, L.R. The transi-
tional elementary school and its
curriculum. Dubuque, Iowa: William
C. Brown, 1966.

King, A.R. and Brownell, J.A. The curric-
ulum and the disciplines of knowledge:
A theory of curriculum practice.
New York: John Wiley and Sons, 1966
(Reprinted in 1976).

Koopman, G.R. Curriculum development. New
York: The Center for Applied Research
in Education, 1966.

Leeper, R.R. (Editor). Curriculum change:
Direction and process. Washington:
Association for Supervision and Curric-
ulum Development, 1966.

Lindvall, C.M. The task of evaluation in
curriculum development projects: A
rationale and case study. Pittsburgh: Learning Research and Development Center, University of Pittsburgh, 1966.

Macdonald J.B. and Leeper, R.R. (Editors).
Language and meaning. Washington:
Association for Supervision and Curriculum Development, National Educational Association, 1966.

Martin, W.T. and Pinck, D.C. (Editors).
Curriculum improvement and innovation: A partnership of students,
school teachers, and research scholars.
Cambridge, Mass.: Robert Bently, 1966.

Matthew, C.V. and Roam, J.E. A curriculum
demonstration program for drop-out-prone
students. Edwardsville: Southern
Illinois University, 1966.

National Education Association. <u>The way</u>
<u>teaching is</u>. Washington: Associa-
tion for Supervision and Curriculum
Development and the Center for the
Study of Instruction, 1966.

Ontario Association for Curriculum Development. <u>Curriculum development in a</u>
<u>dencentralized educational system</u>
(Fifteenth Annual Conference, November, 1966). Toronto: R. Luxford,
Ed., 1966.

Ontario Curriculum Institute. <u>Children,</u>
<u>classrooms, curriculum and change; a</u>
<u>report of the Committee on the Scope</u>
<u>and Organization of the Curriculum</u>.
Toronto: The Ontario Curriculum
Institute, 1966a.

Ontario Curriculum Institute. <u>New dimen-</u>
<u>sions in curriculum development</u>
(Proceedings of the Second International Conference). Toronto: The Ontario Curriculum Institute, 1966b.

Organization for Economic Cooperation and
Development. <u>Curriculum improvement</u>
<u>and educational development: Moder-</u>
<u>nizing our schools</u>. Paris: Organi-
zation for Economic Cooperation and
Development, 1966.

Parker, J.C. and Rubin, L.J. <u>Process as</u>
<u>content: Curriculum design and the</u>
<u>application of knowledge</u>. Chicago:
Rand McNally, 1966.

Ragan, W.B. and Stendler, C.B. <u>Modern</u>
<u>elementary curriculum</u> (Third Edition).
New York: Holt, Rinehart and Winston, 1966.

Robison, H.F. (Editor). <u>Precedents and</u>
<u>promise in the curriculum field</u>.
New York: Teachers College Press, 1966.

214

Rosenbaum, D.S. and Toepfer, C.F. Curriculum planning and school psychology: The coordinated approach. Buffalo, New York: Hertillon Press, 1966.

Sachs, B.M. The students, the interviews, and the curriculum. Boston: Houghton Mifflin, 1966.

Sand, O. and Wilson E. Innovation in planning school curricula. Washington: National Education Association, 1966.

Saylor, J.G. and Alexander, W.M. Curriculum planning for modern schools. New York: Holt, Rinehart and Winston, 1966.

Scriven, M. The methodology of evaluation (Publication 110 of the Social Science Consortium). Washington: U.S. Department of Health, Education, and Welfare, 1966.

Seguel, M.L. The curriculum field: Its formative years. New York: Teachers College, Columbia University Press, 1966.

Swenson, G. and Keys, D. Providing for flexibility in scheduling and instruction. Englewood Cliffs, New Jersey: Prentice-Hall, 1966.

Taylor, P.H. Purpose and structure in the curriculum (Inaugural address). England: University of Birmingham, 1966.

U.S. National Science Foundation. Course and curriculum improvement projects: mathematics, science, engineering. Washington: National Science Foundation, 1966.

Unruh, G.G. and Leeper, R.R. Influences
in curriculum change. Washington:
Association for Supervision and
Curriculum Development, 1966.

1967

Aceland, R. A move to the integrated
curriculum. Exeter, England: University of Exeter, 1967.

Alexander, W.M. (Editor). The changing
secondary school curriculum: Readings. New York: Holt, Rinehart
and Winston, 1967.

Alpren, M. (Editor). The subject curriculum: Grades K-12. Columbus, Ohio:
Charles E. Merrill, 1967.

American Educational Research Association
Monograph Series on Curriculum Evaluation, Number 1. Perspectives of
curriculum evaluation (by R.W.
Tyler, R.M. Gagne and M. Scriven).
Chicago: Rand McNally,
1967.

Anderson, W.G. What are the subject
matter boundaries? Danville, Illinois: Interstate Printers and
Publishers, 1967.

Association for Supervision and Curriculum
Development. Curriculum materials.
Washington: National Education
Association, 1967.

Beauchamp, G.A. and Beauchamp, K.E. Comparative analysis of curriculum systems. Wilmette, Illinois: The Kagg
Press, 1967.

Berman, L.M. (Editor). The humanities and
the curriculum. Washington: Associa-

216

tion for Supervision and Curriculum
Development, 1967.

Bishop, L.J. Collective negotiation in
curriculum and instruction. Washington: Association for Supervision and
Curriculum Development, 1967.

Burnham, B. New designs for learning:
Highlights of the reports of the
Ontario Institute 1963-1966. Toronto: University of Toronto Press,
1967.

Conner, F. and Ellena, W. Curriculum handbook for school administrators. Washington: American Association of School
Administrators, 1967 (Also 1973).

Cooperative Curriculum Project. Tools of
curriculum development for the
church's educational ministry. Anderson, Indiana: Warner Press, 1967.

Davis, R.B. The changing curriculum: mathematics. Washington: Association for
Supervision and Curriculum Development,
1967.

Fantini, M.D. and Weinstein, G. Toward a
contact curriculum. New York: Anti-
Defamation League of B'nai B'rith, 1967.

Florida State Department of Education.
Report on strategies for curriculum
change. Tallahassee, 1967.

Gagne, R.M. The conditions of learning.
New York: Holt, Rinehart and Winston,
1967.

Glaser, R. Adapting the elementary school
curriculum to individual performance.
Pittsburgh: Learning Research and
Development Center, University of
Pittsburgh, 1967.

Great Britain School Council. The new curriculum: A presentation of ideas,
experiments and practical developments
(Selected from Schools Council Publications over the past three years). London: Her Majesty's Stationery Office,
1967.

Kerr, J.F. The problem of curriculum reform.
Leicester, England: Leicester University Press, 1967.

Leeper, R.R. (Editor). Humanizing education: The person in the process.
Washington: Association for Supervision and Curriculum Development, 1967.

Michaelis, J.U., Grossman, R.H., and Scott,
L.F. New designs for elementary cur-
riculum and instruction. New York:
McGraw-Hill, 1967.

Minnesota, University of. Working clinic
in modern curriculum (Addresses).
Minnesota: University of Minnesota,
1967.

National Education Association, Center for
the Study of Instruction. Rational
planning in curriculum and instruction: Eight essays. Washington:
National Education Association, 1967.

Neagley, R.L. and Evans, N.D. Handbook
for effective curriculum development.
Englewood Cliffs, New Jersey: Prentice-Hall, 1967.

Newfoundland Teachers Association, Curriculum Seminar. The curriculum
process--A basis for action. St.
John's Newfoundland: Newfoundland
Teachers Association, 1967.

School Health Education Study. Health education: A conceptual approach to curriculum design: K-12. St. Paul, Minnesota: Minnesota Mining and Manufacturing
Company Education Press, 1967.

Schools Council. Curriculum development:
Teacher's group and centers. Working
Paper Number 10. London: Her Majes-
ty's Stationery Office, 1967.

Sullivan, E.V. Piaget and the school curriculum: A critical appraisal.
Ontario: Ontario Institute for Studies in Education, Bulletin Number 2,
1967.

Tewksbury, J.L. Nongrading in the elementary school. Columbus, Ohio: Charles
E. Merrill, 1967.

Theory into Practice. Curriculum theory
development: Work in progress (J.
Frymier, Editor). Volume 6, Number 4,
October, 1967. Ohio State University, 1967.

Van Til, W., Vars, G.F., and Lounsbury, J.H.
Modern education for the junior high
school years (Second Edition). Indianapolis: Bobbs-Merrill, 1967.

Venable, T.C. Philosophical foundations of
the curriculum. Chicago: Rand-
McNally, 1967.

Verduin, J.R. Cooperative curriculum
improvement. Englewood Cliffs, New
Jersey: Prentice-Hall, 1967.

Wahle, R.P. (Editor). Toward professional
maturity of supervisors and curriculum
workers. Washington, D.C.: ASCD, 1967.

Wheeler, D.K. Curriculum process. London:

University of London Press, 1967 (Also
1971 by University of London Press--
Unibooks).

Wilhelms, F.T. (Editor). Evaluation as
feedback and guide. 1967 Yearbook.
Washington: Association for Supervision and Curriculum Development,
1967.

1968

Alexander, W.M., et al. The emergent middle school. New York: Holt, Rinehart and Winston, 1968.

Allen, E.D. The changing curriculum:
Modern foreign language. Washington:
Association for Supervision and Cur-
riculum Development, 1968.

Bangs, F.K. and Hillestad, M.C. Curricular
implications of automated data pro-
cessing for educational institutions.
Boulder, Colorado: University of
Colorado, 1968.

Beauchamp, G.A. Curriculum theory. Wilmette, Illinois: The Kagg Press,
1968.

Beck, R.H., et al. Curriculum imperative:
Survival of self in society. Uni-
versity of Nebraska, Department of
Secondary Education, 1968.

Beckner, W. and Cornett, J.D. The secondary school curriculum. Columbus,
Ohio: Charles E. Merrill, 1968.

Berman, L.M. New priorities in the curriculum. Columbus, Ohio: Charles E.
Merrill, 1968.

Cave, R.G. All their future. Harmonds-
worth: Penguin, 1968.

Centre for Curriculum Renewal and Educa-

220

tional Development Overseas. Modern
curriculum developments in Britain.
London: The Centre, 1968.

Dearden, R.F. The philosophy of primary
education. London: Routledge and
Kegan Paul, 1968.

Dressel, P.L. College and university curriculum. Berkeley, California: Mc-
Cutchan, 1968.

Education Development Center. African
education programme. Essex: E.T.
Heron, 1968.

Frazier, A. The new elementary school.
Washington: Association for Supervision and Curriculum Development,
1968.

Great Britain Schools Council. Practical
support for curriculum change; the
young school leaver. London: Her
Majesty's Stationery Office, 1968.

Grobman, H.G. Evaluation activities of
curriculum projects: A starting
point. Chicago: Rand McNally, 1968.

Heller, R.W. and Rosenthal, A.M. (Editors).
The child and the articulated cur-
riculum. New York: Western New York
Study Council, 1968.

Jackson, P.W. Life in classrooms. New
York: Holt, Rinehart and Winston,
1968.

Jarvis, O.T. and Wootton, L.R. The elementary school and its curriculum. Iowa:
William C. Brown, 1968.

Johnson, H.T. Foundations of curriculum.
Columbus, Ohio: Charles E. Merrill,
1968.

Karplus, R. (Editor). What is curriculum evaluation? Six answers. Berkeley, California: Science Curriculum Improvement Study, University of California, 1968.

Keith, L.G., Blake, P., and Tiedt, S. Contemporary curriculum in the elementary school. New York: Harper and Row, 1968.

Kerr, J.F. (Editor). Changing the Curriculum. London: University of London Press, 1968.

Kopp, H.G. (Editor). Curriculum: Cognition and content. Washington: Alexander Graham Bell Association for the Deaf, 1968.

Leeper, R.R. (Editor). Curriculum decisions: Social realities. Washington: Association for Supervision and Curriculum Development, 1968.

Maclure, J.S. Curriculum innovation in practice. Report of the Third International Curriculum Conference. London: Her Majesty's Stationery Office, 1968.

Martinson, R.A. Curriculum enrichment for the gifted in the primary grades. Englewood Cliffs, New Jersey: Prentice-Hall, 1968.

Nisbet, S. Purpose in the curriculum. London: University of London Press, 1968 (Second Edition).

Ontario Association for Curriculum Development. Reconciliation of means and ends in education (R. Luxford and K. Pold, Editors). Toronto: Ontario Association for Curriculum Development, 1968.

Short, E.C. and Marconnit, G.D. (Editors).
    Contemporary thought in public school
    curriculum. Dubuque, Iowa: William
    C. Brown, 1968.

Sowards, G.W. and Scobey, M.M. The chang-
    ing curriculum and the elementary
    teacher (Second Edition). Belmont,
    California: Wadsworth, 1968.

Steeves, F.L. (Editor). The subjects in
    the curriculum: Selected readings.
    New York: Odyssey Press, 1968.

Thomas, R.M., Sands, L.B., and Brubaker,
    D.L. Strategies for curriculum
    improvement: Proposals and proce-
    dures. Boston: Allyn and Bacon,
    1968.

Trump, J.L. and Miller, D.F. Secondary
    school curriculum improvement:
    Proposals and procedures. Boston:
    Allyn and Bacon, 1968.

Unruh, G.G. and Leeper, R.R. (Editors).
    Influences in curriculum change.
    Washington: Association for Super-
    vision and Curriculum Development,
    1968.

Witt, P.W.F. (Editor). Technology and
    the curriculum. New York: Teachers
    College Press, 1968.

1969

American Educational Research Association.
    Curriculum. Review of Educational
    Research (39), June, 1969.

Anderson, V.E. Curriculum guidelines in
    an era of change. New York: Ronald
    Press, 1969.

Association for Supervision and Curriculum
Development (W.H. Beatty, Editor).
Improving educational assessment and
an inventory of measures of affective
behavior. Washington: The Association, 1969.

Bar, M.R. (Editor). Curriculum innovation
in practice in relation to colleges
of education. Report of the study
conference at Edge Hill College of
Education: Ormsirk, Lancashire,
1969.

Bent, R.K. and Unruh, A. Secondary school
curriculum. Lexington, Mass.: D.C.
Heath, 1969.

Cassidy, H.G. Knowledge, experience and
action: An essay on education. New
York: Teachers College Press, 1969.

Crary, R.W. Humanizing the school: Curriculum development and theory. New
York: Random House, 1969.

Dragositz, A. (Editor). Curriculum innovations and evaluation. Proceedings
of Association for Supervision and
Curriculum Development pre-conference
seminar, March, 1968. Princeton, New
Jersey: Educational Testing Service,
1969.

Ellis, E.V. The role of the curriculum
laboratory in the preparation of
quality teachers. Tallahassee,
Florida: Florida A and M University
Foundation, 1969.

Frazier, A. (Editor). A curriculum for
children. Washington: Association
for Supervision and Curriculum Development, 1969.

Frost, J.L. and Rowland, G.T. Curriculum
for the seventies. New York: Houghton Mifflin, 1969.

Grobman, H. Evaluation activities of
curriculum projects. London: McGraw-
Hill, 1969.

Guttchen, R.S. and Bandman, B. (Editors).
Philosophical essays on curriculum.
Philadelphia: J.B. Lippincott, 1969.

Gwynn, J.M. and Chase, J.B. Curriculum
principles and social trends (Fourth
Edition). New York: Macmillan, 1969.

Hamilton, N.K. and Saylor, J.G. (Editors).
Humanizing the secondary curriculum.
Washington: Association for Supervision and Curriculum Development,
1969.

Hass, G. Curriculum and instruction prac-
tices for continuous learner progress.
Clearwater Research and Development
Council, 1969.

James, H.T., et al. The schools and the
challenge of innovation. Washington:
Committee for Economic Development,
1969.

Jones, H.L. (Editor). Curriculum development in a changing world. Syracuse:
School of Education, Syracuse University, 1969.

Joyce, B. Alternative models of elementary
education. Waltham, Mass.: Blaisdell
Publishing Company, 1969.

Larson, M.E. Review and synthesis of
research: Analysis for curriculum
development in vocational education.
Columbus, Ohio: Center for vocational
and Technical Education, 1969.

Meeker, M.N. The structure of intellect: Its interpretation and uses. Columbus, Ohio: Charles E. Merrill, 1969.

Morphet, E.J. Designing education for the future. New York: Scholastic (Seven Volumes), 1966-69.

Ohliger, J. (Editor). Project to train teachers in adult basic education curriculum development, July 21-August 8, 1969; final report. Columbus, Ohio: Center for Adult Education, College of Education, Ohio State University, 1969.

Payne, A. The study of curriculum plans. Washington: National Education Association, 1969.

Phillips, C.M. Changes in subject choice at school and university. London: Weidenfeld and Nicolson, 1969.

Popham, W.J., et al. Instructional objectives. Chicago, Illinois: Rand McNally, 1969.

Rogers, L.R. Use of organized knowledge. Clearwater, Florida: Florida Educational Research and Development Council, 1969.

Rubin, L.J. (Editor). Life skills in school and society. 1969 Yearbook. Washington: Association for Supervision and Curriculum Development, 1969.

Rudd, W.G.A. Curriculum innovation: Regional and local efforts in curriculum practice. England: Edge Hill College of Education, 1969.

Schwab, J.J. College curriculum and student protest. Chicago: University of Chicago Press, 1969.

Skolnick, I.H. A guide to curriculum construction for the religious school. Chicago, Illinois: Chicago College of Jewish Studies Press, 1969.

Springer, U.K. Recent curriculum developments in France, West Germany and Italy: A study of trends at the middle level of education. New York: Teachers College, Columbia University Center for Education in Industrial Nations, 1969.

Stockmeyer, E.A.K. Rudolf Steiner's curriculum for Waldorf schools. London: Rudolf Steiner Press, 1969.

Symmes, S.S. (Editor). Developmental economic education programs: Handbook for curriculum change; guidelines. New York: Joint Council on Economic Education, 1969.

Tyler, R.W. Basic principles of curriculum and instruction (Reprint). Chicago: University of Chicago Press, 1969.

Vars, G.F. (Editor). Common learnings: Core and interdisciplinary team approaches. Scranton, Pennsylvania: International Textbook Company, 1969.

Walton, S.F. The Black curriculum. East Palo Alto (Nairobi): Black Liberation Publishers, 1969.

Wilson, J. Moral education and the curriculum. Oxford: Pergamon Press, 1969.

CHAPTER VIII

CURRICULUM LITERATURE AND CONTEXT:

1970-1979

Contextual Reminders

The fact that this book was written in 1978 and 1979 presents two problems that are particularly significant to this chapter. The first involves the difficulty of maintaining a detached perspective in order to see events with enough objectivity to determine whether they should be permanently associated with the Seventies or whether they were ephemeral. The second problem is simply the fact that all of the data are not yet available, let alone analyzed and interpreted. Nevertheless, problems often carry subtle advantages. Though it is difficult to maintain detachment, productive insights often come from involvement. The events of the Seventies are fresh in our minds, and mere reminders can set in motion reconstructions of them that are more vivid than an extensive catalog of historical highlights. At the same time we must await the distance of history that tempers knowledge drawn from interaction with events to produce insight about what, in fact, constitutes the influential forces of the decade.

The Seventies began amid problems of the Vietnam War, its protest movements, stories of its near completion, stories of troop increases, and with rumors of peace talks. Finally, in 1975, the United States forces withdrew and the South Vietnamese surrendered. A war that lingered for nearly fifteen years, that ended the lives of over 55,000 persons from the United States and over a million Vietnamese, a war that cost the United States over 140 billion dollars was cver.

Vietnam was not the only bastion of violence
in the Seventies. Civil war in Nigeria left countless Biafrans homeless and starving. Bombings and
sabotage plagued Northern Ireland for much of the
decade. Israeli and Egyptian forces continued an
ebb and flow of negotiation and conflagration throughout the decade. It reached a culmination in peace
talks initiated by United States President Carter,
an endeavor that resulted in granting the 1978
Nobel Prize for Peace to leaders Sadat of Egypt and
Begin of Israel. The early Seventies brought the
creation and tragedy of Bangladesh. In 1972, on
the other side of the globe, Juan Peron returned to
Argentina after seventeen years in exile; and in
1973 Salvadore Allende of Chile, the first elected
Marxist president in the Western Hemisphere, was
assassinated in a coup d'etat. Two years before,
Idi Amin seized power through another coup in Uganda.
In 1974 still another army coup overthrew Portugese
dictator, Marcello Caetano. In Ethiopia in the same
year, the half century rule of Haile Selassie was
ended, and in Greece the vote was against allowing
the return of exiled King Constantine II. Movement
toward autonomy was pursued by French separatists
in Canada at mid-decade. Racial riots plagued South
Africa, and civil war in Angola led to communist
victories there. Economic disputes raged over
fishing rights in the "cod war" between Iceland and
Britain in 1976. The above is merely a sample.

From 1977 through 1979, it is not difficult to
recall stress, conflict, and aggression that mention
of the following places brings to mind: riots in
Cairo, Muslim terrorists in Washington, D.C., massacre
in Ethiopia, coup in Pakistan, conflagration between
Libya and Egypt, coup in Thailand, apartheid policy
enforcement in South Africa, Somalian expulsion of
Soviets and Cubans, guerrilla attacks in Nicaragua,
military coup in Afghanistan, guerrilla warfare in
Rhodesia, Eritrean secessionist fighting in Ethiopia,
and riots leading to the departure of the Shah of
Iran.

Disaster and death were by no means solely
due to human impingement as evidenced by the
following: a 1970 tidal wave that killed
100,000 and left a million homeless in Pakistan;
a 1970 earthquake in Peru that killed over 50,000
and left 800,000 homeless; a 1971 tidal wave that
killed over 15,000 in India; 1972 earthquakes
that killed 5,000 in Iran and 10,000 in Nicaragua;
a 1974 hurricane in Honduras that killed 8,000
and left over 300,000 homeless; a 1976 earthquake
that killed 665,000 in Tangshan, China and three
others that took 22,000 lives in Guatemala City,
8,000 in the Philippines, and 4,000 in Turkey; and
a Romanian earthquake in 1977 that killed over
1,000 and left 20,000 homeless. As pervasive as
these were, they do not set the Seventies apart
from other decades in magnitude of natural disaster.

At the same time that conflict, frustration,
and tragedy pervaded much of the Seventies, so
did conflict resolution and frequent attempts to
produce policy that would prevent impingement of
humans on one another. The Vietnam War was
terminated at least on a large scale. Communist
China was finally admitted to the United Nations
in 1971 and Taiwan withdrew. Colonial posses-
sions continued to become a relic of past times,
yet according to some, economic colonialism was
increasing. In 1972 the USA and USSR reached an
agreement to stop the nuclear arms race. In the
same year President Nixon made visits to China
and the USSR. A new era of diplomatic and economic relations with China ensued. Despite
continued outbreaks of violence that shocked the
1972 Olympic Games in Munich, Israeli and Egyptian attempts to negotiate peace were manifest.
In 1974 the United States and USSR agreed to
limit armaments. By the end of the decade,
trade agreements that involved various combinations of the major economic powers of the world
(e.g., the United States, the USSR, Japan, Germany, Communist China, England, and France)
increased markedly. Continued inflation and its

ever-present threat of recession and depression continued to mount. The portent and potential of unprecedented power in a kind of "inter-corporationalism" waxed strong as discussion of internationalism waned.

Reflecting a bit on internationalism, the Seventies were a time that marked transition for national leaders. Foremost among these was the unprecedented exit of a United States president, Richard Nixon, and numerous high officials from office amid the possibility of impeachment during the Watergate scandal in 1974. Nixon was succeeded and subsequently pardoned of all crime by Gerald Ford. Of at least equal impact on the other side of the world in 1976 came the end of an era: the deaths of Chairman Mao Tse-tung and Premier Chou En-lai, authors of the cultural revolution in Communist China. In the final years of the decade China moved into a state of increased acceptance of and by other powers in international economy. Elsewhere world leaders were also in transition: Egypt's Abdul Nasser died in 1970, succeeded by Anwar Sadat; Kurt Waldheim of Austria succeeded Burma's U Thant at the helm of the United Nations in 1971; the deposition of Ethiopia's Haile Selassie by the army in 1974; the death of France's President Georges Pompidou and the resignation of Israeli Prime Minister Golda Meir, both in 1974; the end of the eleven year rule of Indira Gandhi in India in 1977; the 1978 succession of Popes with the death of Pope Paul VI, followed by the election of Pope John Paul I, his subsequent death approximately a month later, followed by the election of Pope John Paul II and his memorable visits throughout the world; the 1979 exit of the Shah of Iran amid riot and turmoil there, and the subsequent holding of American hostages.

In quite another domain, activities in the traditional arts of architecture, painting, music, and literature continued to be plentiful. Determination of the greatest among the contributions, however, is particularly difficult

232

without the advantage of retrospect. In any
event, the prominent names of the times invoke
reflection on the immediate past in these areas:
in architecture, Kevin Roche, Minoru Yamasaki,
Bruce Graham, Welton Becket, Mitchell Giurgola,
Roger Taillibert; in sculpture, Armans Vaillan-
court, Alexander Calder, Don Thibodeaux; in
music, Shostakovich, Henze, Janacek, Pendericki,
Bennet, Ligeti, Nono, Menotti, Cage, Kirchner,
Emerson; and in literature, John Updike, Gore
Vidal, Graham Greene, Mary McCarthy, Herman
Wouk, Frederick Forsyth, Joseph Heller, Vladimir
Nabokov, Saul Bellow, Agatha Christie, Alexander
Solzhenitsyn, Arthur Miller, Harold Pinter,
Evelyn Waugh, James Michener, Kurt Vonnegut, Jr.,
and Jorge Luis Borges.

It was a time of the skyscraper, and the
competition to build a taller one, a time of
outdoor art forms in the city, a time when novels
depicted the excitement and insight to be found
in the ordinary as well as in the sophisticated
and renown. Moreover, it was a time when the
popular arts continued to emerge as legitimate
expressions of the plights, impediments, ideals,
and aspirations of the public, not always a
national public but one for whom nationalism
was less important. The art of advertising,
the art of rock music, the art of the comic strip,
the art of popular periodicals, the art of television, and the art of the sports world all spoke
to the everyday interests of everyperson. Personkind found kinship in these, perhaps less
sophisticated, portrayals of human experience.
The Seventies solidified an era that Robert Theo-
bald called the communication era, a shift beyond
the age of industrialization.[1] Perhaps even more
wholly than the other popular arts was the continued use of film to represent human activity.
The variety of societal ills, fantasies, ideals,
and individual feelings portrayed in the following films attests to the film, the popular film
as well as the art film, as full-fledged literature: Patton, Women in Love, Klute, The French

Connection, The Prime of Miss Jean Brodie, Caba-
ret, The Godfather, Midnight Cowboy, Billy Jack,
Jaws, A Touch of Class, The Sting, Harry and
Tonto, One Flew Over the Cockoo's Nest, Alice
Doesn't Live Here Anymore, Conrak, Day for Night,
Walking Tall, Network, Rocky, Annie Hall, Oh
God, Star Wars, Close Encounters of a Third Kind,
Julia, Superman, Kramer vs. Kramer, Being There,
and such television films as Upstairs, Downstairs,
Roots, and The Duchess of Duke Street. The
emergent sophistication and the widespread appeal
of the popular arts today contribute in their own
way to a representation of what the Greeks called
paideia, a source of evidence about the modern
character and the ideals it epitomizes.

Sciences and technology, too, corroborate
progress into the communications era. Computers,
cybernetics generally, revolutionized the business world and the realm of the media. The space
race continued and contributed directly and indirectly to the communications revolution. China
entered that race in 1970 with the launching of
their first satellite, the same year that communication expertise enabled the United States to
recover an explosion ridden spacecraft, Apollo
13, from its orbit around the Moon. A Soviet
spacecraft, Mars III, successfully landed on
Mars, and a United States craft, Mariner 9,
orbited that planet in 1971. The same year saw
American astronauts drive a vehicle on the lunar
surface, while the next year brought the establishment of astronomical observatories on the
Moon. In 1973 dockings were made with United
States space station, Skylab, while Russian
scientists sent four unmanned spacecrafts to
Mars. The next year Mariner 10 brought photographs of Mercury to United States scientists,
and in 1975 Viking I transmitted pictures of
the Martian surface to Earth.

Funding was gradually reduced for the
exploration of space. Nevertheless, other
scientific and technological achievements continued, having pervasive implications: artifi-

234

cial tissue was used as a substitute for skin by Japanese scientists in 1973, male birth control pills were developed in 1977 by United States researchers; the Alaskan pipeline began operation in the same year; in 1978 Rand Corporation representatives reported plans for a coast-to-coast subway that would take only twenty-one minutes; also in 1978 David M. Rorvik published a book asserting that a successfully cloned human being had been achieved, an assertion that was clearly not unquestioned; the same year, however, brought the clearly documented birth of a test-tube baby who was fertilized outside of the body and nurtured in laboratory conditions. Not all scientific discovery pointed directly to human advance. Studies aired in 1979 showed with increased assurance that smoking was etiological in varieties of respiratory diseases, cancer, heart disease, and certain types of birth defects. In addition, many studies pointed to the augmented devastation of the environment by human and industrial waste and the exploitation of natural and human resources.

The Seventies also issued in attempts to correct misuses of the biosphere that were amplified by scientific research. Increased attention to the environment resulted in striving to prevent, for example, litter and excess use of gasoline. Massive attempts to correct ecological problems were set in motion by corporations, their foundations, and governmental agencies.

The burgeoning inequities of city life often brought economic crises; a federal loan staved off the economic collapse of New York City. Civil rights for Blacks continued as a goal, accompanied in the United States by Native American Indian calls for equality, as evidenced by a demonstration at Wounded Knee, South Dakota in 1973. Equal rights for other racial and ethnic groups became prominent areas of concern, protest and legislation. Throughout the decade equal rights for women were furthered in social, economic, occupational, and political areas throughout the world due to the hard work of this movement. As early as 1970 England's parliament ruled that women should receive equal payment for equal work. Gay rights, the rights of the elderly, the rights of children, and the rights of the mentally and physically handicapped began to be given increased magnification in public consciousness in many parts of the globe. Yet, equality was far from adequately defined, much less actualized in these domains. By the end of the decade recession was pounding at the door; the price of gold and other standards of economic value soared, and the heated quest for oil could be felt deeply in the purses of middle and lower class persons throughout the world.

The Seventies moved personkind closer to the stars, closer to an understanding of the intricate make-up of humans themselves, closer to self-reflection through the media of popular arts, and closer to consciousness that might realign the "have-muches" with the "have-lesses." The decade brought us closer with each other through a transition to communication systems that implode our neurons with information and saturate our ephemeral realms with a dissonance and consonance of impressions and images wrought by increased proximity to one another. With all of this came massive problems of decision and responsibility about what constitutes just action, of what constitutes the best of human-ness. With these problems, and they are indeed pervasive, came equally massive potential for human growth. There was even a question posed that according to many scientists, ranks among the most imaginatively provocative of all time; to wit, Professor Gerard O'Neill of the Physics Department at Princeton University advocated serious consideration of the following:

> In the long run is a planetary surface, any planetary surface, really the right place for an expanding technological civili-zation?[2]

236

He urged consideration of the social, political, physical, cultural, ethical, and educational advantages of small communities of human beings traveling in self-sustaining environments through space. Provocative? Most certainly. Imaginative? Without doubt. Possible? Some scientists indicated that it was! Would not implications for education and curriculum be indeed profound?

Curriculum Thought and Literature

The late Sixties and early Seventies were crisis-riddled times. They were also times of immense potential. Scientists, citizens groups, individual citizens, even politicians, and persons from many avenues of life witnessed and called for change in policies regarding the environment, technological developments, consumerism, employment practices, women's rights, racial and ethnic rights, corporate power, international relations, and activities of politicians. Much of the widespread critique that began in the counter-culture of the Sixties had now infused the mainstream of the Seventies. Overt protests were less frequent, but heated demand for equity left few spheres untouched, often scathed, by demands for accountability.

Education was far from immune to these occurrences. The protest literature[3] of schooling in the Sixties, e.g., writings by Herb Kohl, George Dennison, Jonathan Kozol, and John Holt were granted a bit more scholarly legitimation after the appearance of Charles Silberman's Crisis in the Classroom (1970). Some of the public and profession alike may have had little trouble ignoring the counter-culture educational writing; some deemed the free schools and the free classrooms as an anomaly perpetuated by teachers of the "hippy" persuasion though others were markedly influenced. But the appearance of Silberman's book brought credence to the idea that schools were educationally bankrupt. After all, Silberman was an already highly regarded

237

sociologist and his research was not of the first person variety as was much of the counter-culture educational literature. Silberman generalized, and that is the kind of knowledge that social behaviorists throughout the world of social science had programmed the public to value with receptivity.

Unlike social behaviorist writing, the writing style of counter-culture educators was intuitive and usually based on in-depth interaction with small numbers of situations, a long way from the kind of objectivity and generalization that the dominant notion of science taught people to appreciate. This issue will be rejoined in the discussions of curriculum contributions by Schwab, Pinar, Reid, Apple, Greene, and others who utilized alternative orientations to curriculum inquiry. For now, it is sufficient to emphasize that both the counter-culture educators and Silberman helped revive interest in and set precedent for new dimensions and the experiential tradition. Both kindled criticism that extinguished the flame of trust that the public had in its schools during the Fifties and early Sixties.

The foregoing is symptomatic of a larger issue. The advance of communication made it increasingly impossible to view education of the Seventies apart from its context within social and political happenings. In previous decades there had been considerable lag. Pressures for accountability hit schools during the same time period that similar demands impaled other major institutions. Schools, however, were more obviously under public control and it was not difficult to manipulate funding strings for schooling and research at all levels.

The "golden days" of educational funding were soon a prized relic of the past. So was unquestioned faith in public schools. Yet publication and research in the Seventies was not dormant. There was a rise in the number of smaller funding agencies, which for a while could be combined with funding that lingered from massive programs of the late Sixties. There was also the perennial lag from submission of scholarly works to publication. Therefore, it is not surprising that the above factors, the growing number of curricularists and an increased emphasis on publication as a symbol of professional worth, forged a total number of curriculum volumes in the Seventies that exceeded those of the Sixties by over 100 books.

Curriculum, as a subset of educational studies, became enmeshed in a context of sociopolitical forces that affected its practice, accountability, and scholarship. The multiplicity of forces upon curriculum research and practice in the Seventies was indeed widespread and disjointed. The scope of such forces can only be sampled; other historical sources treat them more fully.[4] Here, they are noted primarily for their impact on curriculum thought.

Large scale empirical studies also carried considerable influence. Many curricularists interpreted the Coleman Report to indicate that school curriculum, instruction, and the like had little impact on achievement. The socio-economic status of the home was touted as the critical variable in predicting achievement. The International Educational Assessment, a survey of education in approximately twenty nations, brought a curricular conclusion, thought simplistic or at least common-sensical by some; that the best indicator of what students will learn in schools is that to which they were exposed. Moreover, studies indicated that the duration of exposure was critical, thereby leading to a multiplicity of studies of time on task in the several academic areas. National Assessment of Educational Progress (another major involvement on behalf of Ralph Tyler) sought to determine skill and knowledge levels of Americans at specified age intervals. As with standardized achievement tests, such information often triggered heated school criticism if "norms" were not "met." It was clear that, with both scholars and the public, empirical studies that portrayed data quantitatively were deemed the most defensible kind of contribution.

Other kinds of contributions were, however, beginning to edge their way into educational scholarship. A movement in educational history, labeled revisionism, seemed to stem from increased consciousness of the plight of non-white, non-Anglo, non-Germanic racial and ethnic groups in America's history. No one remained sacrosanct from the criticism of this inquisition by revisionist educational historians.[5] Even John Dewey, foremost among philosophers who influenced curriculum writers, was among those accused of paving the way to subjugation of lower socio-economic classes and ethnic and racial minorities.

Toward the end of the decade, concern for a branch of sociological and philosophical inquiry that evolved in Britain began to look seriously at the kind of knowledge perpetuated by dominant social classes in advanced industrial society. Since Thomas Kuhn impacted the research community with his The Structure of Scientific Revolutions,[6] the idea that the conventional paradigm of scholarship in any given era is not the only possibility began to surface more fully. Moreover, the epistemological base that pervaded scholarship in any era could no longer be viewed wholly as a universal and objective language for inquiry, though any system of rules sustains a sort of objectivity. Instead, the widely accepted social science paradigm was realized to be the dominant paradigm among alternative possibilities. Dominance in this case depended upon a composite of ideological, economic, intellectual, and socio-political forces that were too often beyond scholars' control if not their consciousness.

In this critical vein the curriculum literature of the Seventies began with Joseph Schwab's
small but influential book, The Practical: A
Language for Curriculum (1970), made visible a
year earlier as an article by the same title in
School Review.[7] Schwab argued that the curriculum field was moribund, dying by adherence to a
mode of inquiry that did not suit the task of
improving schools. His critique focused on the
assumptive bases of the language or principles
of research. Drawing upon the Aristotelian
distinction between theoretic and practical
epistemological bases, Schwab argued that the
current theoretic or social-science paradigm
is largely irrelevant to the task of improving
curricular practice in schools. He advocated
that scholarly endeavor must be changed to the
practical paradigm, a mode of inquiry that seems
archetypical of Dewey. Whereas the problem
source of theoretic research resides in concep-
tualizations of researchers, that of the practical is in events and situational conflicts. The
method of inquiry of the theoretic paradigm is
induction, assuming the possibility of objectivity and the virtual absence of a Heisenbur-
gian uncertainty principle. On the contrary,
the practical assumptions hold that illuminating insight stems from interaction with problematic arenas rather than induction upon them.
Moreover, the subject matter of theoretic
inquiry is universals and its end is the production of publishable knowledge, while the practical takes a subject matter that is unique to
situations, that acknowledges the need to see
an interdependence of causal factors that are
not generalizable but are necessary knowledge
for promoting an end of decision and action that
rectifies specific problems.

In later articles, Schwab[8] called for eclectic arts that matched or tailored theoretic
knowledge to situations and generated additional courses of action for application in the
plethora of circumstances where theoretic knowledge did not apply. He also bolstered his contextual position by calling for a study of

241

curriculum that was based on no less than
deliberation that illuminated the interdependence of five commonplaces of curricular
experience: subject matter, learners, teachers, curricular decision or policy, and milieu.
Interactions among these factors in problematic
classroom encounters create the curricula that
actually occur there. Salient writings by
Schwab were collected and discussed by Westbury
and Wilkof (1978). Schwab's work stimulated
increased attention to the nature of curriculum
problems and ways in which they could be studied. At the end of the decade, W.A. Reid raised
provocative questions and arguments about the
overarching problem of how to best think about
curriculum (1978), and contributed to curricular
policy studies by drawing upon both rationalist
and humanist methodologies.

Schwab's critique and proposal were not
alone in the turn taken by curriculum writers
in the Seventies; namely, the reconceptualists.
The roots of the latter are phenomenological,
existential, psychoanalytic, and Marxist. The
similarity between Schwab and the reconceptualists of the late Seventies is infrequently noted,
and seldom seen as having similar intellectual
roots. More will be said later in this chapter
about reconceptualist positions. Suffice it
to note here that much of it spurred humanist
concerns, i.e., such positions represent a new
variety of the humanist orientations proposed
in the early Sixties, e.g., the 1962 ASCD Yearbook,
and articles by such scholars as James B. Macdonald and Dwayne Huebner. It became quite clear
that these perspectives were growing.

These orientations, however, were clearly
overshadowed by the preponderance of extant
theoretic bias in the dominant brand of social
behaviorist curriculum thought. Nevertheless,
those of a humanistic ilk were loosely linked
together by assumptions that acknowledged the
following: the centrality of situational problems; a necessary interactivity with environ-

242

ments for knowledge creation; a dialectical dialogue among persons for the exchange and growth
of knowledge; an emphasis on persons as whole
beings in the state of becoming or growing; the
need to tie institutionalized learning to larger
community functioning; the concomitant priority
of interest or a Deweyan psychological organization of subject matter; acceptance of a variety
of alternative and defensible ways of knowing;
and the importance of acknowledging and fostering
individuality. Such assumptions describe the
character of a new variation, perhaps a profound
one, in the experientialist line of curriculum
thought. This listing of assumptions is not
intended to be exhaustive; neither is it intended to suggest criteria to which a given author
must adhere to be considered part of this rebirth
of experientialism.

The idea that the above group was a loosely
knit category should be re-emphasized. In practice-focused literature the sources seldom were
acknowledged to be in the curriculum domain.
Instead of using curriculum, most bear titles that
referred to humanistic education or teaching,
affective education, confluent education, open
education, personalized education, values clarification, etc. Some curriculum authors, however,
can be identified with similar interpretations
of experientialist proposals for and reports about
practice. Examples of these include: Bremer and
Van Moschzisher (1971), Buffie and Jenkins (1971),
Featherstone (1971), Kopp and Zufelt (1971), Manning (1971),Dale (1972), Miller (1972), Harmin,
Kirschenbaum, and Simon (1973), Silberman (1973),
Goodlad, et al. (1974), Holly (1974), Kopp and
Zufelt (1974), Murphy (1974), Hollaway (1975),
UNESCO (1975), Fantini (1976), Frazier (1976),
Margolin (1976), Berman and Roderick (1977), Olsen
and Clark (1977), Jelinek (1978) and Weston
(1978). Quite obviously some of these citations
are not directly curricular; however, they are
included here as sources of marked influences on
or reflections of curriculum thought and practice. Indeed disjointed in both origins and

243

advocacies, these sources represent important kinds of experiential contributions.

Having considerable impact on curriculum thought and literature, but as yet little if any on schooling in the Seventies, was a group noted earlier as the reconceptualists. This group,whose curricular roots trace, among others, to Macdonald and Huebner, and to their mentor Virgil Herrick, tends to be grounded in the humanities and in philosophy. Tenets of their writings are not dissimilar to much that is basic to Schwab's practical, Dewey's instrumentalist progressivism, and the practice-focused humanists. Yet, part of their origin is decidely different; it was given a conceptual unification in the work of William Pinar. The visibility of unification was spearheaded by Pinar through books in 1974, 1975, and 1976 (with Grumet) through annual conferences beginning in 1973 at the University of Rochester, and through the inauguration of The Journal of Curriculum Theorizing in 1979. Other writers,notably, John S. Mann, Michael Apple, Madeleine Grumet, Henry Giroux, Janet Miller, Paul R. Klohr, Alex Molnar, Max van Manen, David C. Williams, and George Willis are sometimes associated with this "movement." The publication of Macdonald and Zaret's Schools in Search of Meaning (1975) by the Association for Supervision and Curriculum Development, Qualitative Evaluation: Concepts and Cases in the Curriculum (1978) by George Willis, and Ideology and Curriculum (1979) by Michael Apple helped to characterize the movement's several directions.

A similarity of intellectual roots enables clarification of reconceptualist origins. Existential literary sources, e.g., Sartre, Camus, Kafka and others combined with the work of such continental philosophers as Maurice Merleau-Ponty and most notably Jurgen Habermas. Certain reconceptualists also rely substantially upon the work of Basil Bernstein and other sociologists of knowledge from Britain and the conti-

244

nent. Recommended as an introduction to such
sources are Michael F.D. Young's Knowledge and
Control (1971) and P.W. Musgrave's Knowledge,
Curriculum, and Change (1973). Some of the
reconceptualist literature is woven within a
fabric of neo-Marxian thought known as critical
theory. Although one can turn to original works
by Habermas for background, one could study a
fine secondary source such as Thomas McCarthy's
The Critical Theory of Jurgen Habermas (Cambridge: The MIT Press, 1978).

Practical application is not ignored by
reconceptualists as evidenced by their frequent
citation of Paulo Freire's The Pedagogy of the
Oppressed (1970). In this work, for example,
Freire reported on work with oppressed peasants
from Brazil. He related his avoidance of the
usual impediments associated with superior and
inferior roles in teaching-learning situations
by engaging the peasants in dialogue that
accented the worth of all involved and used the
opportunity to mutually overcome weaknesses and
synthesize strengths. In Toward a Poor Curriculum (1976), by Pinar and Grumet, practical as
well as philosophical application was made of
certain central ideas in reconceptualist thought.
Poor, as used by these authors, referred to a
curriculum that is stripped of distracting
accouterments, a curriculum of inner human feeling that emerges as the course of the learning
journey evolves. Experiencing that curriculum
was described as follows: regressive, i.e.,
sensitization to one's past self; progressive,
i.e., projection of one's future self; analytic,
i.e., sensitization to intricacies of one's
present; and a continuously evolving synthesis
of the three that accumulates toward self-
actualization. A summary and extension of
Pinar's position and his interpretation of its
relation to other extant positions in the
curriculum field may be found in his "State of
the Art" address at the 1978 annual conference
of the American Educational Research Association, subsequently published in Educational

245

Researcher.[9] One final point is in order; namely, that there are marked differences among writers who have been, from time to time, given the reconceptualist label. It is dangerous to cast writers of rich variation in one mold simply because they differ from dominant orientations. I suspect that Pinar and others would agree with this point.

Michael Apple and others have contributed repeatedly to the literature on hidden curriculum, noted earlier as a topic sparked by Philip Jackson in his Life in Classrooms (1968). Though not among the reconceptualist authors, Braun, Overly, and Snyder each produced works in 1970 that acknowledged the importance of hidden curriculum. Thus, it can be seen that while the curriculum reconceptualists represent a major movement in the experientialist position, they are quite different in origin from other curriculum writers of the past three decades, including other experientialists. Nevertheless, their interpretations of critical theory and its emphasis on dialectical synthesis is, I submit, closer to Deweyan roots than I have thus far seen acknowledged in reconceptualist writing. Dewey's version of science was quite thoroughly practical and humanistic. It can be argued, however, that it was not emancipatory in either the political or epistemological sense as advocated among reconceptualists.

A book that is not easy to categorize is Eisner's The Educational Imagination (1979). It tends to be experientialist more than social behaviorist or intellectual traditionalist. Yet, it stems from different origins. While Dewey and his followers stemmed from pragmatic philosophy and while reconceptualists stemmed from continental phenomenology, existentialism and psychoanalysis, Eisner's roots are in the arts. He advocated curricular content that reflects critical perception and alternative modes of representation as central or basic to education. He offered qualitative modes of evaluation that are analogous to functions of critics and connoisseurs in the arts.

Moving now to other curriculum orientations
of the Seventies, it seems pertinent to emphasize that, by comparison, the reconceptualist
position was not characterized by the quantity
of production created by either the social behaviorists or authors of synoptic texts, i.e.,
those who by now could be labeled intellectual
traditionalists within curriculum inquiry itself.
Let us look at several groups within this rather
massive category.

Authors of synoptic texts, it should first
be recalled, often emerged from Deweyan roots.
Captivated with the desire to induct novice
curricularists into the field, they produced
encyclopedic renditions of curriculum knowledge.
Their subtopics are now quite familiar: foundations, purposes, development, design, implementation, evaluation, organization, instruction,
materials, and change, etc. Desirous too, of
helping budding curricularists become able to
influence practice, they provided guidelines,
often calling them principles. Surely, they
must have known that such recipes would scarcely
equip readers to exercise Deweyan intelligence.
Yet, what alternative did they have, given their
limited exposure to would-be curricularists?
All of this combined with a zealous drive by
synoptic text writers to insure that future
curricularists would be aware of recent curriculum innovations and requisite rhetorics.

Thus, one form of synoptic text conveyed
the message that future curricularists must be
readied for uncertain futures when they would be
preparers of curricular experiences that could
either help or hinder children and youth to deal
with life. At a time when rapid technological
advance may have been confused with personal
instability, many general texts appeared that
emphasized innovation and preparation for unknown
futures. The synoptic text continued, modified
by a "we must ready ourselves!" furor. It seemed

247

that such emphasis on novel aspects of curriculum knowledge helped to legitimate curriculum as an area of study that was almost continuously progressing. It is debatable if this was, in fact, a warranted form of legitimation. The following are examples of curriculum books that promoted the novelty of curriculum thought; they are accompanied by key words from their titles that help to characterize this orientation: from 1970, Billett (improving), Burns and Brooks (changing), Doll (improvement), Feyereisen (renewal), Foshay (invention), Frymier and Hawn (improvement), Hicks, et al. (new), Shuster and Ploghoft (emerging); from 1971, Alexander and Saylor (tomorrow), Oliver (improvement); from 1972, Lee and Lee (tomorrow), Organization of Economic Cooperation and Development (the eighties and onwards); from 1973, Beck, Cook and Kearney (modern), Inlow (emergent), Morley (modern); from 1974, Hass, et al. (new); from 1977, Oliver (improvement); and from 1978, Steeves and English (changing), and from 1979 Trump and Miller (improvement). This type of emphasis in curriculum books diminished as the Seventies progressed.

Synoptic texts, generally, waned in the Seventies especially in view of the increasing number of curriculum books produced. Yet, some continued to appear, serving as introductions or overviews of the general area of curriculum study and development. They constituted a second form of synoptic text. Prominent examples include: Bell (1971), Cave (1971), Christine and Christine (1971), Nicholls and Nicholls (1972 and 1978), Firth and Kimpston (1973), Owen (1973), Hass, et al. (1974), Saylor and Alexander (1974), Stenhouse (1975), Tanner and Tanner (1975), Unruh (1975), Barrow (1976), Jenkins and Shipman (1976), Zais (1976), Chandra (1977), Hass (1977), Kelly (1977), McNeil (1977), Gress and Purpel (1978), Lawton, et al. (1978), and Taylor and Richards (1979). These texts, with few exceptions, differed in one important way from synoptic texts of the past. While those

of the Seventies often did attempt to be encyclopedic, at least in the sense of sampling a
variety of major issues, they did not contain
the massive lists of principles or guidelines
that served as prescriptions for practice. The
texts by Bell, Cave, Firth and Kimpston, Owen,
Tanner and Tanner, Lawton, Barrow, Jenkins and
Shipman, Stenhouse, Taylor and Richards and Zais
tended to be more oriented to incisive analysis
than many earlier synoptic texts. In addition, the
Tanner and Tanner (1975 and 1980) and Zais (1976)
texts contained elaborate sections on the history
of contributions to curriculum thought and action.

Also noteworthy was a continuation of synoptic texts that dealt with curriculum at separate
levels of schooling   Among these were the following treatments: at the secondary school level,
Beckner and Cornett (1972), Clark, et al. (1972),
Trump and Miller (1979); at the elementary level,
Lavatelli, Kaltsounis, and Moore (1972), Rodgers
(1975), Wiles and Bondi (1979); at the early childhood level, Parker (1972), Cook and Doll (1973),
Margolin (1976), Seefeldt (1976), Jones (1977);
and at a level that emphasized the newly evolving
middle school and the adolescent years as well as
the junior high, Kindred and Wolotkiewicz (1976),
Curtis and Bidwell (1977), Lounsbury and Vars
(1978).

Another type of emphasis on the "novel" in
curriculum writing of the Seventies differed from
the synoptic type discussed above. It dwelt on
the process of change or innovation and to a
frequent extent on case studies of change.
Examples of this kind of contribution include:
Lawler (1970), Pharis, et al. (1970), Skeel and
Hagen (1971), Hoyle (1972), Hoyle and Bell (1972),
Leithwood and Russell (1972), Mayhew and Ford
(1973), Dickson and Saxe (1974), Kingston (1974),
Regan and Leithwood (1974), Wass (1974), Goodlad
(1975), Harris, et al. (1975), Reid and Walker
(1975), Roberts (1975), Leithwood and Clipsham
(1976), MacDonald and Walker (1976), and Werner
(1979).

Finally, still another type of emphasis on the "novel" dealt with different types of schools and ways in which the curriculum of schools might be selected and organized. Such writings included both proposals and reports, usually taking the form of commentary rather than quantitative research. Sources in this domain were quite varied as illustrated by the following: Turner (1971) on schools that liberated learning; Wilson (1971) on curricula that provided for varieties of avenues to knowledge acquisition; Miller (1972) on secondary curriculum based on humanities; Purpel and Belanger (1972) on several kinds of curricula that evolved during the period of cultural revolution in the Sixties; Saylor (1972) on a call for future-oriented schools; Trump and Miller (1972) on organizational plans that influenced modular scheduling; Frymier (1973) on processes for creating schools of tomorrow; Moffett (1973) on student-centered curricula; Silberman (1973) on open education; Talmage (1975) on organization in individualized education systems; Michaelis, et al. (1975) on different conceptions of curriculum and instruction for elementary schooling. Frazier (1976) on strategies for teaching that involved mastery, adventure, and association; Kauffman (1976) on developing programs that are based on teaching about the future; Frymier (1977) on a special style of individualization; Oliver (1977) on minicourses; Shane (1977) on futures approaches; Holt (1978) on the common curriculum in comprehensive schools; Bloomer and Shaw (1979) on constraints on innovative curricular organization; and Egan (1979) on development as a key factor in curricular selection and organization.

Many of the above variations of emphasizing the novel in curriculum (i.e., the outgrowths of synoptic texts, the procedures and cases, and the proposals for new kinds of curricular organization) combined with the traditional synoptic texts to produce a phenomenon that, itself, should be admitted as a school of curriculum thought. A glance at this combined array of sources seems disparate indeed. However, most of the viewpoints expressed grew out of a long tradition of curricular thought aimed at helping schools. Many writers of such literature were formerly teachers and administrators, and they perceived their role as proposers of ways for schools to overcome problems by replacing old curricular patterns with new ones. Producers of synoptic texts and their descendents who promoted the novel were, as noted earlier, a new brand of traditionalists. This is not to imply that they were intellectual traditionalists who were characterized earlier in the book as purveyors of watered down liberal arts knowledge and skills that re-surfaced during the mental discipline period and dominated most elementary and secondary schools throughout the Twentieth Century. Yet, producers of synoptic texts were "traditionalists" of another ilk, one that grew as the curriculum field itself grew in tandem with the rise of universal schooling.

Curriculum knowledge became a more recognized kind of knowledge as the century progressed and as books called curriculum books were produced in greater numbers. During the Thirties, the synoptic text emerged as a catalogue, sometimes as creator of "up-to-date" curriculum knowledge. It became a tradition, a growing compendium of thoughts by an equally growing number of curricularists. The thoughts were sometimes based on research, sometimes on philosophical argument, and ever-increasingly were built into a cacophony of ideas from experientialist, social behaviorist, and intellectual traditionalist thought. Almost invariably, these combinations were directed as prescriptions for schools. For many years the literature distilled the thoughts into "principles" or guidelines to be followed or kept in mind by those who developed curriculum in schools. In the Seventies less of the guidelines appeared. They were replaced with discussions of issues and the usual presentation of a patchwork of ideas, practices from the recent

251

past, and highlights of other ideas that were considered novel.

Thus, the mainstream of curriculum literature that reached a pinnacle in the synoptic texts of the Fifties and Sixties was, in fact, the creation of a tradition, an "intellectual tradition" of knowledge in curriculum. While the sources of this knowledge were rather diverse, the primary source was schooling itself. This seldom took the form of systematic research into schooling; instead, it was acquired through involvement in schooling. Initially, many curriculum writers were school teachers, later perhaps curriculum consultants or administrators in schools. Sooner or later they became associated with colleges and universities and taught school persons, consulted with schools, and wrote about schools. Their experiential base, much of their knowledge, was derived from schools instead of from academic disciplines. Although they seldom perpetuated the substance of the intellectual traditionalist persuasion, they did help to perpetuate the form in which it continuously occurred, the school as an institution. Thus, I believe they can be fairly, not pejoratively, called a new breed of intellectual traditionalist.

Let us now look at experientialist and social behaviorist thought as it appeared in the Seventies. Roots of experientialism can be traced through Dewey and Herbart to Froebel, Pestalozzi, Comenius, Erasmus, the humanist revival in the Renaissance, and to classical study of humanities. Some reconceptualists of the Seventies refurbished experientialist lines of thought by drawing upon intellectual roots in literary sources within the humanities. Experientialists who were more oriented to schools than the reconceptualists continued advocacy of curricular styles manifested by followers of Dewey. Both persuasions are included in examples that follow and tendencies toward the existential, phenomenological, psychoanalytic, and humanistic can be detected. Examples

252

include Association for Supervision and Curriculum Development (1970) emphasis on nurturing humaneness; Braun's (1970) emphasis on curriculum not as the plan but as occurrences resulting from planning; Freire's (1970) advocacy of interpersonal dialogue; Nerbovig's (1970) continuation of the unit approach to developing integrated curriculum; Weinstein and Fantini's (1970) integration of humanistic and affective activities within accepted modes of objectives and curriculum activities; Bremer and Van Moschzisher's (1971) description of the dissolving of barriers between school and community in the education of youth; Buffie and Jenkins' (1971) continuance of the idea of nongradedness; Kopp and Zufelt's (1971) advocacy of personally tailored curricula; Manning's (1971) interpretation of humanism; Walton's (1971) version of integrated curricula in British primary settings; Dale's (1972) interpretation of learning environments; Thelen's (1972) interpenetration of curriculum and instruction with a sense of aims tempered by a union of action and inquiry; Moffett's (1973) student-centered emphasis; Silberman's (1973) presentation of varieties of perspectives on open classrooms; UNESCO's (1977) case study of integrated curriculum development; Bowers' (1974) existential perspective on teaching, learning, and policy that can invoke a curriculum of dialogues among teachers and students that is basic to democratic action; Holly's (1974) argument that curricular experiences should go beyond developing basic competencies in skills to inspire such necessities for democracy as self-realization and liberation; Haigh's (1975) interpretation of curriculum integration; Hendricks and Fadiman (1975) on curriculum that engages human beings in encounters through such new modes of communication as meditation, fantasy, altered states of consciousness, and Eastern thought/action; Holloway's (1975) humanistic orientation to problem-solving; UNESCO's (1975) experiential curriculum that involved perception, communication, and action; Timmerman's (1976) version of curriculum integration for teenagers; Berman and Roderick's

253

(1977) process-oriented curriculum that focused
on decision-making, communication, and "peopling"
for the enhancement of living; Olsen and Clark's
(1977) stress on the importance of relating
curriculum to life; Greene's (1978) analysis of
landscapes for learning; Reid's (1978) humanistic
extrapolation of the practical; Overly's (1979)
call for lifelong learning; Egan's (1979) argument
for the dynamic interdependence between development
and curriculum; and Bremer's (1979) union of education and art to evolve a conception of community
education that conceives of the public as curriculum.

The social behaviorists were, at the same
time, by no means idle. Charged with the widespread acceptance of social science methodology
that stemmed from involvement of social scientists in curriculum projects during the Sixties,
curricularists of this persuasion continued to
dominate scholarly endeavors. Their propensity
to measure stemmed from roots in a Thorndikian
faith in quantitative measurement and a Skinne-
rian search for objective and observable facts
of human and animal activity. This orientation
involved a behavioristic quest for causal relationships, a logical positivistic faith in the
potential for explanation and pieces of insight
in minute but tested conclusions that had the
potential to gradually build the puzzle of any
aspect of knowledge or action.

In short, faith was manifest in the Hobbesian declaration that saw explanation of human
behavior as a legitimate object of scientific
inquiry. Such a faith helped trigger the
evolution of modern political science and the
diversified social sciences. It should be
noted that this conception of scientific
methodology was quite different from that advocated by Dewey. Instead of holding to the
situational orientation of a Deweyan application
of scientific method, modern social behaviorists,
imbued with social science methodology, adhered
stringently to the Baconian faith that the

254

accumulation and recording of instances would
eventually elucidate the form of nature; thus,
it would enhance and direct technological advance
commensurate with it. Applications of this
faith were exemplified in curriculum practice by
skills management systems. It was assumed that
atomistic specifications of objectives and competencies could be organized to construct systems of concepts that were technologically sound
strategies for schools to use in their effort to
foster human betterment.

The emphasis on combinations of competencies, behavioral objectives, computerization,
systematic needs assessments, attempts to com-
bine elements of the humanistic with the
behavioristic, and much rhetoric from systems
theory and management theory pervaded the literature of the Seventies: Ammerman (1970), Bernabei and Leles (1970), Feyereisen (1970), Harnack (1970), Drumheller (1971), Eisele (1971),
Kapfer (1971), Utz (1971), Drumheller (1972),
Havenstein (1972), Razik (1972), Vargas (1972),
Baker and Popham (1973), Ogletree and Hawkins
(1973), Stradley (1973), Gilchrist, et al. (1974),
Rowntree (1974), Beauchamp (1975), English and
Kaufman (1975), Hug (1975), Mager (1975), and
Casciano-Savignano (1978).

Mager's (1975) work deserves special note
because of its impact on curriculum technology.
His emphasis is derived from his concern for
training programs in such areas as business,
industry, and the military. His work represents
an orientation that looks at performance results
of prespecified tasks as a curricular end, and
is much different from a Deweyan conception of
growth or from a liberal education. The business ethic is also captured by English (1978)
in an emphasis on quality control in curriculum,
but the point emphasized demonstrates the need
to go beyond mere quantitative representations
of efficacy in curriculum.

A decline of technological emulation in curriculum books can be seen in the second half of the decade. Most of the above works were application-oriented; though they sometimes involved scholarly research. Although such writing had rather widespread application or rhetoric, in practice there was a decided absence of curriculum research that convincingly supported it. Moreover, proponents of social behavioristic applications of curriculum were not alone in the curriculum field. Educational researchers who favored empirical or behavioristic methodologies dominated educational scholarship in the Seventies. Many of the field's journals published material of that genre with considerable exclusiveness. The fact that graduate students were increasingly trained in statistical methodologies and research design of greater sophistication speaks to the same point. In this context, all schools of curriculum thought met criticism for the preponderance of "armchair speculation" and the lack of "scientific" research to support their proposals. It was argued by many who espoused social behaviorist methodologies that little generalized evidence existed to support the efficacy of many means-ends assertions in curriculum literature.

Behind the research efforts of these new social behaviorists was the desire to empirically substantiate facts about learners, the learning process, learning conditions, causal factors in learning acquisition, curricular means and ends and inputs and outputs. Scholarly journals took a decided stance toward publication of research that quantitatively documented findings about the above and related matters. Great numbers of educational research studies and journal articles reflected this social science orientation. Some offered important curriculum implications, but few appeared directly from within general curriculum circles. Studies of the behaviorist variety were more frequently found in the area of curriculum evaluation, about which more will be said presently.

Books about curriculum research, however, tended to be more situational, analytic, and interpretative than behaviorist. They tended more toward the conceptual and/or prescriptive than the empirical and experimental, although some embraced both. Examples of books on curriculum research include: Johnston and Burns (1970) on applications of research findings to elementary school curriculum; Lavatelli (1970) on applications of Piagetian research to early childhood curricula; Taylor (1970) on analyses of ways teachers plan courses; Dahllof (1971) on grouping patterns, content validity, and analyses of factors in curriculum process; McClure (1971) on field studies in curriculum development; Smith and Keith (1971) on their analysis of organizational factors in an innovation; Grobman (1972) on decision aspects of developmental curriculum projects; Harrow (1972) on a continuation of Bloom's and Krathwohl's styles of taxonomical objectives into the psychomotor domain; Lundgren (1972) on research into curriculum process begun by Dahllof that led to the identification of theoretical constructs, referred to as _frame factors_, that govern curriculum acquisition; Derr (1973) on a taxonomical representation of a social domain of educational purposes; Taylor and Walton (1973) on several perspectives on curriculum research, innovation, and change; Shipman, Bolam, and Jenkins (1974) on a case study of curriculum change; Taylor and Holley (1974) on a case study of the English "sixth form"; Botel and Botel (1975) on a critical appraisal of taxonomical approaches to the classification of objectives; Eaton (1975) on a survey of uses of curricular terminology; Musgrave (1975) on a presentation of curriculum studies that combined empirical investigation with philosophical and social analysis; Reid and Walker (1975) on case studies in curriculum innovation; Stenhouse (1975) on practice-oriented research perspectives for the curriculum makers; Rudduck and Kelly (1976) on the problem of dissemination; Hamilton, et al. (1977) on modes of illuminating curricular phenomenon without the usual recourse to numbers; Reid (1978) on ways to think about and deal with curricular problems; Willis (1978) on qualitative approaches to curriculum research and evaluation; Apple (1979) on investigation of kinds of knowledge and class relationships perpetuated by curriculum; Schaffarzick and Sykes (1979) on research and experience that wrought value-laden curriculum issues; Goodlad and associates (1979) on the exploration of curriculum practices in schools; and Bremer (1979) on research as a community and personal form of artful growth.

The work of Dahllof and Lundgren on frame factors is a fine example of combining social science methodology and sound theory construction for practical use. Related to time-on-task studies noted earlier, their treatment of frame factors sometimes serves as a theoretical basis for such studies. It can be given practical interpretation since allotment of time, levels of objectives, and teaching methods are frame factors over which teachers can exert control. Such frame factors as student intelligence, student achievement level, class size, length of school year, location of school in community, grouping of students into classes, and curriculum policy requirements are among those that remain beyond the control of individual teachers but exert marked impact on the kind and quality of knowledge that students acquire from curricular experience (Dahllof 1971, Lundgren 1972).

Another area of curriculum inquiry is closely allied with the social behaviorist mode of research. This is the area of curriculum evaluation, an area that often epitomized the theoretic mode of scientific study characterized above more fully than did books on curriculum research in the 1970's. Sometimes considerable overlap exists between curriculum research and evaluation. Curriculum evaluation books, as noted above, were of considerable variety and

were often far removed in style from behavioristic assumptions; case study approaches are
prime examples. Variety, too, exists among
major curriculum evaluators as can be realized
easily through familiarization with work by
Baker, Bloom, Cronbach, Dahllof, Eash, Ebel,
Eisner, Gagne, Goodlad, Kallos, Lundgren, Parlett, Popham, Provus, Scriven, Stake, Stenhouse,
Stufflebeam, Talmage, Tyler, Walker, Westbury,
and Willis. Although all did not author books
on curriculum evaluation in the Seventies, these
researchers authored articles, headed research
agencies, spearheaded notable studies, and/or
promoted styles of evaluation used by governmental and private agencies that provided cur-
riculum-related funding.

Examples of books that directly related
evaluation with curriculum include: Lindvall
and Cox (1970), Wiseman and Pidgeon (1970), Olson
and Richardson (1972), Taylor and Cowley (1972),
Weiss (1972), Wiseman and Pidgeon (1972), Great
Britain Schools Council (1973a and 1973b), Greene
(1973), Payne (1974), Worner (1973), Zenger and
Zenger (1973), Shipman, Bolam, and Jenkins
(1974), Case and Lowry (1975), Stenhouse (1975),
Hamilton (1976), Mathews (1976), Tyler, Klein,
et al. (1976), Bellack and Kliebard (1977),
Hamilton, et al (1977), Lewy (1977), Willis
(1978), and Eisner (1979).

Among the above,several should be given
special note. Taylor and Cowley (1972) present
a fine sample of writings on curriculum evaluation, while Bellack and Kliebard (1977) provide
pieces that provoke broad perspectives on a more
wholistic conception of curriculum evaluation.
The books by Hamilton, et al. (1977), Willis
(1978), and Eisner (1979) provide alternatives
to social behavioristic interpretations of
research. They offer modes of illumination of
curricular phenomena that go beyond what Hamilton
and his colleagues call the numbers game by exam-
ining methods that are naturalistic, literary, and

259

artistic; thus, providing what Willis called
qualitative evaluation. The need for such scholars was pointed to by Wilson (1971) who argued
that through their quite limited notion of scientific study, curriculum researchers often missed
a good deal of intellectual growth during the
Fifties and Sixties. Curriculum and evaluation
research lagged considerably behind orientations
to inquiry in psychology, philosophy, and natural
science. Methods employed in such areas acknowledged the value of personal, situational, intuitive, interactive, and emotional avenues to knowing.

Though this myopia of perspectives in curriculum research was widespread, it was not omni-
present. Stake, Eisner, and others argued on
numerous occasions for intuitive or artistic
human judgment as legitimate knowledge. Both the
dominant form of social behaviorist evaluation
and the qualitative styles that emerged to counter
or complement it were, in part, products of
increased demand for school accountability. Some
argued that defensible evaluation is the necessary
starting point for curriculum development processes. To know what occurred, what currently
exists, was deemed by some to be a crucial prerequisite for deciding what should be. Many
argued that current modes of evaluation inade-
quately portrayed extant happenings in perspective.
Such arguments were sometimes based on the superficiality of analytic categorization schemes.
An even more penetrating criticism was that knowledge of what is was assumed to be sufficient for
determining what should be. Questions of what
should be are, of course, ethical or normative at
their base. Empirical data may be necessary but
are insufficient bases for curricular prescription.
Prescription necessarily builds on the ethical and
aesthetic purposiveness.

That defensible purposes need to be a paramount curriculum development concern rekindled
another focus in curriculum literature. Authors

who emphasized purposes frequently tended to use sophisticated theoretical and philosophical tools. Writings of Freire (1970), Pinar (1974, 1975, 1976) Macdonald and Zaret (1975), and Greene (1978) provided phenomenological and existential perspectives on purposes of both educational activity and research. Schwab (see Westbury and Wilkof, 1978) and Reid (1978) offered contributions that called for practical inquiry and action. Armentrout (1971), Krug (1972), and Wilhelms (1972) provided elaborations on purposes and content geared specifically to America's educational future. Levit (1971), Martin (1970), and Jenkins, et al. (1972) produced collections of readings about curriculum drawn from philosophy of education that represented an array of philosophic styles, especially that of analytic philosophy.

Jenkins' work was quite different in that his book was part of a set designed to introduce students to several spheres of curriculum thought, and as such, provided more than the usual magnitude of contextual explanation of excerpts presented. The nature of objectives and theoretical perspectives in educational literature 1955-1970 was provocatively explored by Morris (1972) with a distinctively British flavor. This relation of philosophy to curriculum was examined by Dixon (1972), and applications of curriculum theory were discussed by Garcia (1973). White (1973) took a serious look at implications of a compulsory curriculum with a British frame of reference, while Broudy (1974) provided a similar service in America, though both offered a much broader view than within nationalistic confines.

The relation of philosophy and theory continued to be explored on a rather large scale. Holly (1974) probed beyond conventional notions of curriculum to suggest modes of secondary education that contribute to a philosophy of general human growth and well-being. Beauchamp produced a third edition of his Curriculum Theory in 1975,

261

continuing his systems oriented approach which now included an example of propositions in that type of curriculum theorizing. In 1977, Mauritz Johnson augmented a combination of his analytic approaches to curriculum theory in the elaborate Intentionality in Education. Analytic philosophy applied to curriculum was also provided by P.H. Hirst in a set of papers (1975) that addressed the relation of knowledge and curriculum. Sidney Hook produced another set of papers in the same year that argued in favor of curricula that fostered general education. Barrow (1976) provided a common sense based philosophy for liberal education. I.K. Davies (1976) produced a more highly technological treatment of objectives.

A sample of papers presented at a 1976 curriculum theory conference in Milwaukee provided an array of views on curriculum theory that demonstrated purpose, perceptiveness, and disagreement in curriculum theory (Molnar and Zahorik, 1977). In 1978, Brent provided a text called Philosophical Foundations for the Curriculum; in it he illustrated at least two points. The first was the growing importance perceived for philosophical analysis as a basis for curriculum, and second, the concomitant notion that it was one of several bases necessary for curriculum inquiry. In the same year Michael Schiro provided a well-organized treatment of curriculum relative to four ideological bases: scholar academic, social efficiency, child study, and social reconstructionist. His analysis provides the curriculum student or scholar with a good deal of conceptual background for evaluating both the rationale and implications of each.

The notion was clear that defensible conceptions of curriculum needed to grow from a complex context. That it could not derive from philosophical or theoretical discourse alone became blatantly clear as educators tried, often in vain, to align curriculum with conditions of students

262

en masse. It could not be done without a broader base of knowledge derived from several disciplines and from practical settings. To this end three categories of literature emerged that: (1) discussed curriculum implications of the changing and pluralistic culture; (2) continued the trend of foundational studies in education by embracing curricular dimensions of them; and (3) exposed and analyzed influences of political and ideological factors on curriculum thought and practice.

Books that responded to cultural changes by providing their implications for curriculum include the following: Browne and Ambrosetti (1970 and 1972) on popular culture; Dunfee (1970) on ethnic groups and their values; the Schools Council for Curriculum and Examinations (1971) on early school leavers; Purpel and Belanger (1972) on the cultural revolution and its values; Wootton and Reynolds (1972, 1974, 1977) on a variety of social trends; Ford (1973) on Black history and culture; Ahlum and Fralley (1974) on the feminist movement and its values; Way (1974) on Spanish-speaking students; Newman (1975) on citizen action; Barnes (1976) on the impact of communications; Newton (1976) on Black history and culture; Langenbach and Neskora (1977) on day care situations; Lesser (1977) on television; Robinson and Wilson (1977) on extending economic ideas in the curriculum; The Carnegie Foundation (1978) and Levine (1978), both on increased concern for college curriculum; Hefley (1978) on textbook controversies emphasizing legal perspectives; Jelinek (1978) on curricular responses to several critical social realities; Becker (1979) on curriculum in a global age; Jelinek (1979) on curriculum amid fluctuating educational values and an emerging category of books on curriculum for special education that illustrates the evolving character of that field of education, e.g., Sniff (1973), Fredericks (1978), Wechman (1979), and Rumanoff (1979).

Becker (1979) illustrates the growing importance attributed to international cooperation. This orientation toward increased emphasis on pluralism took form in curriculum literature through the rare appearance of studies that compared curricula from different countries, or proposals for curricula that provided increased international understanding. Miel and Berman (1970) exemplify the latter, while the former was attempted by Beauchamp and Beauchamp (1972) and by Taylor and Johnson (1974). Additional reports on and proposals about curricula in other nations were provided by the following: Achtenhagen and Meyer (1970), Janzen (1970), UNESCO (1971), Hawes (1972), Seminar in Southeast Asia (1972), Holmes and Ryba (1973), Netherlands (1973), Center for Educational Research and Innovation (1975), Kallos (1975), UNESCO (1975), Posner and de Keijzer (1976), UNESCO (1976), Curriculum Development Center for Malaysia (1978), and Musgrave (1979). Among these, Kallos should be noted for his argument that America is too unaware of research and theory in both highly and less developed cultures. Max van Manen[10] should also be noted here for his attempt to convey work associated with the Utrecht School in the Netherlands to American scholars.

It is interesting to note that, perhaps due to increased communication technology, the Seventies was the first decade in which curriculum books were co-edited by American and British educators, and that a sizeable number of books appeared that included chapters or articles written by authors from different countries. Furthermore, most of these writings were by British, American, Australian, and Canadian authors. As for other countries, the works of Dahllof, Kallos, and Lundgren from Sweden were also visible in the curriculum literature of America. Representation here by curricularists from other countries was indeed lacking. Funds for translating prominent works not written in English provided one major obstacle, but the tendency toward scholarly isolation is hardly

defensible. It should be noted that throughout
the history of curriculum literature, aside from
a scattering of representation from the British
Isles, sparse reference was given to curricularists from other nations in American curriculum
literature. References to such monumental
educational scholars as Herbart, Froebel, Pestalozzi, and Montessori were prevalent as expected, but references to non-English contemporaries
other than Piaget were, overall, strikingly
absent. By comparison with previous decades,
the appearance of a few English translations
of non-English curriculum authors may constitute a positive step for the Seventies, albeit
a small one.

In addition to literature that sprung from
changing and pluralistic culture through treatments of current issues and international perspectives, a second kind of text provided a broadly based context for curriculum study from the
foundations of education. Usually, <u>foundations
of education</u> referred to an introduction to
knowledge derived from such areas as sociology,
anthropology, history, philosophy, and/or psychology that served as a basis for the study of
education. Curriculum books, particularly those
of the synoptic variety, usually contained sections
with brief versions of such background. A rather
elaborate example of educational foundations for
curriculum development and thought was presented
in the first parts of Smith, Stanley, and Shores
(1950 and 1957). Most texts treated the topic
more briefly. In the Seventies, entire books came
to be published that explored foundational assumptions of curriculum issues. Examples of such
books include: Short (1970), Olson (1971), Whitfield (1971), Zais (1976), Brent (1978), and
Schiro (1978). Though often criticized as
ahistorical by its own members, curriculum writers
of the Seventies[11] did begin to seriously look at
their own past. This was well exemplified by the
History of Education Society's (1971) review of
changes in curriculum, Elson's (1972) study of

textbooks, the ASCD Yearbook at the bicentennial which was edited by O.L. Davis (1976), and Rudolph's history of undergraduate college curriculum (1978). It was also exemplified by the founding of the Society for the Study of Curriculum History under the direction of Laural Tanner[12] in 1977.

A third way that curriculum writers responded to cultural change provided a perspective that was quite new in curriculum literature. This orientation was concerned with political and ideological forces that shaped both schooling, curriculum studies, and curriculum implementation. Some of the authors in this group held that action and decision of educators was determined by factors such as social class, socioeconomic levels, and values implicit in ideological contexts in which schools are embedded. Furthermore, they argued that curriculum could not be planned through purely rational activity, that political factors were ever dominant, and that such documents as the "Tyler rationale" were indeed too rational.

Criticism emerging from such standpoints as these can be found in the work of the following authors: Freire (1970) on power granted to the role of teacher; Young (1971) on the impact of dominant social class ideologies; ASCD (1971) on the influence of bureaucracy and freedom on schooling, with special note given to Kliebard's piece on curriculum theory; Gracey (1972) on a study of bureaucratic influences on elementary curriculum; Seaman, Esland, and Gosin (1972) on relationships between ideology and innovation; Lawton (1973) on interactivity among educational theory, social change, and curriculum planning; Musgrave (1973) on relations among change, knowledge, and curriculum; the 1974 ASCD Yearbook on projections about education in an open society; Bowers (1974) on existential problems of freedom and literacy in relation to curriculum, teaching, and social policy; Speiker (1974) on

266

determining reliability of practical community
involvement in curriculum planning; Taylor, et al.
(1974) on an analysis of purposes, power, and
constraint in curriculum planning; Kallos (1975)
on comparisons of curriculum research orientations
of Americans and Europeans; Lawton (1975) on
influences of class and culture on curriculum,
contending that such influences are minimal;
Cremin (1976) on the need to perceive and deal
with an interaction of the many educative forces
that actually and potentially guide the public;
Pring (1976) on relationships between schooling
and knowledge; Reynolds and Skilbeck (1976) on
cultural impact on curriculum and classroom life;
Taylor and Tye (1975) on social determinants of
school and curriculum; Comer (1977) on several
interdependent forces that influence curriculum;
Eggleston (1977) on sociological perspectives
of curriculum issues; Claydon, Knight, and Rado
(1978) on the implications of pluralistic culture
and society on curriculum; Nelson (1978) on legal
influences upon and ramifications of curriculum;
Bremer (1979) on curriculum as an outgrowth of
community; Apple (1979) on the relationship
between school knowledge and ideology; and
Schaffarzick and Sykes (1979) on value conflicts
and curriculum.

The majority of books that treated ideological and sociological interpretations of
curriculum emphasized large scale influences
that socio-economic class has on schooling,
curriculum, the kind of knowledge distributed,
and the way it is received. Other noted scholars,
e.g., Decker Walker, Herbert Kliebard, Michael
Kirst, William Pinar, Barry Franklin, Steven
Selden, and William Doll have pointed to the
importance of political factors in curriculum
research, decision, and implementation.

Despite the philosophic debates (the arguments
about the proper kind of research methodologies,
the role of ideology in dictating kinds of knowledge distributed by schools, and the political

267

forces in curricular decision-making), as laudable as all of these concerns were, school administrators and teachers were paid to do their jobs now. Although they likely knew well that their decision and action were clouded by political and other influences, students arrived daily, and activities needed to be provided for them. These teachers and administrators needed help, yet they had little time to receive it. Therefore, as in prior decades, curriculum scholars produced books for practitioners on curriculum administration, leadership, supervision, and teaching. They tended to be how-to books about curriculum design, implementation, and materials. Publishers added to this style of literature by providing reappearances of "time honored" texts in second, third, and even more editions, i.e., texts that demand by scholars and practitioners alike recalled.

Such books tended, like the synoptic texts of previous decades, to oversimplify complex matters. Yet, some deemed oversimplification to be more productive than no information at all. It was unlikely that most practitioners would be in positions to be provided with complex and lengthy arguments. The fleeting now was to be attended. Thus, it was the prime goal of many authors to influence those who directly affect children and youth in schools. If they hadn't the time to be thoroughly saturated, it was assumed that brief introductions should lead them to the richness of curriculum considerations. This must have been the line of thought of many who valiantly strove to aid schools through literature directed to practice. Books of this type appeared on several topics.

Attempts to generate administrative and supervisory influence through the formal organization of schools brought such curriculum books on administration, leadership, and supervision as: Lewis and Miel (1972), Olson and Richardson (1972), Conner and Ellena (1973), Ellena (1973), Greene (1973), Stradley (1973), Worner (1973), Kopp and Zufelt (1974), Tankard (1974), Newfield (1975), Staples, et al. (1975), Speiker (1976), Van Geel (1976), Gran (1977), Rubin (1977b), Rubin (1977c), and Speiker (1977).

Books on curriculum design provided another attempt by scholars to influence practice. They provided means for course developers to systematically consider necessary elements and relationships for building curricula. As can be detected readily, the levels of rigor and practicality are considerably varied among these sources: Burns and Brooks (1970), Kemp (1971), Merritt and Harris (1972), Michaelis, Grossman, and Scott (1975), Davies (1976), Gow (1976), McNeil (1976), Sockett (1976), Gower and Scott (1977), Hannah and Michaelis (1977), Johnson (1977), Posner and Rudnitsky (1978). The latter was offered, stemming from a conceptual orientation similar to Johnson (1977), for teachers who wished to carefully design courses. It was analytic and precise, and it acknowledged the importance of teachers in the curriculum development process.

Other authors also regarded teachers as central to curriculum making and implementation as evidenced by the following books: Beechhold (1971), Burdin and McAulay (1971), Christine and Christine (1971), Gracey (1972), Merritt and Harris (1972), Nicholls and Nicholls (1972), Hughes (1973), Blazier (1974), Murphy (1974), Hendricks and Fadiman (1975), Frymier (1977), Marbach (1977), Joyce (1978), Nicholls and Nicholls (1978), and Postman (1979). Postman's Teaching as a Conserving Activity is a partial sequel to his popular Teaching as a Subversive Activity (with C. Weingartner, Delacorte Press, 1969). Both provided educators with philosophy and practical ideas to create curricula that liberate students from the tyranny of the present.

It seems strange, insofar as school books and other teaching materials have been the

269

prime guidepost of much teaching, that curriculum literature would not contain many elaborate treatments and reviews of much materials. Books on this topic are indeed scarce; some did appear in the Seventies: Seferian and Cole (1970), Elson (1972), Zenger and Zenger (1973), Farguhar (1974), Tyler, Klein, et al. (1976), and Hefley (1978). Those who are interested in this topic are advised to consult evaluation studies by EPIE which involve the careful review of materials and their implementation. Curriculum Review is a Chicago based journal that serves educational practitioners and decision-makers by providing assessments of textbooks and other curriculum materials for use in schools.

In addition to the plethora of new books that focused on change, still others were revised and/or re-published in the Seventies, hailing that many readers saw in them a high degree of perennial value. Prominent among them were: Ragan and Shepherd (1971 and 1977), Miel (1972), Trump and Miller (1972), Doll (1974 and 1978), Anderson and Macdonald, on the works of Virgil Herrick (1975), Beauchamp (1975), Foshay, reprints of his more influential articles (1975), Mager (1975), King and Brownell (1976), Shuster and Ploghoft (1977). It should also be noted that such publishers as the Arno Press, the Greenwood Press, AMS, and others produced a large number of reprints of educational classics that are difficult to obtain in the original. Reprints of such authors as Dewey, Rugg, Kilpatrick, Hopkins, Counts, Bobbitt, Charters, and others should be of considerable interest to curriculum scholars of today. Many of the books that have recent reprints are noted parenthetically in the bibliographical sections of this book.

As can be detected early from the foregoing, the Seventies, like the Sixties, brought a landslide of curriculum books. The increased modeling of educational scholarship after that in the social and natural sciences brought with it an

270

equation of publication, status, and worthiness in the research community. Hence, the upsurge of new journals, the expansion of old ones, and the pressure to contribute to them were massive indeed. This communication barrage was accompanied by the emergence of computerized clearing houses, e.g., ERIC, in which can be found papers presented at conferences, various other manuscripts and research reports.

The breadth of curriculum information was too great for any one curriculum scholar to fathom. Thus, as was done in the Sixties but with even greater fervor, curriculum scholars of the Seventies took it upon themselves to search out part of the literature, select some of the best writings, and compile books of readings.

A significant variation on the collections of readings emerged in the Seventies. Some books of readings were designed to provide contrast and commentary. Contrast was provided by careful categorization of the articles selected, often to represent major lines of curriculum thought and/or activity (e.g., Eisner and Vallance, 1974). Commentary by the editor(s) frequently clarified similarities and differences among selected authors and sharpened problematic areas that needed further study. Further, both the new and traditional collections of readings helped to shape the major concerns of the field by their topical organization. For example, Bellack and Kliebard (1977) organized selections in four major groupings: (1) perspectives on how curriculum problems should be studied, (2) relationships between knowledge and curriculum, (3) perspectives on curriculum evaluation, and (4) relationships between change and curriculum.

Other fine collections of curriculum articles include: Hass, et al. (1970), Martin (1970), Eisner (1971), Hillson and Hyman (1971), Hooper (1971), Leeper (1971), Levit (1971),

271

McClure (1971), Parlardy (1971), Van Til (1971), Alexander (1972), Heidenreich (1972), DeCarlo and Madon (1973), Edward (1974), Hass, et al. (1974), Van Til (1974), Curriculum Design and Development Course Team (1975 and 1975), Taylor and Tye (1975), Petty (1976), Rubin (1977a, 1977b, and 1977c), Willis (1978), Taylor and Reid (1979), and Schffarzick and Sykes (1979).

While some of these readings provided an overview as a main objective, some focused on particular areas such as elementary education, secondary education, criticism of curriculum, evaluation, and the problem of knowledge; nevertheless, each provided numerous perspectives within a domain identified. Further, it should be noted that while all of the above were collections, several contain a large proportion of articles that appear for the first time, e.g., Willis (1978), Rubin (1977a,b,c), and McClure (1971).

Finally, several books went beyond the presentation of selected articles to a considerable extent. By virtue of carving new territory in conceptions of evaluation, Willis (1978) did this. In an attempt to identify five conflicting conceptions of curriculum development, Eisner and Vallance (1974) went beyond usual collections. They identified curriculum as: (1) the development of cognitive processes, (2) technology, (3) consumatory experience, (4) a springboard to social reconstruction, and (5) academic rationalism. Orlosky and Smith (1978) coupled elaborate excerpts from influential curriculum writings with a considerable amount of commentary that tied related writings together and provided interpretation, criticism, and analysis at the same time.

It is interesting to note that Orlosky and Smith (1978) identified five general topics of concern that were not wholly dissimilar from

272

those of Bellack and Kliebard (1977), noted earlier. These included: (1) an overview of curriculum study, (2) styles of curriculum theory, (3) operational concepts and principles, (4) curriculum change, and (5) evaluation. Under the topic of curriculum theory styles, they presented four: humanistic, disciplinary, technological, and futuristic. The latter are similar to categories advanced by Eisner and Vallance. The point here is that dissimilarity does not reign omnipotent in curriculum categorization schemes.

Perhaps the most ambitious efforts to catalog, interpret, and criticize major curriculum ideas, proposals, and practices are two sets of books produced in Britain. The first was developed in conjunction with the Open University. Published first by the Open University Press and later made available in America by Harper and Row, the initial version consisted of nine books containing seventeen units on curriculum context, design, and development. Both British and American scholars are broadly represented. Excerpts are provided along with substantial interpretation and criticism. The Open University Press also published a set of units in 1976; these are listed together under the authorship of that press in a large citation in the bibliographical section of this chapter.

The other elaborate set of curriculum perspectives is provided in a five volume set under the general editorship of David Jenkins. It was published in 1976 by Open Books with an overall title of Curriculum Studies. The five books are: Curriculum: An Introduction by Jenkins and Shipman, Designing the Curriculum by Sockett, Changing the Curriculum by MacDonald and Walker, Curriculum Evaluation by Hamilton, Knowledge and Schooling by Pring, and Culture and the Classroom by Reynolds and Skilbeck. Each book is quite thorough in introducing salient contributions for topics addressed.

Each book is concise and well-referenced. Together they form a commendable introduction to curriculum thought through the mid-Seventies.

In addition to collections and sets of curriculum books, one can become acquainted with curriculum literature by surveying bibliographies in major books, especially those of the synoptic variety. Two books appeared in the Seventies that directly treat bibliographical material: Tyler's (1970) annotated guide to selected literature,and Brickman's (1974 and 1976) bibliographical essays on curriculum and instruction. For more brief overviews of recent curriculum writing,the reader might turn to the American Educational Research Association "State of the Art" addresses by John McNeil and William Pinar[13], Decker Walker's review of curriculum writing in the Review of Research in Education,[14] and Philip Jackson's 1979 overview and critique of recent curriculum research and theory.[15]

Contributions to the Seventies were monumental in quantity; at the same time new quality was witnessed in the curriculum literature. If escalation and variety of contributions are indicators, it would seem that the label of moribund, placed on the field at the onset of the Seventies, has been somewhat overcome.

It is patent that a field's worth cannot be judged by quantity of production alone. We need to seriously reflect on many questions. The defensibility of such reflection is greatly increased if it is rooted in knowledge of former endeavors--scholarly and practical. How do the contextual events and prevailing values of a time period shape the growth of curriculum thought and literature? What is the quality and worth of the accumulated curriculum literature? What aspects of it fit together in meaningful ways? What aspects are independently worthwhile? Does curriculum scholarship offer something of direct

274

benefit to schooling or other educational enter-
prises? To what extent does the literature
contain ideas, proposals, and a record of practices that are inert and should be discarded?
Does it contain ideas, proposals, practices, and
imaginative projections that can clarify and
direct intelligent and effective curriculum activity in the future? Does it educate? As Dewey
described education,[16] does it give meaning to
experience and help to direct the courses of
subsequent experiences in curriculum inquiry and
action?

Speculations on questions of this kind are
presented in the Conclusion. Moreover, they are
questions for all who would embark on next stages
of the journey portrayed in the foregoing chapters, i.e., the ongoing curriculum of curriculum
inquiry.

Notes

[1]Theobald, Robert. *An Alternative Future for
America's Third Century*. Chicago: The Swallow
Press, 1976.

[2]This question was used to focus much of the
discussion on a NOVA television special entitled
The Final Frontier. A transcript is available
from NOVA, Box 1000, Cathedral Station, Boston,
MA, 02118 ($2.00).

[3]Silberman's book is included in the bibliography. Others among this popular protest
literature were not explicitly curriculum writings, but had important relevance to curriculum
matters. Examples include: Dennison, G. *The
Lives of Children*. New York: Random House, 1969;
Holt, J. *How Children Fail*. New York: Delta,
1964; Kohl, H. *36 Children*. New York: Signet,
1968; Kozol, J. *Death at an Early Age*. Boston:
Houghton Mifflin, 1967.

[4]See for example: Tyack, D.B. The One Best
System: A History of American Education. Cam-
bridge: Harvard University Press, 1974; and
Butts, R.F. Public Education in the United
States: From Revolution to Reform. New York:
Holt, Rinehart and Winston, 1978.

[5]Examples include: Bowles, S. and Gintis, M.
Schooling in Capitalist America. New York:
Basic Books, 1975; Greer, C. The Great School
Legend. New York: Basic Books, 1972; Karier,
C.J., Violas, P., and Spring, J. Roots of
Crisis. Chicago: Rand McNally, 1973; Katz, M.
Class, Bureaucracy, and Schools. New York:
Praeger, 1971; Sharp, R. and Green, A. Education
and Social Control. London: Routledge and Kegan
Paul, 1975; Spring, J. Education and the Rise of
the Corporate State. Boston: Beacon, 1972.
For a bit of counterpoint readers should see:
Burnett, J.R. John Dewey and the Ploys of
Revisionism. Educational Considerations. Winter
1980, 7(2), 2-8.

[6]Kuhn, T.S. The Structure of Scientific
Revolutions. Chicago: University of Chicago
Press, 1970.

[7]The practical: A Language for Curriculum.
School Review. November, 1969, 78, 1-23.

[8]See: The practical: Arts of Eclectic.
School Review. August, 1971, 79(4), 493-542;
and The Practical 3: Translation into Curriculum. School Review, August, 1973, 81(4),
501-22, both by Schwab. These and other essays
by Schwab are presented by Westbury and Wilkof
(1978) with an excellent introduction to Schwab's
work. Schwab's perspective on research is related to similar orientations in: Schubert, W.H.
Recalibrating Educational Research Toward a Focus
on Practice. Educational Researcher. January
1980, 9(1), 17-24 and 31.

[9]See: Pinar, W.F. Notes on the Curriculum Field 1978. Educational Researcher. September, 1978, 7(8), 5-12. For a critical review of reconceptualist literature see: van Manen, M. Reconceptualization in Curriculum Inquiry. Curriculum Inquiry. Winter 1978, 8(4), 365-375.

[10]Van Manen, M. A Phenomenological Experiment in Educational Theory: The Utrecht School. Paper presented to the Annual Meeting of the American Educational Research Association, Toronto, March 1978. Also note the many Dutch and German sources mentioned in the bibliography of his paper. Subsequently revised and published as: An Experiment in Educational Theorizing; The Utrecht School. Interchange, 1978-79, 10(1), 48-66.

[11]See discussions in the Preface and Introduction to this book, and note "5" in the Introduction.

[12]The Society for the Study of Curriculum History was founded in New York in 1977. Its first three annual meetings were held in Toronto in 1978, San Francisco in 1979, and Boston in 1980. Proceedings of these meetings have been discussed for publication.

[13]Both were published in Educational Researcher, September 1978, 7(8): Notes on the Curriculum Field, 1978, by William F. Pinar, and Curriculum--A Field Shaped by Different Faces, by J.D. McNeil.

[14]See: Decker Walker's Toward Comprehension of Curricular Realities, a chapter in Review of Research in Education. (Edited by Lee Shulman) Itasca, Illinois: F.E. Peacock, 1976, v. IV, pp. 268-308.

[15]Jackson, P. The Curriculum and Its Discontents. Invited address for Division B (Curriculum and Objectives) of the American Educational Research Association, San Francisco, April 10, 1979.

16
In <u>Democracy and Education</u>, Dewey described education as follows: "We thus reach a technical definition of educaton: It is that reconstruction of reorganization of experience which adds to the meaning of experience, and which increases ability to direct the course of subsequent experience." Dewey, John. <u>Democracy and Education</u>. New York: Macmillan, 1916 and 1944, p. 76 of the 1966 Free Press paperbound edition.

Bibliography of Curriculum Books,
1970-1979

1970

Achtenhagen, F. and Meyer, H. Curriculum
revision. Muchen: Kosel, 1970.

Ammerman, H.L. Systematic approaches for
identifying and organizing content for
training programs. Alexandria, Virginia: Human Resources Research Organization, 1970.

Association for Supervision and Curriculum
Development (M.M. Scobey and G. Graham,
Editors). To nurture humaneness: Com-
mitment for the '70's: Yearbook.
Washington, D.C.: The Association,
1970.

Bernabei, R. and Leles, S. Behavioral objectives in curriculum and evaluation.
Dubuque: Kendall/Hunt, 1970.

Billett, R.O. Improving the secondary-school
curriculum: A guide to effective curriculum planning. New York: Atherton
Press, 1970.

Braun, S.J., et al. Curriculum is what hap-
pens; planning is the key. Washington:
National Association for the Education
of Young Children, 1970.

Browne, R.B. and Ambrosetti, R.J. Popular
culture and curricula. Bowling Green,
Ohio: Bowling Green University Popular
Press, 1970.

Burns, R.W. and Brooks, G.D. (Editors).
Curriculum design in a changing society.
Englewood Cliffs, New Jersey: Educa-
tional Technology Publishers, 1970.

Carr, W.G. (Secretary General). Values and the curriculum. A report of the Fourth International Curriculum Conference. Washington: National Education Association, 1970.

Dillon, E.J., Heath, E.J., and Biggs, C.W. Comprehensive programming for the success of learning. Columbus, Ohio: C.E. Merrill, 1970.

Doll, R.C. Curriculum improvement: Decision-making and process (Second Edition). Boston: Allyn and Bacon, 1970.

Dunfee, M. Ethnic modifications of the curriculum. Washington: National Education Association, 1970.

Exeter Curriculum Conference Report. Curriculum development. England: University of Exeter, 1970.

Feyereisen, K., Fiorino, A.J., and Nowak, A.T. Supervision and curriculum renewal: A systems approach. New York: Appleton-Century-Crofts, 1970.

Foshay, A.W. Curriculum for the seventies: An agenda for invention. Washington: National Education Association (CSI), 1970.

Freire, P. Pedagogy of the oppressed. New York: Herder and Herder, 1970.

Frymier, J.R. and Hawn, H.C. Curriculum improvement for better schools. Worthington, Ohio: Charles A. Jones, 1970.

Gattegno, C. What we owe children: The subordination of teaching to learning. New York: Outerbridge and Dienstfrey, 1970.

Grobman, H.G. Developmental curriculum projects: Decision points and processes. Itasca, Illinois: F.E. Peacock, 1970.

Harnack, R.S. Evaluation of an innovation-- Computer based curriculum planning. Buffalo: SUNY at Buffalo, 1970.

Hass, G., Wiles, K., and Bondi, J. (Editors). Readings in curriculum. Boston: Allyn and Bacon, 1970.

Hicks, W.V., Houston, W.R., Cheney, B.D., and Marquard, R.L. The new elementary school curriculum. New York: Van Nostrand Reinhold Company, 1970.

Howson, G. (Editor). Developing a new curriculum. London: Heineman, 1970.

Janzen, H. Curriculum change in a Canadian context. Toronto: Cage Educational Publications, 1970.

Johnston, A.M. and Burns, P.C. Research in elementary school curriculum. Boston: Allyn and Bacon, 1970.

Lavatelli, C.S. Piaget's theory applied to an early childhood curriculum. Boston: American Science and Engineering, Incorporated, 1970.

Lawler, M.R. (Editor). Strategies for planned curricular innovation. New York: Teachers College Press, Columbia University, 1970.

Lindvall, C.M. and Cox, R.C. Evaluation as a tool in curriculum development. Chicago: Rand McNally, 1970.

Martin, J.R. (Editor). Readings in the philosophy of education: A study of the

curriculum. Boston: Allyn and Bacon,
1970.

Miel, A. and Berman, L. Educating the young
people of the world. Washington:
Association of Supervision and Curriculum Development, National Education
Association, 1970.

Myers, D.A. Decision making in curriculum
and instruction. Dayton, Ohio: Institute for Development of Educational
Activities, 1970.

Nerbovig, M. Unit planning: A model for
curriculum development. Worthington,
Ohio: A. Jones Publishing, 1970.

Neufeld, K.A. (Editor). Invitational Conference on Elementary Education, Third,
Banff, Alberta, 1969. Individualized
curriculum and instruction; proceedings.
Edmonton: The University of Alberta,
Department of Elementary Education,
1970.

Overly, N.V. (Editor). The unstudied curriculum: Its impact on children.
Washington: Association for Supervision
and Curriculum Development, 1970.

Pharis, W.L., Robison, L.E., and Walden,
J.C. Decision making and schools for
the seventies. Washington: National
Education Association, 1970.

Pritzkau, P.T. On education for the authen-
tic. Scranton, Pennsylvania: International Textbook Company, 1970.

Schwab, J.J. The practical: A language for
curriculum. Washington: National
Education Association, 1970.

Seferian, A. and Cole, H.P. Encounters in
thinking: A compendium of curricula
for process education. Buffalo: Creative Education Foundation, 1970.

Short, E.C. (Editor). A search for valid
content for curriculum courses. Toledo,
Ohio: College of Education, University of Toledo, 1970.

Shuster, A.H. and Ploghoft, M.E. The emerging elementary curriculum (Second Edition). Columbus, Ohio: Charles E.
Merrill, 1970.

Silberman, C.E. Crisis in the classroom: The
remaking of American education. New
York: Random House, 1970.

Snyder, B.R. The hidden curriculum. New
York: Knopf, 1970.

Taylor, P.H. How teachers plan their courses.
London: The National Foundation for
Educational Research in England and Wales,
1970.

Tyler, L. A selected guide to curriculum
literature: An annotated bibliography.
Washington: National Education Association, 1970.

Weinstein, G. and Fantini, M. Toward a humanistic education: A curriculum of
affect. New York: Praeger, 1970.

Wiseman, S. and Pidgeon, D. Curriculum evaluation. England: Slough National Foundation for Educational Research in England
and Wales, 1970.

283

1971

Alexander, W.M. and Saylor, J.G. The high
school today and tomorrow. New York:
Holt, Rinehart, and Winston, 1971.

Armentrout, W.W. (Editor). What should the
purposes of American education be?
Dubuque, Iowa: Kendall/Hunt, 1971.

Association for Supervision and Curriculum
Development. Freedom, bureaucracy and
schooling (V.F. Haubrich, Editor). 1971
Yearbook. Washington: The Association,
1971.

Beechhold, H.F. The creative classroom.
New York: Charles Scribner's Sons,
1971.

Bell, R. (Editor). Thinking about the curriculum. Bletchley, Bucks, England:
The Open University Press, 1971.

Bishop, L.K. and Hartley, H.J. (Editors).
Individualizing educational systems, the
elementary and secondary school: Implications for curriculum, professional
staff, and students. New York: Harper
and Row, 1971.

Bremer, J. and Van Moschzisher, M. The school
without walls. New York: Holt, Rinehart,
and Winston, 1971.

Buffie, E.G. and Jenkins, J.M. (Editors).
Curriculum development in non-graded
schools: Bold new venture. Bloomington: Indiana University Press, 1971.

Burdin, J.L. and McAulay, J.D. Elementary
school curriculum and instruction:
The teacher's role. New York: Wiley,
1971.

Cave, R.G. An introduction to curriculum
development. London: Ward Lock Educational, 1971.

Chai, Hon-Chan. Planning education for a
plural society. UNESCO Unipub, 1971.

Charters, W.W. Curriculum construction
(Reprint). New York: Arno Press,
1971.

Christine, C.T. and Christine, D.W. Practical guide to curriculum and instruction. West Nyack, New York: Parker
Publishing Company, 1971.

Connelly, F.M., et al. (Editors). Elements
of curriculum development. Toronto:
Ontario Institute for Studies in Education, 1971.

Dahllof, U.S. Ability grouping, content
validity and curriculum process analysis. New York: Teachers College,
Columbia University, 1971.

Drumheller, S.J. Handbook of curriculum
design for individualized instruction:
A systems approach. Englewood Cliffs,
New Jersey: Educational Technology
Publishers, 1971.

Eisele, J.E., Bianchi, G.B., et al. Computer
assisted planning of curriculum and
instruction. Englewood Cliffs, New
Jersey: Educational Technology Publishers, 1971.

Eisner, E.W. (Editor). Confronting curriculum reform. Boston: Brown and Company, 1971.

Featherstone, J. Schools where children
learn. New York: Liveright Publishing Company, 1971.

Hathaway, W.E. A network-based approach to curriculum development. Edmonton, New Brunswick: The Author, 1971.

Hillson, M. and Hyman, R.T. (Editors). Changes and innovation in elementary and secondary organization: Selected readings. New York: Holt-Rinehart-Winston, 1971.

History of Education Society. The changing curriculum. London: Methuen Company, 1971.

Hooper, R. (Editor). The curriculum: Context, design and development. Edinburgh: Oliver and Boyd, 1971.

Hunt, F.J., et al. Social science and the school curriculum. Sydney: Angus and Robertson, 1971.

Kapfer, M.B. Behavioral objectives in curriculum development. Englewood Cliffs, New Jersey: Educational Technology Publications, 1971.

Kemp, J.E. Instructional design: A plan for unit and course development. Belmont, California: Fearon, 1971.

Kopp, O.W. and Zufelt, D.L. Personalized curriculum: Method and design. Columbus, Ohio: Merrill, 1971.

Leeper, R.R. (Editor). Curricular concerns in a revolutionary era. Washington: Association for Supervision and Curriculum Development, 1971.

Levit, M. (Editor). Curriculum: Readings in the philosophy of education. Urbana, Illinois: University of Illinois Press, 1971.

McClure, R.M. Field studies in curriculum development. Washington: National Education Association, 1971a.

McClure, R.M. (Editor). The curriculum: Retrospect and prospect. The Seventieth Yearbook of the National Society for the Study of Education: Part I. Chicago: The University of Chicago Press, 1971b.

Manning, D. A humanistic curriculum. New York: Harper and Row, 1971.

National Education Association Staff Report. Schools for the Seventies and beyond: A call to action. Washington, D.C.: National Education Association, 1971.

Oliver, A. Curriculum improvement. New York: Dodd, Mead and Company, 1971.

Olson, W.C. Psychological foundations of the curriculum. Nendeln, Liechtenstein, 1971.

Parlardy, J.M. (Editor). Elementary school curriculum--An anthology of trends and challenges. New York: Macmillan, 1971.

Ragan, W.B. and Shepherd, G.D. Modern elementary curriculum (Fourth Edition). New York: Holt, Rinehart and Winston, 1971.

Richmond, K.W. The school curriculum. London: Methuen and Company, 1971.

Schools Council for Curriculum and Examinations (Editors). Choosing a curriculum for the young school leaver. Englewood Cliffs, New Jersey: Scholastic Book Services, 1971.

Skeel, D.J. and Hagen, O.A. The process of curriculum change. Pacific Palisades, California: Goodyear Publishing Company, 1971.

Smith, L.M. and Keith, P.M. Anatomy of educational innovation: An organizational analysis of an elementary school. New York: Wiley, 1971.

Tanner, D. Secondary curriculum: Theory and development. New York: Macmillan, 1971.

Turner, J. Making new schools: The liberation of learning. New York: David McKay Company, 1971.

UNESCO. Curriculum revision. Nendeln, Liechenstein: Kraus Reprint, 1971.

Utz, R.T. and Leonard, L.D. A competency based curriculum. Dubuque, Iowa: Kendall/Hunt Publishing Company, 1971.

Van Til, W. (Editor). Curriculum: Quest for relevance. Boston: Houghton Mifflin, 1971.

Walton, J. The integrated day in theory and practice. London: Ward Lock Educational, 1971.

Whitfield, R. (Editor). Disciplines of the curriculum. London: McGraw-Hill, 1971.

Wilson, L.C. The open access curriculum. New York: Allyn and Bacon, 1971.

Wright, B.A, Camp, L.T., Stosberg, W.K., Fleming, B.L. The elementary school curriculum--Better teaching now. New York: Macmillan, 1971.

Young, M.F.D. (Editor). Knowledge and control: New directions for the sociology of education. London: Collier-Macmillan, 1971.

1972

Alexander, W.M. (Editor). Changing secondary school curriculum: Readings (Second Edition). New York: Holt, Rinehart and Winston, 1972.

Beauchamp, G.A. and Beauchamp, K.E. Comparative analysis of curriculum systems (Second Edition). Wilmette, Illinois: The Kagg Press, 1972.

Beckner, W. and Cornett, J.D. The secondary school curriculum, content and structure. Scranton, Pennsylvania: Intext Educational Publishers, 1972.

Browne, R.B. and Ambrosetti, R.J. (Editors). Popular culture and curricula. Bowling Green, Ohio: Bowling Green University Press, 1972.

Clark, L.H., Klein, R.L. and Burks, J.B. The American secondary school curriculum (Second Edition). New York: Macmillan, 1972.

Dale, E. Building a learning environment. Bloomington, Indiana: Phi Delta Kappa, 1972.

Dixon, K. (Editor). Philosophy of education and the curriculum. Oxford, New York: Pergamon Press, 1972.

Drumheller, S.J. Teacher's handbook for a functional behavior-based curriculum. Englewood Cliffs, New Jersey: Educational Technology Publications, 1972.

289

Eastern Regional Institute for Education. How to get new programs into elementary schools. Englewood Cliffs, New Jersey: Educational Technology Publications, 1972.

Eisenberg, J.A. and MacQueen, G. Don't teach us that! Don Mills, Ontario: Paper Jacks, 1972.

Elson, R.M. Guardians of tradition. Lincoln: University of Nebraska Press, 1972 (A reprint of 1964 version).

Engle, S. and Longstreet, W.S. A design for social education in the open curriculum. New York: Harper and Row, 1972.

Gracey, H.L. Curriculum or craftsmanship: Elementary school teachers in a bureaucratic system. Chicago: University of Chicago Press, 1972.

Grobman, H. Developmental curriculum projects: Decision points and processes. Itasca, Illinois: F.E. Peacock, 1972.

Harrow, A.J. A taxonomy of the psychomotor domain; A guide for developing behavioral objectives. New York: David McKay, 1972.

Havenstein, A.D. Curriculum planning for behavioral development. Worthington, Ohio: Charles A. Jones, 1972.

Hawes, H.W. Planning the primary school curriculum in developing countries. Paris: UNESCO, 1972.

Heidenreich, R.R. (Editor). Current readings in improvements in curriculum. Arlington, Virginia: College Readings, 1972.

Hoyle, E. Problems of curriculum innovation II. Bletchley, Bucks, England: The Open University Press, 1972.

Hoyle, E. and Bell, R. Problems of curriculum innovation I. Bletchley, Bucks, England: The Open University Press, 1972.

Jenkins, D., et al. Curriculum philosophy and design. Bletchley, Bucks, England: The Open University Press, 1972.

Krug, M.M. (Editor). What will be taught: The next decade. Itasca, Illinois: F.E. Peacock, 1972.

Lavatelli, C.S., Kaltsounis, T., and Moore, W.J. Elementary school curriculum. New York: Holt, Rinehart and Winston, 1972.

Lee, J.M. and Lee, D.M. Elementary education: Today and tomorrow (Second Edition). Boston: Allyn and Bacon, 1972.

Leithwood, K.A. and Russell, H.H. Planned educational change; developing an operational model. Peterborough: Ontario Institute for Studies in Education, Trent Valley Centre, 1972.

Lewis, A.J. and Miel, A. Supervision for improved instruction: New challenges and new responses. Belmont, California: Wadsworth Publishing Company, 1972.

Lundgren, U.P. Frame factors and the teaching process: A contribution to curriculum theory and theory on teaching. Stockholm: Almqvist and Wiksell, 1972.

Maclure, S. Styles of curriculum development. Washington, D.C.: Organization for Economic Cooperation and Development, 1972.

Merritt, J. and Harris, A. Curriculum design and implementation. Bletchley, Bucks, England: The Open University Press, 1972.

Miel, A. and Associates. Cooperative procedures in learning. Westport, Connecticut: Greenwood, 1972 (Reprint of 1952 edition).

Miller, B. The humanities approach to the modern secondary school curriculum. New York: Center for Applied Research in Education, 1972.

Morris, B. Objectives and perspectives in education: Studies in educational theory (1955-1970). London: Routledge and Kegan Paul, 1972.

Nicholls, A. and Nicholls, S.H. Developing a curriculum: A practical guide. London: Allen and Unwin, 1972.

Olson, A.V. and Richardson, J. Accountability: Curricular applications. San Francisco, California: Intext Educational Publishers, 1972.

Ontario Association for Curriculum Development. Relevance in the curriculum. Twentyfirst Annual Conference (S. Dubois, Editor). Toronto: Ontario Association for Curriculum Development, 1972.

Organization of Economic Cooperation and Development, Center for Educational Research and Innovation. The nature of the curriculum for the Eighties and onwards. Paris: Organization of Economic Cooperation and Development, 1972.

Parker, R.K. (Editor). The preschool in action: Exploring early childhood programs. Boston: Allyn and Bacon, 1972.

292

Purpel, D. and Belanger, N. (Editors).
Curriculum and the cultural revolution.
Berkeley, California: McCutchan Pub-
lishing Company, 1972.

Raynor, J. and Grant, N. Patterns of curriculum. Bletchley, Bucks, England:
The Open University Press, 1972.

Razik, T.A. Systems approach to teacher
training and curriculum development:
The case of developing countries.
Paris: UNESCO, 1972.

Rubin, L.J. Curriculum and instruction study
guide. Fort Lauderdale, Florida: Nova
University Press, 1972.

Saylor, J.G. (Editor). The school of the
future, now. Washington: Association
for Supervision and Curriculum Development, 1972.

Seaman, P., Esland, G., and Gosin, B. Innovation and ideology. Bletchley, Bucks,
England: The Open University Press,
1972.

Segal, R. Got no time to fool around: A
motivation program for education.
Philadelphia: Westminster Press, 1972.

Seminar on strategies for curriculum development in Southeast Asia. Glugor, Penang,
Malaysia, 1972.

Shipman, M. and Raynor, J. Perspectives on
the curriculum. Bletchley, Bucks,
England: The Open University Press,
1972.

Taylor, P.A. and Cowley, D.M. (Editors).
Readings in curriculum evaluation.
Dubuque, Iowa: William C. Brown, 1972.

Thelen, H. Education and the human quest: Four designs for education. Chicago, Illinois: University of Chicago Press, 1972.

Trump, J.L. and Miller, D.F. Secondary school curriculum improvement (Second Edition). Boston: Allyn and Bacon, 1972.

Vance, B. Teaching the prekindergarten child: Instructional design and curriculum. Belmont, California: Brooke-Cole, 1972.

Vargas, J.S. Writing worthwhile behavioral objectives. Scranton, Pennsylvania: Harper and Row, 1972.

Weiss, J. Curriculum evaluation: Potentiality and reality. Toronto: Ontario Institute for Studies in Education, 1972.

Wilhelms, F. What should schools teach? Bloomington, Indiana: Phi Delta Kappa, 1972.

Wiseman, S. and Pidgeon, D. Curriculum evaluation. Briston, England: J.W. Arrowsmith, 1972.

Wootton, L.R. and Reynolds, J.C. (Editors). Trends influence curriculum. New York: MSS Information, 1972.

1973

Baker, E.L. and Popham, W.J. Expanding dimensions of instructional objectives. Englewood Cliffs, New Jersey: Prentice-Hall, 1973.

Beck, R.H., Cook, W.W., and Kearney, N.C.

Curriculum in the modern elementary
school. Englewood Cliffs, New Jersey:
Prentice-Hall, 1973.

Center for Educational Research and Innova-
tion. Styles of curriculum development.
Paris: Organization for Economic
Cooperation and Development, 1973.

Conner, F. and Ellena, W. Curriculum handbook for school administrators. Washington: American Association of School
Administrators (Second Edition), 1973.

Cook, R.C. and Doll, R.C. The elementary
school curriculum. Boston: Allyn and
Bacon, 1973.

DeCarlo, J.E. and Madon, C.A. (Editors).
Innovations in education for the Seven-
ties: Selected readings. New York:
Behavioral Publications, 1973.

Derr, R.L. A taxonomy of social purposes of
public schools. New York: David
McKay, 1973.

Educational Technology Reviews Series,
(Twelve Volumes) Various Titles Relating to Curriculum Development. Englewood Cliffs, New Jersey: Educational
Technology Publications, 1973.

Ellena, W.J. Curriculum handbook for school
executives. Arlington, Virginia: American Association of School Administrators,
1973.

Firth, G.R. and Kimpston, R.D. The curricular continuum in perspective. Itasca,
Illinois: F.E. Peacock, 1973.

Ford, N.A. Black studies: Threat or challenge. London: Kennikat Press, 1973.

Frymier, J.R. A school for tomorrow. Berkeley, California: McCutchan Publishing, 1973.

Garcia, D.S. Curriculum theory and application. Manilla: Alemar-Phoenix, 1973.

Goodlad, J.I. and Shane, H.G. (Editors). The elementary school in the U.S. Seventy-Second Yearbook of National Society for the Study of Education: Part II. Chicago: University of Chicago Press, 1973.

Great Britain Schools Council. Evaluation in curriculum development: Twelve case studies. London: Macmillan, 1973a.

Great Britain Schools Council. Pattern and variation in curriculum development projects. Houndmills, Busingstoke, Hampshire: Macmillan Education, Ltd., 1973b.

Greene, G.G. Accountability in the elementary school curriculum. Dubuque: Kendall/Hunt, 1973.

Harmin, H., Kirschenbaum, H., and Simon, S. Clarifying values through subject applications for the classroom. Minneapolis: Winston Press, 1973.

Hemphill, J.K. and Roseman, F.S. Educational development: A new discipline for self-renewal. Eugene, Oregon: Center for the Study of Educational Administration, 1973.

Holmes, B. and Ryba, R. (Editors). Curriculum development at the second level of education. Papers read at the fourth general meeting, Prague: Comparative Education Society in Europe, 1973.

Hughes, P.W. (Editor). The teacher's role in curriculum design. Sydney: Angus and Robertson, 1973.

Hyman, R.T. (Editor). Approaches in curriculum. Englewood Cliffs, New Jersey: Prentice-Hall, 1973.

Inlow, G. The emergent in curriculum (Second Edition). New York: John Wiley and Sons, 1973.

Lawton, D. Social change, educational theory, and curriculum planning. London: University of London Press, 1973.

Lewy, A. Using experts' judgements in the process of curriculum evaluation. Los Angeles: UCLA Graduate School of Education, 1973.

Mayhew, L.B. and Ford, P.J. Changing the curriculum. San Francisco, California: Jossey-Bass, 1973.

Moffett, J. A student-centered language arts curriculum, grades K-13: A handbook for teachers. Boston: Houghton-Mifflin, 1973.

Morley, F.P. A modern guide to effective K-12 curriculum planning. West Nyack, New York: Parker Publishing, 1973.

Musgrave, P.W. Knowledge, curriculum and change. Carlton: Melbourne University Press, 1973.

Netherlands Workshop on Curriculum Research, Vierhouten, Netherlands. Curriculum research and development. The Hague: Netherlands Foundation for Educational Research, 1973.

Ogletree, C.J. and Hawkins, M. Writing
instructional objectives and activities
for modern curriculum. New York: MSS
Information Corporation, 1973.

Owen, J.G. The management of curriculum
development. Cambridge: University
Press, 1973.

Robertson, J.H. Courses of study. Folcroft,
Pennsylvania: Folcroft Library Editions, 1973.

Silberman, C.E. (Editor). The open classroom reader. New York: Vintage
Books, 1973.

Sniff, W.F. A curriculum of the mentally
retarded young adult. Springfield,
Illinois: Charles C. Thomas, 1973.

Stradley, W. Administrator's guide to an
individualized performance results
curriculum. New York: Center for
Applied Research in Education, 1973.

Taylor, P.H. and Walton, J. (Editors). The
curriculum: Research, innovation, and
change. London: Ward Lock Educational, 1973.

Trump, J.L. and Miller, D. Secondary school
curriculum improvement: Challenges,
humanism, accountability (Second Edition). Boston: Allyn and Bacon, 1973.

White, J.P. Towards a compulsory curriculum.
London: Routledge and Kegan Paul,
1973.

Worner, R.B. Designing curriculum for educational accountability: From continuous progress education through PPBS.
New York: Random House, 1973.

Zenger, S. and Zenger, W. Writing and evaluating curriculum guides. Belmont, California: Fearon, 1973.

1974

Ahlum, C. and Fralley, J.M. (Editors). Feminist resources for school and colleges: A guide to curriculum materials. Old Westbury, New York: Feminist Press, 1974.

Association for Supervision and Curriculum Development. Education for an open society. 1974 Yearbook. (Edited by Della-Dora, D. and House, J.E.), 1974.

Blazier, W.H. Lights! Action! Camera! Learn! Allison Park, Pennsylvania: Allison, 1974.

Bowers, C.A. Cultural literacy for freedom: An existential perspective on teaching, curriculum and school policy. Eugene, Oregon: Elan Publishers, Inc., 1974.

Brickman, W.W. Bibliographical essays on curriculum and instruction. Folcroft, Pennsylvania: Folcroft Library Editions, 1974 (Reprint of 1948 edition).

Broudy, H.S. General education: The search for a rationale. Bloomington, Indiana: Phi Delta Kappa Educational Foundation, 1974.

Cawelti, G. Vitalizing the high school: A curriculum critique of major reform proposals. Washington: Association for Supervision and Curriculum Development, 1974.

Cross, K.P., et al. Planning non-traditional programs: An analysis of the issues for

post-secondary education. San Francisco: Jossey-Bass, 1974.

Dickson, G.E. and Saxe, R.E. Partners for
educational reform and renewal. Berkeley, California: McCutchan, 1974.

Doll, R.C. Curriculum improvement: Decision
making and process (Third Edition).
Boston: Allyn and Bacon, 1974.

Edward, C.H. (Editor). Readings in curriculum: A process approach. Champaign,
Illinois: Stipes, 1974.

Eisner, E.W. and Vallance, E. (Editors).
Conflicting conceptions of curriculum.
Berkeley, California: McCutchan, 1974.

Faculty of Education, British Columbia University. Program development in education (monograph). British Columbia:
British Columbia University, 1974.

Farguhar, E.E. Curriculum materials. Washington: Association for Supervision and
Curriculum Development, 1974.

Gilchrist, R.S., et al. Curriculum development: A humanized systems approach.
Belmont, California: Fearon, 1974.

Goodlad, J.I., et al. Toward a mankind
school. New York: McGraw-Hill, 1974.

Hass, G., Bondi, J. and Wiles, J. (Editors).
Curriculum planning--A new approach.
Boston: Allyn and Bacon, 1974.

Holly, D. Beyond curriculum: Changing secondary education. Frogmore, St. Al-
bans, Herts: Paladin, 1974.

Kingston, . Compulsory education and curriculum revision. Exeter, England:

300

University of Exeter School of Education, 1974. (Partial citation was only
one found).

Kopp, O.W. and Zufelt, D.L. Personalized
curriculum through excellence in leadership. Danville, Illinois: Interstate,
1974.

Macintosh, H.G., et al. Toward a freer curriculum. London: University of London
Press, 1974.

Murphy, R. Imaginary worlds: Notes on a new
curriculum. New York: Virgil Books,
1974.

Ontario Association for Curriculum Development. Action and reaction in the curriculum. Twenty-second Annual Conference. Ottawa: Ontario Association
for Curriculum Development, 1974.

Open Curriculum Conference (First), St.
Louis (L. Hotter, Editor). New York:
Division of Research, National League
for Nursing, 1974.

Payne, D.A. (Editor). Curriculum evaluation:
Commentaries on purpose, process, pro-
duct. Lexington, Massachusetts: D.C.
Heath, 1974.

Pinar, W. (Editor). Heightened consciousness,
cultural revolution, and curriculum
theory. Berkeley, California: McCutchan, 1974.

Regan, E.M. and Leithwood, K.A. Effecting
curriculum change: Experiences with
the conceptual skills. Toronto:
Institute for Studies in Education,
1974.

Rowntree, D. Educational technology in curriculum development. London: Harper and
Row, 1974.

Saylor, J.G. and Alexander, W.M. Planning
curriculum for schools. New York: Holt,
Rinehart and Winston, 1974.

Schools Council Research Service. Evaluation
in curriculum development: Twelve case
studies. New York: APS Publishers, 1974a
(Also by Macmillan Education, Ltd.,
London, 1973).

Schools Council Research Service. Pattern and
variation in curriculum development projects. New York: APS Publishers, 1974b
(Also by Macmillan Education, Ltd.,
Hampshire, 1973).

Shipman, M.D., Bolam, D., and Jenkins, D.R.
Inside a curriculum project; a case
study in the process of curriculum
change. Scranton, Pennsylvania: Barnes
and Noble, 1974 (Also by Methuen, London, 1974).

Speiker, C.A. A study to determine the
reliability of community involvement in
curriculum planning. Minneapolis:
University of Minnesota, 1974.

Tankard, G.G. Curriculum development: An
administrators guide. West Nyack, New
York: Parker, 1974.

Taylor, P.H. and Holley, B.J. The English
sixth form: A case study in curriculum
research. London: Routledge and Kegan
Paul, 1974.

Taylor, P.H. and Johnson, M. (Editors).
Curriculum development: A comparative
study. Windsor: NFER, 1974.

302

Taylor, P.H., Reid, W.A., Holley, B.J. and
Exon, G. Purpose, power, and constraint
in the primary school curriculum. London: Macmillan Education, Ltd., 1974.

Van Til, W. (Editor). Curriculum: Quest for
relevance (Second Edition). Boston:
Houghton Mifflin, 1974.

Wass, H., et al. Humanistic teacher education:
An experiment in systematic curriculum
innovation. Fort Collins, Colorado:
Shields Publishing Company, 1974.

Way, R.V. Adapting the curriculum of an
elementary school to serve the language
needs of Spanish speaking children. San
Francisco, California: R & E Research
Associates, 1974.

Wootton, L.R. and Reynolds, J.C. (Editor).
Trends influence curriculum (Second
Edition). New York: MSS Information
Corporation, 1974.

Yarbrough, V.E., et al. (Editors). Readings
in curriculum and supervision. New
York: MSS Information Corporation,
1974.

1975

Anderson, D.W. and Macdonald, J.B. (Editors).
Strategies in curriculum development:
The works of Virgil E. Herrick. Westport, Ct.: Greenwood, 1975 (Reprint of
1965 Edition).

Beauchamp, G.A. Curriculum theory (Third
Edition). Wilmette, Illinois: The
Kagg Press, 1975.

Botel, M., and Botel, N. A critical analysis
of the taxonomy of educational objectives.
Washington, D.C.: Curriculum Development
Associates, 1975.

Case, P.N. and Lowry, A.M. Evaluation of alternative curricula. Chicago: American Library Association, 1975.

Centre for Educational Research and Innovation. Handbook on curriculum development. Paris: Organization for Economic Cooperation and Development, 1975.

Curriculum Design and Development Course Team. Curriculum design. New York: Halsted Press, 1975.

Curriculum Design and Development Course Team. Curriculum innovation. New York: Halsted Press, 1975.

Eaton, J.M. An abc of the curriculum. New York: Longman, 1975.

English, F.W. and Kaufman, R.A. Needs assessment: A focus for curriculum development. Washington: Association for Supervision and Curriculum Development, 1975.

Foshay, A.W. Essays on curriculum: Selected papers. New York: Teachers College, Columbia University, 1975.

Fullan, M. and Promfret, A. Review of research on curriculum implementation. Toronto: Department of Sociology of Education, Toronto Institute for Studies in Education, 1975.

Glatthorn, A.A. Alternatives in education: Schools and programs. New York: Dodd Mead and Company, 1975.

Goodlad, J.I. The dynamics of educational change: Toward responsive schools. New York: McGraw-Hill, 1975.

304

Great Britain Schools Council. The whole curriculum. Working Paper 53. London:
Evans/Methuen, 1975.

Haigh, G. Integrate: Curriculum integration in the school. New York: Beekman, 1975.

Harris, A., Lawn, M., and Prescott, W.
Curriculum innovation. New York: John
Wiley; A Halsted Press Book, 1975.

Hendricks, G. and Fadiman, J. (Editors).
Transpersonal education: A curriculum
for feeling and being. Englewood
Cliffs, New Jersey: Prentice-Hall
(Spectrum Books), 1975.

Hirst, P.H. Knowledge and the curriculum:
A collection of philosophical papers.
London: Routledge and Kegan Paul,
1975.

Hollaway, O. Problem solving: Toward a more
humanizing curriculum. Philadelphia,
Pennsylvania: Franklin, 1975.

Hook, S.(Editor). The philosophy of the curriculum: The need for general education. Buffalo, New York: Prometheus
Books, 1975.

Hug, W.E. Instructional design and the media
program. Chicago: American Library
Association, 1975.

Kallos, D. Curriculum and teaching: An un-
American view. Lund, Sweden: Institute of Education, 1975.

Lawton, D. Class, culture and the curriculum.
London: Routledge and Kegan Paul, 1975.

Macdonald, J.B. and Zaret, E. (Editors).
Schools in search of meaning. Washington:
Association for Supervision and Curric-
ulum Development, 1975.

Mager, R.F. Preparing instructional objectives (Second Edition). Belmont, California: Fearon, 1975.

Martin, J.R. Choice, chance, and curriculum (Boyd H. Bode Memorial Lecture Series: Number Three). Columbus, Ohio: Ohio State University Press, 1975.

Mayer, W.V. (Editor). Planning curriculum development (With examples from projects for the mentally retarded). Boulder, Colorado: Biological Sciences Curriculum Study, 1975.

Michaelis, J.U., Grossman, R.H., and Scott, L.F. New designs for elementary curriculum and instruction (Second Edition). New York: McGraw-Hill, 1975.

Musgrave, P.W. (Editor). Contemporary studies in the curriculum. Sydney: Angus and Robertson, 1975.

Newfield, J.W. Information demands of curriculum supervisors: Final report, part I. (NIE Project Number G-74-0056). New Orleans, September 30, 1975.

Newman, F.M. Education for citizen action: Challenge for the secondary curriculum. Berkeley: McCutchan, 1975.

Pinar, W. (Editor). Curriculum theorizing: The reconceptualists. Berkeley: California: McCutchan, 1975.

Ponder, G.A. and Davis, O.L. (Editors). Curriculum perspectives. Austin, Texas: Texan House, Incorporated, 1975.

Reid, W.A. and Walker, D.F. (Editors). Case studies in curriculum change. London: Routledge and Kegan Paul, 1975.

306

Roberts, A. (Editor). Educational innovation: Alternatives in curriculum and instruction. Boston: Allyn and Bacon, 1975.

Rodgers, F.A. Curriculum and instruction in the elementary school. New York: Macmillan, 1975.

Rogers, V.R. and Church, B. Open education: Critique and assessment. Washington: Association for Supervision and Curriculum Development, 1975.

Schaffarzick, J. and Hampson, D.H. (Editors). Strategies for curriculum development. Berkeley, California: McCutchan, 1975.

Staples, I.E. (Editor). Impact of decentralization on curriculum: Selected viewpoints. Washington: Association for Supervision and Curriculum Development, 1975.

Stenhouse, L. Introduction to curriculum research and development. New York: Holmes and Meier, 1975.

Talmage, H. (Editor). Systems of individualized education. Berkeley, California: McCutchan, 1975.

Tanner, D. and Tanner, L. Curriculum development: Theory into practice. New York: Macmillan, 1975.

Taylor, P.H. (Editor). Aims, influence and change in the primary school curriculum. Windsor, Berkshire: NFER Publishing Company, 1975.

Taylor, P.H. and Tye, K.A. (Editors). Curriculum, school and society: An introduction to curriculum studies. Atlantic Highlands, New Jersey: Humanities Press, 1975.

Thompson, K. and White, J. Curriculum development: A dialogue. London: Pitman, 1975.

307

UNESCO. An experience-centered curricu-
     lum: Exercises in perception, commu-
     nication, and action (Educational
     Studies and Document Set Number Seven-
     teen). New York: Unipub, Incorporated,
     1975.

University of London Institute of Education.
     The curriculum. The Doris Lee Lectures
     delivered at the Institute of Education,
     University of London. London: Univer-
     sity of London Institute of Education,
     1975.

Unruh, G.G. Responsive curriculum development:
     Theory and action. Berkeley, California:
     McCutchan, 1975.

Warwick, D. Curriculum structure and design.
     Mystic, Ct.: Lawrence Verry, Incor-
     porated, 1975.

1976

Barnes, D. From communication to curriculum.
     New York: Penguin Books, Ltd., 1976.

Barrow, R. Common sense and the curriculum.
     Hamben, Connecticut: Shoe String Press,
     1976.

Brickman, W.W. Bibliographical essays on cur-
     riculum and instruction. Folcroft,
     Pennsylvania: Folcroft, 1976.

Cremin, L.A. Public Education. New York:
     Basic Books, Incorporated, 1976.

Curriculum Design and Development Course
     Team (Open University). Curriculum
     design. New York: Halsted Press, 1976.

Curriculum Design and Development Course
     Team (Open University). Curriculum

innovation. New York: John Wiley and
Sons, Incorporated, 1976.

Davies, I.K. Objectives in curriculum design.
New York: McGraw-Hill, 1976.

Davis, O.L. (Editor). Perspectives on curriculum development 1776-1976. 1976
Yearbook. Washington: Association of
Supervision and Curriculum Development,
1976.

Fantini, M.D. (Editor). Alternative education: A source book for parents,
teachers, students, and administrators.
Garden City, New York: Doubleday, 1976.

Frazier, A. Adventuring, mastering, asso-
ciating--New strategies for teaching
children. Washington, D.C.: Association
for Supervision and Curriculum Development, 1976.

Gow, D.T. Design and development of curriculum materials; Volume I: A self-
instructional text; Volume II: Instructional design articles. Pittsburgh:
University Center for International Studies, University of Pittsburgh, 1976.

Great Britain Schools Council. Curriculum in
the middle school years. London: Methuen
Educational and Evans Brothers, 1976.

Hamilton, D. Curriculum evaluation. London:
Open Books, 1976.

Jenkins, D. and Shipman, M.D. Curriculum: An
introduction. London: Open Books, 1976.

Kane, J. (Editor). Curriculum development in
physical education. New York: Beekman
Publishers, 1976.

309

Kauffman, D.L., Jr. Teaching the future:
A guide to future-orientated education.
Palm Springs, California: ETC Publica-
tions, 1976.

Kindred, L.W. and Wolotkiewicz, R.J., et al.
The middle school curriculum: A prac-
titioner's handbook. Boston: Allyn and
Bacon, 1976.

King, A.R., Jr. and Brownell, J.A. Curriculum
and the disciplines of knowledge: A
theory of curriculum practice (Reprint
of 1966 Edition). Huntington, New York:
Krieger, 1976.

Leithwood, K.A., Clipsham, J.S., et al. Planning curriculum change: A model and
case study. Toronto: Ontario Institute
for Studies in Education, 1976.

MacDonald, B. and Walker, R. Changing the
curriculum. London: Open Books, 1976.

McNeil, J.D. Designing curriculum: Self-
instructional modules. Boston: Little,
Brown and Company, 1976.

Margolin, E. Young children: Their curriculum and learning processes. New York:
Macmillan, 1976.

Mathews, J. Examinations: Their use in
curriculum evaluation and development.
London: Evans/Methuen Educational, 1976.

Newton, J.E. Curriculum evaluation of black
studies in relation to student knowledge
of Afro-American history and culture.
San Francisco, California: R & E
Research Associates, 1976.

Open University Press (England). Curriculum
design and development: Unit 1-2, Scope

310

of curriculum study; Unit 3-4, Culture
ideology and knowledge; Units 5-8, The
child, the school, and society; Case
Study 1, Tanzania: Education for self-
reliance; Unit 9-10, Towards the whole
curriculum; Unit 11-13, Curriculum
organization; Unit 14-15, Design issues;
Unit 16-18, Rationality and artistry;
Unit 19-21, Curriculum evaluation; Case
Study 3, Stantonbury Campus; Unit 22-23,
Innovation--problems and possibilities;
Unit 24-26, Supporting curriculum development; Case Study 5, Portrait of Coun-
testhorpe College; Case Study 6, Library
Guide--using the literature; Case Study
4, A middle school. London: Open University Press, 1976.

Petty, W.T. (Editor). Curriculum for the modern elementary school. Chicago: Rand
McNally and Company, 1976.

Pinar, W.F. and Grumet, M.R. Toward a poor
curriculum: Introduction to the theory
and practice of currere. Dubuque,
Iowa: Kendall/Hunt Publishing Company,
1976.

Posner, A. and De Keijzer, A.J. China: A
resource and curriculum guide (Second
Edition). Chicago: University of
Chicago Press, 1976.

Pring, R. Knowledge and schooling. London:
Open Books Publishing, Ltd., 1976.

Reynolds, J. and Skilbeck, M. Culture and the
classroom. London: Open Books Publishing, Ltd., 1976.

Rudduck, J. and Kelly, P. The dissemination
of curriculum development (Wrigley, J.
and Sparrow, F., Editors). New York:
Humanities Press, 1976.

311

Seefeldt, C. (Editor). Curriculum for the
preschool-primary child: A review of
the research (New Edition--Elementary
Education Set). Columbus, Ohio:
Charles Merrill, 1976.

Sockett, H. Designing the curriculum. London: Open Books, 1976.

Speiker, C.A. (Editor). Curriculum leaders:
Improving their influence. Washington:
Association for Supervision and Curric-
ulum Development, 1976.

Tawney, D. Curriculum evaluation today:
Trends and implications. London:
MacMillan, 1976.

Timmerman, T. Finding a way: Integrated
curriculum for the pre-teen. Amherst,
Massachusetts: Kandala, 1976.

Tyler, L.L., Klein, M.F., et al. Evaluating
and choosing curriculum and instructional
materials. Los Angeles: Educational
Resource Associates, 1976.

UNESCO. Co-operation in curriculum explorations: Report of a high-level personnel
exchange workshop. New York: Unipub,
1976.

Van Geel, T. Authority to control the school
program. Lexington, Massachusetts:
Lexington Books, 1976.

Zais, R.S. Curriculum: Principles and foundations. New York: Thomas Y. Crowell,
1976.

1977

Bellack, A.A. and Kliebard, H. (Editors).
Curriculum and evaluation. New York:
McCutchan, 1977.

312

Berman, L.M. and Roderick, J.A. Curriculum--
Teaching the what, how, and why of
living. Columbus, Ohio: Charles E. Merrill, 1977.

Bruner, J. The process of education (Revised). Cambridge: Harvard University
Press, 1977.

Chandra, A. Curriculum development and
evaluation in education. Mystic, Connecticut: Verry, 1977.

Comer, J.P. Forces affecting curriculum.
Washington: Association for Supervision
and Curriculum Development, 1977.

Curriculum Design and Development Course
Team (The Open University). Curricu-
lum design. New York: John Wiley and
Sons, Incorporated, 1977.

Curtis, T.E. and Bidwell, W.W. Curriculum
and instruction for emerging adolescents. Reading, Massachusetts: Addison-Wesley, 1977.

Edward, C.H. (Editor) Readings in curriculum: A process approach. Danville,
Illinois: Stipes, 1977.

Eggleston, J. The sociology of the school
curriculum. London: Routledge and
Kegan Paul, 1977.

Frymier, J. Annehurst curriculum classification system: A practical way to individualize instruction. Bloomington, Indiana: Kappa Delta Pi, 1977.

Gower, R.R. and Scott, M.B. Five essential
dimensions of curriculum design: A handbook for teachers. Dubuque, Iowa: Ken-
dall-Hunt, 1977.

313

Gran, E. Notes from a board of education: Ways to individualize your basic program. Amherst, Massachusetts: Mandala, 1977.

Hamilton, D., MacDonald, B., King, C., Jenkins, D., Parlett, M. (Editors). Beyond the numbers game: A reader in educational evaluation. Berkeley: McCutchan, 1977.

Hannah, L.S. and Michaelis, J.U. Comprehensive framework for instructional objectives: A guide to systematic planning and evaluation. Reading, Massachusetts: Addison-Wesley, 1977.

Hass, G. (Editor). Curriculum planning: A new approach (Second Edition). Boston: Allyn and Bacon, 1977.

Johnson, M. Intentionality in education. Albany, New York: Center for Curriculum Research and Services, 1977.

Jones, D.M. Curriculum targets in the elementary school. Englewood Cliffs, New Jersey: Prentice-Hall, 1977.

Kelly, A.V. The curriculum: Theory and practice. New York: Harper and Row, 1977.

Langenbach, M. and Neskora, T.W. Day care: Curriculum considerations. Columbus, Ohio: Merrill, 1977.

Lesser, H. (Editor). Television and the preschool child: A psychological theory of instruction and curriculum development. New York: Academic Press, 1977.

Lewy, A. Handbook of curriculum evaluation. New York: Longman, Incorporated, 1977.

314

McNeil, J.D. Curriculum: A comprehensive
introduction. Boston: Little, Brown
and Company, 1977.

Marbach, E.S. Creative curriculum: Kindergarten through grade three. Provo,
Utah: Brigham Young University Press,
1977.

Molnar, A. and Zahorik, J.A. (Editors).
Curriculum theory. Washington: Asso-
ciation for Supervision and Curriculum
Development, 1977.

Oliver, A.I. Curriculum improvement: A
guide to problems, principles, and
process (Second Edition). New York:
Harper and Row, 1977a.

Oliver, A.I. Maximizing minicourses: A
curriculum alternative. New York:
Teachers College, Columbia University,
1977b.

Olsen, E.G. and Clark, P.A. Life-centering
education. Midland, Michigan: Pendell
Publishing Company, 1977.

Open University Press (England). Curriculum
design and development: Unit 17-18,
Innovation, the school and the teacher;
Unit 29-30, Innovation, the school and
the teacher, two. London: Open University Press, 1977.

Ragan, W.B. and Shepherd, G.D. Modern elementary curriculum (Fifth Edition). New
York: Holt, Rinehart and Winston, 1977.

Robinson, K. and Wilson, R. (Editors). Extending economics within the curriculum.
London: Routledge and Kegan Paul, 1977.

Rubin, L. (Editor). <u>Curriculum handbook:
Administration and theory</u>. Boston:
Allyn and Bacon, 1977a.

Rubin, L. (Editor). <u>Curriculum handbook:
The disciplines, current movements and
instructional methodology</u>. Boston:
Allyn and Bacon, 1977b.

Rubin, L. (Editor). <u>Curriculum handbook: The
disciplines, current movements, instructional methodology, administration, and
theory</u> (Abridged Edition). Boston: Allyn
and Bacon, 1977c.

Shane, H.G. <u>Curriculum change toward the
twenty-first century</u>. Washington:
National Education Association, 1977.

Shuster, A.H. and Ploghoft, M.E. <u>The emerging elementary curriculum</u> (Third Edition). Columbus, Ohio: Merrill, 1977.

Speiker, C. <u>Standards and guidelines for the
evaluation of graduate programs preparing curriculum leaders</u>. Washington:
Association for Supervision and Curriculum Development, 1977.

UNESCO. <u>Integrated approach to curriculum
development in primary education in
Sri-Lanka</u>. New York: Unipub, 1977.

Wootton, L.R. and Reynolds, J.C. <u>Trends and
issues affecting curriculum</u>. Washington,
D.C.: University Press of America, 1977.

<u>1978</u>

Bourne, P. and Eisenberg, J. <u>Social issues in
the curriculum: Teaching Canadian literature in high school</u>. Toronto: Ontario
Institute for Studies in Education, 1978.

316

Brent, A. Philosophical foundations for the curriculum. Winchester, Massachusetts: Allen and Unwin, 1978.

Carnegie Foundation for the Advancement of Teaching. Missions of the college curriculum. San Francisco: Jossey-Bass, 1978.

Casciano - Savignano, C.J. Systems approach to curriculum and instructional improvement. Columbus, Ohio: Merrill, 1978.

Claydon, L. Knight, T. and Rado, M. Curriculum and culture: Schooling in a pluralist society. Winchester, Massachusetts: Allen and Unwin, 1978.

Curriculum Design and Development Course Team. Curriculum innovation. New York: Halsted Press, 1978.

Curriculum Development Centre of Malaysia. Studies of curriculum development centers. New York: Unipub, 1978.

Doll, R.C. Curriculum improvement: Decision making and process (Fourth Edition). Boston: Allyn and Bacon, 1978.

English, F.W. Quality control in curriculum development. Washington, D.C.: American Association of School Administrators, 1978.

Fredericks, H.D.B., et al. The teaching research curriculum for moderately and severely handicapped. Springfield, Illinois: Charles C. Thomas, 1978.

Greene, M. Landscapes of learning. New York: Teachers College Press, 1978.

317

Gress, J.R. and Purpel, D.E. (Editors). Curriculum: An introduction to the field. Berkeley: McCutchan, 1978.

Hefley, J. Textbooks on trial. Milford, Michigan: Mott Media, 1978.

Holt, M. The common curriculum: Its structure and style in the comprehensive school. London: Routledge and Kegan Paul, 1978.

Jelinek, J.J. (Editor). Improving the human condition: A curricular response to critical realities: 1978 Yearbook. Washington: Association for Supervision and Curriculum Development, 1978.

Joyce, B. Selecting learning experiences: Linking theory and practice. Washington, D.C.: Association for Supervision and Curriculum Development, 1978.

Lawton, D., Gordon, P., et al. Theory and practice of curriculum studies. London: Routledge and Kegan Paul, 1978.

Levine, A., et al. Handbook on undergraduate curriculum. San Francisco: Jossey-Bass, 1978.

Lounsbury, J.H. and Vars, G.F. A curriculum for the middle school years. New York: Harper and Row, 1978.

Nelson, M. Law in the curriculum. Bloomington, Indiana: Phi Delta Kappa, 1978.

Nicholls, A. and Nicholls, H. Developing a curriculum: A practical guide (Second Edition). London: Allen and Unwin, 1978.

Orlosky, D.E. and Smith, B.O. Curriculum

318

development: Issues and insights.
Chicago: Rand McNally, 1978.

Posner, G.J. and Rudnitsky, A.N. Course
design: A guide to curriculum development for teachers. New York: Longman,
1978.

Reid, W.A. Thinking about the curriculum:
The nature and treatment of curriculum
problems. London: Routledge and Kegan
Paul, 1978.

Rudolph, F. Curriculum: A history of the
American undergraduate course of study
since 1636. San Francisco: Jossey-
Bass, 1978.

Schiro, M. Curriculum for better schools:
The great ideological debate. Englewood Cliffs, N.J.: Educational Technology Publications, 1978.

Steeves, F.L. and English, F.W. Secondary
curriculum for a changing world. Columbus, Ohio: Charles E. Merrill, 1978.

Taylor, P.H. The English sixth form: A case
study in curriculum research. Boston:
Routledge and Kegan Paul, 1978.

Westbury, I. and Wilkof, N.J. (Editors).
Science, curriculum, and liberal education: Selected essays, Joseph J. Schwab.
Chicago: University of Chicago Press,
1978.

Weston, P.B. Framework for the curriculum.
New York: Humanities Press, 1978.

Willis, G. (Editor). Qualitative evaluation:
Concepts and cases in curriculum
criticism. Berkeley: McCutchan Publishing Company, 1978.

319

1979

Apple, M.W. Ideology and curriculum. London: Routledge and Kegan Paul, 1979.

Becker, J.M. Schooling for a global age. New York: McGraw Hill, 1979.

Bloomer, M. and Shaw, K.E. Constraint and innovation: The content and organization of schooling. New York: Pergamon, 1979.

Bremer, J. Education and community. Shepparton (Australia): Waterwheel Press, 1979.

Egan, K. Educational development. New York: Oxford University Press, 1979.

Eisner, E. The educational imagination: On the design and evaluation of school programs. New York: Macmillan, 1979.

Goodlad, J.I. and Associates. Curriculum inquiry: The study of curriculum practice. New York: McGraw, 1979.

Hug, W.E. 40 years of research in curriculum and teaching. New York: Teachers College, Columbia University, 1979.

Jelinek, J.J. (Editor). Education in flux: Implications for curriculum development. Tempe, Arizona: Professors of Curriculum and Arizona State University, 1979.

Musgrave, P.W. Society and the curriculum in Australia. Winchester, Massachusetts: Allen and Unwin, 1979.

Ogletree, E.J. (Editor). Introduction to Waldorf education. Curriculum and methods. Washington, D.C.: University Press of America, 1979.

320

Overly, N.V. (Editor). Lifelong learning: 1979 Yearbook. Washington, D.C.: Association for Supervision and Curriculum Development, 1979.

Postman, N. Teaching as a conserving activity. New York: Delacorte Press, 1979.

Richmond, K.W. The school curriculum. London: Methuen, 1979.

Rumanoff, L.A. A curriculum model for individuals with severe learning and behavior disorders. Baltimore: University Park, 1979.

Schaffarzick, J. and Sykes, G. (Editors). Value conflicts and curriculum issues. Berkeley, California: McCutchan, 1979.

Taylor, P.H. and Reid, W.A. (Editors). Curriculum, culture, and classroom: Trends in curriculum studies. New York: Humanities, 1979.

Taylor, P.H. and Richards, C.M. An introduction to curriculum studies. New York: Humanities Press, 1979.

Trump, J.L. and Miller, D.F. Secondary school curriculum improvement: Meeting challenges of the times (Third Edition). Boston: Allyn and Bacon, 1979.

Wechman, P.H. Curriculum design for severely and profoundly handicapped. New York: Human Sciences Press, 1979.

Werner, W. (Editor). Curriculum Canada: Perspectives, practices, prospects. British Columbia: University of British Columbia Center for the Study of Curriculum and Instruction, 1979.

Wiles, J. and Bondi, J. Curriculum develop-
    ment: A guide to practice elementary
    education. Columbus, Ohio: Merrill,
    1979.

CHAPTER IX

CURRICULUM LITERATURE AND ITS AUTHORS:

PROFILE, OBSERVATIONS, AND RECOMMENDATIONS

As I reflect on the foregoing chapters and on the accumulation of work that each citation symbolizes, I am struck with the richness of curriculum study. This richness cannot be captured wholly by categorization. There is always a sense in which every book on the same general topic remains unique. Thus, my categorization schemes are not offered with great rigidity. A large number of books fall in more than one category. That fact is not intended as an inconsistency. Categorization serves great value in pointing to tendencies; yet, any intent to do so must be realized as superficial. If categorization were deemed easy and clear, the study that derives from it would be simplistic. From my perspective, this is certainly not the case with curriculum books.

Though arguments and classifications presented in some books may be criticized as simplistic, the field as a whole is clearly robust. The lack of agreement, definitional and the like, may indeed be attributed to the seriousness with which curriculum scholars take their work rather than to lack of seriousness. Agreement is difficult when issues are treated with much scrutiny, and when matters studied are attributed profound consequences. The writings of most are replete with acknowledgement, for example, of a Deweyan importance to the process of inducting the young into social and cultural life. I argue that it is in this mission that the glory of curriculum inquiry and its applications reside. That curriculum scholars center their concern for this mission almost entirely on schools may be a distinct limitation. Relative costs and benefits of this mission are discussed in paragraphs that follow.

The emergence of curriculum studies as a specialized area of inquiry is, quite obviously, a result of its residence in a particular cultural context. My conviction that this is the case is reflected in each chapter's section entitled Contextual Reminders.

In some instances the connection between social developments and curriculum thought is obvious, e.g.: the growth of science and technology; the existence or lack of prosperity; the perils of war; the priorities of politics; the ebb and flow of economics; and the ideals and propensities of artistic expression. These are reflected in each decade treated. They contributed to the existence, orientation, and evolution of schools, and to the curriculum scholars and practitioners who emerged to serve them. Indeed, they contributed, in fact, to the very emergence of scholars and practitioners to serve schools. (This is, of course, not to deny the role of unique insight by perceptive individuals in the growth of curriculum inquiry).

More social, political, economic, scientific, intellectual, and artistic information is provided in the Contextual Reminders than is directly connected with curriculum literature of the same time periods. The hope here is to encourage others to look more deeply within the fabric of social forces for major threads of influence that contributed to curriculum thought, literature, and practice. More often than not, the influence of such forces is more subtle, diffuse, and pervasive than usually reveals itself.[1] One major purpose of juxtaposing the curriculum literature with contextual information is to ease and encourage further inquiry.

The research done for this book encouraged me to pursue further study as well. It led me to couple focus on curriculum literature with focus on the professoriate that produced it.[2] It led to inquiry into interconnections among

curriculum scholars, i.e., mentor-student relationships.[3] Findings from these studies are
integrated with ideas drawn from work on earlier
chapters of this book.

To this end the present chapter is divided
into three sections. The first section reviews
highlights of the literature and those who
created it. In it I attempt to profile the shape
of curriculum knowledge—its frames, boundaries,
and scope—as it evolved in the literature during
the first eight decades of the Twentieth Century.
The second section consists of several observations and possibilities that emerged as I pursued
the work leading to this book and the related
studies mentioned above. In the third section,
I describe recommendations that I suggest for
creators of next developments in curriculum
scholarship. Such suggestions are offered with
a good deal of humility. They are, however,
derived from my perception of gaps and omissions
in the literature that I have surveyed.

Review and Profile

Each decade brought new form and substance
to curriculum as an area of study. The date 1918
seems to be the most frequently acknowledged
starting point for curriculum studies. It is the
date of both Bobbitt's The Curriculum and the
Cardinal Principles of Secondary Education. This
was indeed a time of emergence for curriculum as
a separate area differentiated within the field of
education. Yet, it is a bit unfair to begin at
1918. Direct roots of the curriculum professoriate can be traced to earlier times. As readers
will readily recall, at least twenty curriculum
books were published between 1900 and 1918. Let
us consider developments of the final years of the
previous century.

In these years we find a combination of
events that included the ever-rising tide of
universal schooling, the academic pronouncements

of the Committees of Ten and Fifteen, and the existence of several fertile coteries of scholarship. Universal schooling heightened the necessity for experts whose sole attention could be devoted to the production of defensible substance for children and youth who were recipients of that schooling. The Committees of Ten and Fifteen encouraged universal schooling to continue the perpetuation of mental disciplines or intellectual traditions, a subject-oriented curriculum that carried more than remnants of faculty psychology. I referred to proponents of this view as intellectual traditionalists.

It seems that certain influential professors at certain American universities grew uneasy about the possibilities for intellectual traditionalist futures for curriculum in the American experiment of universal schooling. These professors cannot be called curriculum professors in a formal way since curriculum had not developed as a professional area of study. Yet these professors shared a concern for the form and substance of education. Students whom they influenced became founders of curriculum study. They originated the curriculum professoriate.

Let us look at a few of the coteries of professors and students that were, perhaps unwittingly, carving out occupational characteristics of the curriculum professoriate near the turn of the century. Let us look, again, at the kinds of books that they produced. Both scholars and their books fall roughly into two camps. The two camps have many variations, but they both offer alternatives to the intellectual traditionalist domination of educational practice. One is oriented to quantitative measurement, behavioristic psychology, and a Hobbesian faith in the science of education. For the convenience of labeling, I have referred to them as social behaviorists. The other group has its roots in philosophy, and is oriented toward a situational and contextual interaction of art

326

and science as it applies to education. I called
this group experientialists.

The origins of the social behaviorist position trace to Wilhelm Wundt at Leipzig, Germany.
E.L. Thorndike's mentor, J. McKeen Cattell, stud-
ied with Wundt as did G. Stanley Hall and Charles
H. Judd. Although Thorndike, Hall, and Judd were
not primarily curriculum scholars, their leadership created many such scholars. Hall influenced
Bobbitt who received his doctorate in 1909 from
Clark University. From there Bobbitt went to the
University of Chicago where Judd had just assumed
leadership, altering the orientation considerably
from the time that Dewey was in command there.
George D. Strayer completed his doctorate under
Thorndike's direction in 1905. Strayer influenced
students at Columbia Teachers College for nearly
forty years. Hollis Caswell and Paul Hanna were
among his prominent students whose influence on
the curriculum professoriate is unquestioned.
They, in turn, influenced many who moved throughout the country.

Experientialist roots can be traced to John
Dewey and Charles De Garmo. At the turn of the
century, when Dewey was at Chicago, Ella Flagg
Young and W.W. Charters studied with him. Later
at Columbia, Kilpatrick not only studied with
Dewey but became a kind of self-appointed inter-
preter of his educational views. De Garmo, who
studied with K.V. Stoy in Germany, brought Herbartian interpretations to America as did Frank and
Charles McMurry. Boyd H. Bode and William Bagley
received doctorates in 1900 at Cornell University-
sity where De Garmo was Professor of Art and
Science of Education. They studied with Edward
Titchener and Charles Tyler. Books such as
Dewey's The Child and the Curriculum (1902) and
McMurry's two volume Course of Study in the
Eight Grades (1906) illustrate experientialist
commitments to child study, primacy of interest
in curricular organization, and an interdependence between living and schooling in the educative process.

327

Books by Bagley, Strayer, Judd, and others often focused on school surveys. This kind of focus helped to gear the emergent area of curriculum study toward schools. This was the case with the mental discipline interpretation of the intellectual traditionalist approach as well; it was furthered by the work of national committees that were mentioned earlier, and perpetuated by the Commission on the Reorganization of Secondary Education (1918). Despite Dewey's holistic treatment of curriculum matters in Democracy and Education (1916) and despite its widespread citation in curriculum books, curriculum writers increasingly geared their writing to schools.

By the mid-1920's the "descendents" of Thorndike and Judd, of Dewey and Herbart, and of the commissions,each formed fairly distinct groupings of curriculum scholars, i.e., social behaviorists, experientialists, and intellectual traditionalists. Curriculum was indeed an identifiable subdivision of educational inquiry. Bobbitt (1915, 1918, 1922, 1924, 1926), Charters (1923), and Snedden (1921, 1927), led the social behaviorists. Dewey (1900, 1902a, 1902b, 1916), Kilpatrick (1918, 1926), Counts (1926), McMurry (1923), and Rugg (1927), led the experientialists.

Professors in both groups tried to apply interpretations of science to curriculum construction, a process that some deemed riddled by unsystematic selection governed by expedience, tradition, and politics. Social behaviorists used a mechanistic, atomistic, measurement style of science. They analyzed activities, translated the findings to curriculum, and sought generalized knowledge. On the contrary, experientialists sought a situational application of science. The educator's job was to read the character of problematic circumstances, project possible courses of action and their probable consequences, and act in such ways that led to growth. Though vague in many respects, professors who wrote in this persuasion tried to describe a

328

complex application of scientific methodology that accounted for uniqueness in situations as well as commonalities among them. Even the more practice-oriented books in this group such as Rugg and Shumaker (1928) tended to be philosophical.

Another kind of curriculum book out-numbered both of these in the Twenties and early Thirties. This was the highly school-oriented text that focused on curriculum in the secondary, elementary, junior high school, etc. Examples include Koos (1920) and Bonser (1920). Others of a similar type dealt with general curriculum procedures and problems, e.g., Meriam (1920), Monroe (1925), Briggs (1926), Harap (1928), Williams (1928), Hopkins (1929), and Lide (1933). Thus, the alternative to social behaviorist and experientialist literature became not so much the old version of intellectual tradition, but a new school-oriented text. The point was to provide guidelines, often called <u>principles</u>, for school people. The curriculum professoriate was grappling with the issue of how to present knowledge about a complex process in <u>one book</u>. Practitioners would be likely to have only one or two courses in curriculum. Somehow the necessary procedures needed to be conveyed in that scope.

By the mid-1930's many members of the professoriate had apparently internalized the guideline approach. Texts contained list after list of "how to's" and "when to's." Many continued to use this recipe-orientation into the Fifties and Sixties. This was the case despite admonitions by such writers as Bode (1927), Rugg-NSSE (1927), and Hopkins (1929) to engage in serious and complex discourse about assumptions that undergird alternative positions on major curriculum questions.

The schools of curriculum thought became less distinct, more conflated with one another. At the same time curriculum study began to embrace more areas: organization, administration, students, teachers, instruction. In a sense, curriculum had returned to its state before it differentiated from education. That is to say, curriculum study expanded to treat almost as many aspects of schooling as did the study of education itself. This expansion of boundaries relative to schooling and the amalgamation of schools of thought are both reflected in the books of "principles" for practitioners.

To this end a new kind of text was produced that was encyclopedic or synoptic in character. Early in this book it was labeled the synoptic text. Through the synoptic text authors attempted to provide procedures for curriculum development as well as distillations of background information on a host of related topics. First examples of these texts were Curriculum Development (1935) by Caswell and Campbell and Foundations of Curriculum Building (1936) by Norton and Norton.

The synoptic text dominated curriculum writing for more than three decades. It is interesting to note that each text seemed to be designed as a "one shot" professional training course in curriculum. Each tried to cover, or sample, the territory. That there is little gradation in level of these texts supports the assumption that just one exposure to curriculum was the usual expectation. Examples include Spears (1940), Gwynn (1943), Burton (1944), Leonard (1946), Stratemeyer (1947), Tyler (1949), Krug (1950), Lee and Lee (1959), Smith, Stanley, and Shores (1950), Ragan (1953), Saylor and Alexander (1954), and Taba (1962).

Caswell and Campbell also produced another kind of curriculum book, Readings in Curriculum Development (1937); from that date to the present, books of readings served as a major means of conveying curriculum knowledge. Usually they included articles that had already achieved prominence in journals. Sometimes they included new articles that were especially prepared for their publications.

Synoptic texts and books of readings were the major type of curriculum books from the Forties through the Sixties. Added to these were monographs and yearbooks of such organizations as the Association for Supervision and Curriculum Development and the National Society for the Study of Education.

In the Sixties the emphasis on structure of disciplines and curriculum projects became manifested in the synoptic and readings texts. Alternative curricula of humanistic education emerged and were reminiscent of the earlier experientialists. Behavioral objectives, competency-based curricula, systems rhetoric, and technological approaches evidenced a resurgence of social behaviorism. Of similar genre,a major alteration that reached fruition in the Sixties was the increased use of social science and behavioristic methodologies that are labeled conceptual-empiricist by Pinar (1975). This is the theoretic research mode that Schwab (1970) called moribund.

The Seventies brought increased diversification of types of curriculum books and a resultant decline in synoptic texts. More attention also was given in America to British, German, Scandinavian, Australian, and Canadian sources. Schwab and others emerged to advocate practical epistemologies and qualitative methodologies that evolved in the mid-Seventies, bringing a revival of philosophic scrutiny and speculation that once characterized a style of study led by Dewey and the Herbartians. Yet, the literature, especially the journals, remained dominated by conceptual analysis and empirical research. The sophistication of conceptual and statistical analysis soared. To some this represented progress,or at least its potential. To others it symbolized slavery to one epistemological orientation and ignorance that others existed.

Observations and Possibilities

Reflection on the curriculum books and their

authors has led to several observations about
characteristics of the curriculum professoriate.
The characteristics are presented here both
chronologically and cumulatively, according to
the following observations: (1) the curriculum
professoriate evolved as an inheritor; (2) it
created and delimited a future course of
inquiry; (3) it grew as a purveyor of schooling;
(4) it became preoccupied with the determination
of the content of school learning; (5) it professed knowledge; (6) it generated knowledge;
and (7) it sought freedom from the boundary of
that knowledge. Let us consider each of these in
a bit more detail.

Inheritors of a Journey

       Probing the roots of curriculum quickly
reveals that concern for curriculum is perennial.
The etymological origins of curriculum as a
chariot race course can be applied metaphori-
cally to the journey of inducting humans into
society. The basic human concern for induction
of new members into adult oriented society
marks a basis of legitimation for curriculum as
a professional domain. The concern is supported
in several modes of representation.

       To trace roots of prominent curriculum scho-
lars to educators of the later Nineteenth Century is only a beginning. For example, a chain
exists from Madeleine Grumet to William Pinar,
Paul Klohr, Harold Alberty, Boyd H. Bode, to
association with Charles De Garmo, who can be
traced to K.V. Stoy and Herbart. Herbart, in
turn, can be traced in a mentor-student network
to Pestalozzi and Fitche, Lessing, Kant, Martin
Knutzen, Christian Wolff, Leibnitz, and more
indirectly to Descartes and to Rousseau, and to
the French Jesuits. All of these wrote covertly,
if not overtly, about education, and concomitantly about curriculum.

They represent a concern shared by philosophers to antiquity. Philosophical grand schemes
amost invariably treat problems associated with
introducing young to the structure, resources, and
functioning of social groups. Whether proposals
or social criticisms, these writings deal not only
with curriculum in a formal educational setting,
but with education as one of many aspects in any
context of social forces. The treatment of curriculum within such a context is part of a tradition of social philosophical writing.

Similarly, one can surely turn to novels,
poetry, plays, biographies, diaries, and other
literary portrayals for curriculum insights.
They illuminate journeys that educate persons.
They portray experiences that enhance and retard
human growth. They deal with growth holistically,
not in cognitive, affective, or psychomotor
segmentations. The point, perhaps an obvious one,
is that a heritage of curriculum literature runs
deeper than the overt occupational characteristics of the curriculum professoriate. It inter-
penetrates literature from Homer to Plutarch, to
Shakespeare, to Dickens, to Tolstoy, to Dostoyevski and Joyce, Hesse and Kafka, Vonnegut and
Borges. Moreover, curriculum has permeated
human concern since young humans were thought to
need induction to a society. Whether such induction pertained to schooling institutions or
whether it pertained to a child following an adult
through daily routine, curriculum was being done.

Thus, those who emerged to be known as a
curriculum professoriate early in the Twentieth
Century were inheritors of a basic human concern.
The informal provision of activities to induct
the young into adult oriented life is a perennial
parental concern. With the growth of complex
social groups it became more formalized in school
institutions. The substance of education and
schooling was represented in the arts, discussed
in philosophy, and criticized in both. In all of
these it was integrated with and contingent upon
living itself. Education was treated as part and

parcel of the journey of living. The emergence
of the educational professoriate brought more
specialized study. Increased specialization,
and change of residence from life at large to
universities, evolved with the emergence of the
curriculum inquiry and development as occupations.

Delimitors of the Journey

The specialization implicit in a curriculum professoriate magnified focus on a concern
that had heretofore been subsidiary. What had
been a concern for induction of the young into
adult-oriented living, a concern expressed
within broad cultural, artistic, and intellectual contexts, became a preoccupation with
schooling as the means of induction that pushed
contextual concerns to the periphery. Books on
curriculum, especially the synoptic texts,
almost invariably treated the larger contextual
forces as mere influences on curriculum, rather
than curriculum as one thread in a fabric of
forces that all influence the induction of the
young into adult life. Specialization was, in
no small measure, dictated by increased pressure
for universal schooling. Specialized inquiry
into curriculum was legitimated so long as it
appeared to contribute to learning substance to
be conveyed by universal schooling. It is ironic
that the curriculum professoriate, a group commissioned to prepare the young to effectively
engage in life as a whole, is the same group that
turned its attention from induction as a function of life holistically to schooling. Put
another way, the historical journey of those
concerned with inducting the young into life
was, in this century, placed in the hands of
curriculum specialists commissioned to introduce the young to effective living via institutions known as schools.

Purveyors of Schooling

The curriculum professoriate emerged in response to universal schooling. In short, if the form was there it needed substance. If the conveyor belts were set in motion something had to be conveyed. It seemed clear that it would be the quasi-classicial subject matter that dominated schooling unless alternatives were offered. If nothing definite was available to convey, caprice would dictate substance. If caprice governed, the message would be the medium itself. Universal schooling would convey the universal need to be schooled. Would this perpetuate a land of students, persons who would be prepared not to be directors of their own curriculum, but to have the curriculum of their learning directed by others? Would the curriculum of schooling become schooling itself? Is this not symbolized by the recent attention attributed to hidden curriculum as discussed earlier?

At the turn of the century there were too few educators who could devote full-time consideration to the content of universal schooling. Some educational scholars centered their concern on the substance of education generally. Such concern had grown from focus on private schooling or informal learning experiences rather than mass schooling. As mentioned earlier, alternatives to intellectual traditionalist interpretations were found in the theory and practice of Herbartians and Dewey, and in the measurement and behaviorism of Thorndike, Judd, and Cattell. Both alternatives were fueled by public sentiments; i.e., social behaviorists by the growing faith in science and technology, and experientialists by faith in individualism, democracy, and reflective science and ethics.

It is clear that the curriculum professoriate was legitimated by the need to create or perpetuate learning substance for universal schooling. Educational scholars (e.g., De Garmo, Dewey, Hall, Judd, and Thorndike) offered alternative orientations to the intellectual traditionalist curriculum that had dominated schooling.

335

Perhaps they saw it as a socially significant venture to do so.

Developers of Curriculum

It was a kind of occupational commission that the curriculum professoriate would develop curriculum. What else could be the purpose of curriculum inquiry than to discover or invent curricula? Curriculum scholars did, on occasion, develop curriculum; they prepared curriculum materials, proposed examples of programs, and surveyed or assessed extant curriculum implementation. It seems, however, that curricularists soon realized that general programs could not be formulated to meet specific needs of unique situations. Therefore, their discussion elevated to a meta-level and addressed the issue of how instead of what.

They decentralized the decision about what learning substance should constitute curriculum of schools. Instead of using their expertise to advocate, they placed advocacy in state and local hands. They attempted to provide "principles" to guide curriculum development to be done by planners in schools. Often this was defended as facilitatory of the democratic ideal of self-determination. Perhaps, too, it was a response to the realization that curriculum development is primarily a practical task. In any event,the curriculum professoriate became known largely as scholars concerned with problems and procedures of pointing the way to sound curriculum development. They were less frequently developers of extant local curricula.

Professors of Curriculum Knowledge

Service to schools was an initial concern of the curriculum professoriate. The widespread existence of normal schools for teacher training set a precedent for service to schools. As cer-

336

tain prominent philosophers, psychologists, and
educators turned their attention and that of
their students to curriculum matters, curriculum
became associated with universities as well.

The role of curriculum workers was altered
by virtue or vice of the professoriate's emergent residence in universities. That faction
of curriculum workers known as professors had
much of their role directed by the system of
rewards and expectations that is incumbent upon
university faculty members. A professoriate
professes by publication as well as by consulting and teaching. Books became a major symbol
of legitimation. Books facilitated teaching
and consulting, but even more, they provided
evidence of scholarly productivity.

As professors of specialized knowledge,
curriculum professors began by publishing an
amalgam of prescriptions and descriptions drawn
from teaching teachers and administrators with
eclectically selected positions from the three
growing orientations: social behaviorist,
experientialist, and intellectual traditionalist.
As late comers to the university scene, it was
doubtless difficult for curriculum professors to
find a body of lore to use as a basis for
subsequent writing. Thus, they chose from a
host of sources that sometimes only held remote
resemblance to their own practical pursuits.

Understandably, a lag persisted between
curriculum and more established areas or disciplines of study. The lag in both methodology
and substance was blatantly evident. Methodolo-
gically, curricularists, like other educational
researchers, emulated social scientists who, in
turn, emulated successors of natural sciences.
When natural scientists moved from heavy reliance
on statistics to formulation of theory, social
scientists gave prime concern to statistics and
educationalists upgraded statistics requirements
for their students. When natural scientists
moved from theory to situational analysis, social

337

scientists began to develop theories, and curricularists expressed a need (Herrick and Tyler,
1950) for theory and speculated about what it
might entail.

Substantively, the case for lag is similar.
Existential psychology and philosophy were made
central philosophical and literary concerns of
Sartre, Camus, Jaspers, Heidegger, Kafka, and
others by the 1920's and 1930's. Yet, it was not
until the 1970's that existential perspectives
were brought to curriculum scholarship in any full
measure.

A point similar to that asked by Harry S.
Broudy[8] is highly relevant. Broudy asked, "What
do professors of education profess?" The academic community at large has, justifiably or not,
asked similar questions of educational scholars
throughout this century. The same is true, of
course, for those who claimed to be curriculum
scholars. Moreover, they asked themselves this
question, as well, as they produced a body of
literature. It was clear that the curriculum
professoriate had to profess to live. Thus,
curriculum scholars needed to develop knowledge.
As they did so, the development of curriculum
itself ironically took a back seat to scholarly
publications.

Generators of Knowledge

If the job of curriculum professors was to
profess knowledge, it was necessary for them to
create a steady flow of it. Furthermore, this
knowledge had to conform to that deemed acceptable in academia. It had to conform to the
epistemology of the day, at least of a nearby
yesterday.

The problem of what kind of knowledge should
be produced plagued curriculum scholars. As
creators of scholarly research, the curriculum
professoriate had to produce empirically warranted

338

descriptions of school phenomena. They had to conform to the <u>theoretic</u> (Schwab, 1970) or <u>conceptual empiricist</u> (Pinar, 1975) epistemologies of the day.[4] Simultaneously, as a professional area of study, it needed to prescribe services to practitioners in schools. Throughout its eighty year history the curriculum professoriate has come under fire for doing too much and too little in both its research and school-based roles. Generally, it has been strong on prescription and weak on description. Authors produced books that reflected this proportion, but by simultaneously attempting to satisfy demands of scholarly description and practical prescription, they provided books that were amalgams of both. Books for practitioners often turned out to be more theoretic and conceptual empiricist; thus, did not meet needs of specific practical problems. Conversely, books for scholars often lacked the rigor, detachment, and generalizability that merit praise by the scholarly community. The domain of curriculum inquiry clearly embraced a set of problems that too few understood and even fewer devoted energies to understand. As a consequence, the books were often criticized by scholars for being superficial and by practitioners for not relating to specific practical concerns.

Despite the criticism, books were a source of legitimation and their production grew steadily as the decades passed. The proliferation of books was indeed great. The growth of the field was cumulative, and more than a bit haphazard. At first, curriculum was acknowledged as a domain important enough to be treated as an educational subdivision deserving attention in its own right. Many early curriculum scholars no doubt relied on traditions embodied in the mental disciplines position that empowered the existence of curriculum workers. Hence, a number of books emerged in the first three decades that quite wholly reflected the intellectual traditionalist orientation. Others relied more on their immediate scholarly ancestors in education, philosophy, and psychology: Thorndike, Strayer, Wundt, Herbart, De Garmo, Dewey, Peirce, James, etc. These scholars were not curricularists, though they markedly influenced the existence of social behaviorist and experientialist curriculum thought.

As the decades progressed more specialized dimensions of curriculum knowledge emerged. At first, these segments included elementary, secondary, and junior high levels of education. Some treated the subject areas separately. A few probed for assumptions behind these prescriptions and descriptions. Others advocated processes or procedures for developing curricula. Still others treated curriculum administration, implementation, materials, and a host of miscellaneous ideas often called problems or issues. Some books provided data, usually of the informal case study or survey variety. A few probed implications for teaching that might be drawn from these prescriptions and descriptions.

By 1950, curriculum knowledge appeared in so many different shapes and styles that it was growing impossible for anyone but a full time curriculum scholar to grasp it as a whole. This was the knowledge that was used to prepare administrators, supervisors, and teachers, not just other scholars. Most administrators, supervisors, and teachers would only take one or two curriculum courses. Thus, synoptic texts were created to provide one-shot orientations, i.e., everything practitioners needed to know about curriculum.

By the Sixties such literature was criticized ferociously as armchair speculation. Even though much was derived from direct involvement in schools, it was not derived in ways deemed defensible through epistemological lenses that had come to dominate educational inquiry. Defensible knowledge needed to take the form of conceptual analysis sanctioned by analytic philosophers, and/or empirical studies sanctioned

340

by social scientists and psychologists. A plethora of studies from both vantage points dominated curriculum writing from the early 1960's to the present.

A Clamor for Freedom

Finally, the Seventies brought a castigation of the epistemological powers that dominated curriculum inquiry. Schwab's critique of the theoretic research paradigm is well known. Other prominent curriculum scholars call vehemently for inquiry that embraces phenomenological, dialectical, existential, literary, psychoanalytic, practical and/or aesthetic sources: Michael Apple, Dwayne Huebner, J.S. Mann, James B. Macdonald, Maxine Greene, Robert Stake, Elliot Eisner, William Pinar, George Willis, C.A. Bowers, Lawrence Stenhouse, William Reid, and others. Although their orientations may differ considerably from one another in many respects, they share an argument for freedom from the chains of domination by one epistemological base. This criticism pertains broadly to the several dimensions of curriculum study: scholarly curriculum inquiry, curriculum development, the content of school curriculum, and the overarching quality of school experience and its relation to living outside of classrooms.

Recommendations

The purpose of studying curriculum history should be able to provide insight that guides the curricular present and future. Knowledge about occupational characteristics of the curriculum professoriate in the past enables the development of directions that it might take in the future. Though the connection is not entirely clear between the work of curriculum scholars and its influence on curriculum implementation by teachers and acquisition by students, I submit that scholarly work should be conducted with the intent of

341

ultimately providing more worthwhile experiences
for teachers and students. Therefore, I will
share five recommendations, though they are
rudimentary, that I offer to the attention of
those who create curriculum literature.

The Search for Origins

The search for origins of the curriculum
professoriate has begun. Several contributions
have appeared in the Sixties and Seventies that
provide steps toward preventing ahistoricism.
This book is an attempt to portray the books produced by curriculum scholars in the Twentieth
Century. It is also an attempt to interpret and
discuss salient contributions. Further, it provides highlights of the socio-cultural context
in which curriculum literature evolved. Finally,
in this concluding chapter, I attempt to connect
fragments of knowledge about the curriculum professoriate and the literature that symbolizes its
work.

The origins, however, run much deeper than
the beginning of books with curriculum in the
title. The roots of curriculum study are portrayed in history, philosophy, and the arts to
antiquity. Their archetypes can be traced to
ordinary family life, social evolution, and the
arts of high culture. Together, these illuminate
perennial interest in the content of the journey
of children and youth as they are inducted into
the culture perpetuated by adults. Literary,
artistic, historical, and philosophical sources
interpret, evaluate, and criticize that journey.
They sometimes propose its reform. It is imperative that those who wish to study curriculum today
learn more of the saga of human concern which, in
part, gave birth to curriculum as a specialized
area of study in our world of specialization.

The Emulation of Origins

The search for roots in many fields today

discredits the long held notion that the growth of knowledge always ferrets out inert ideas and preserves productive ones. Even natural scientists revive documents previously believed to be archaic. Viewed with new perspectives, such documents often reveal method and substance that illuminate current problems.

Curricularists have experienced this, too. Some have begun to realize that while increased curriculum specialization magnified schooling, it clouded a holistic vision of childhood's curriculum to adulthood. Such a vision is portrayed in novels, poetry, film, painting, music, and the performing arts. It is analyzed in psychology, philosophy, anthropology, and history. These and other sources reflect an array of epistemological bases: intuition, empiricism, experience, revelation, reason, authority, utility, and so on. The science of behaviorism does not monopolize the route to curricular wisdom. The richness of perspectives that brought curricular insight before specialization arrived needs to be revitalized. The variety of methodologies in such perspectives should not be ignored.

Speculative endeavor, though today demised, ignited contributions made by recent ancestors of the curriculum professoriate. Fodor describes it well in reference to psychology, noting ancestors who are common to those of the curriculum professoriate.

> There used to be a discipline called speculative psychology. It wasn't quite philosophy because it was concerned with empirical theory construction. It wasn't quite psychology because it wasn't an experimental science. But it used the methods of both philosophy and psychology because it was dedicated to the notion that scientific theories should be both conceptually disciplined and empirically constrained. What speculative

343

psychologists did was this: They
thought about such data as were
available about mental processes, and
they thought about such first-order
psychological theories as had been
proposed to account for the data. They
then tried to elucidate the general
conception of the mind that was implicit in the data and the theories.
Speculative psychology was, by and
large, quite a good thing: William
James and John Dewey were speculative
psychologists and so, in certain of
his moods,was Clark Hull. But it's
commonly said that there aren't any
speculative psychologists any more.[5]

I suggest that the curriculum professoriate
repel pressures to expunge its tendency to engage
in speculation. It needs to resist the force to
increase specialization which limits attention to
schooling alone. I suggest that curriculum scholars advance the emergent tendency to perceive
curriculum broadly, as a function of culture,not
merely of schooling. Prerequisite to doing this,
at least in the process of doing so, curriculum
scholars need to expose the limits and impositions
of the epistemological assumptions that undergird
the several social and behavioral sciences that
direct the course of educational inquiry today.
In 1979, Schwab[6] called for a moratorium on the
prostitution of educators after academic respect-
ability, i.e., to blind adherence to values
implicit in dominant social science methodology.
At the same conference,Michael Scriven[7] challenged
educational researchers to develop research methodologies that are based on epistemological assumptions worthy of emulation by social scientists
themselves.

Applied to curriculum inquiry, I suggest that
the above necessitates the orchestration of many
methodologies. Relevant modes of inquiry and
expression would not be wholly unlike the rich
precedent of illumination of human situations that

344

is available in literature of philosophy, humanities, the arts, religion, technologies, and the professions, as well as social and natural sciences. The striving to understand curricular problems should be taken with no less seriousness than seeking the good, the beautiful, and the true. It should be of utmost seriousness because the induction of children into society and the attempt to reflectively and imaginatively guide their journey toward greater meaning, goodness, and wisdom fully penetrates the great philosophical questions.

The Ideal and the Mundane

The lofty ideals, i.e., the Platonic search for goodness and wisdom that I advocate for curriculum scholarship in the foregoing, is indeed serious. It makes a claim that is similar to Broudy's in his recent critique of what professors of education profess.[8] He invoked Plato's divided line allegory (The Republic, Book VI), and argued that educational scholars seldom move beyond levels two and three, the levels of facts and hypothetical entities or models. It is, in fact, thought presumptuous for them to even claim investigations into level four, the realm of wisdom or intuition with the forms. Rarely, if ever, do curricularists, other educators, and scholars at large directly admit that they engage in pursuit of wisdom, to usurp the title of Abraham Kaplan's recent book.[9] The job of curriculum scholars cannot stop short of this magnitude of inquiry. After all, one must go far to find an endeavor as worthy of seriousness as the study and development of itineraries by which children and youth move toward adult social life.

The import of this endeavor is indeed laudable, indeed admirable, and is I believe, a subtle germ of inspiration that lingers in the hearts and minds of many who are among the curriculum professoriate. It is perhaps this germ of inspiration that enables curriculum professors to create amid some of the

345

more debilitating characteristics of academe.
These rather mundane characteristics, unmentioned
thus far in this book, should be placed in juxta-
position with our loftiest ideals to provide a
balanced view. Curriculum professors are expected
to be first class teachers, consultants, researchers, and authors. They are expected to compete
in productivity with colleagues in other disciplines, have that productivity defined by these
colleagues as publication rather than direct
service to the curricular journey of children and
youth, and have their work and ability in the
academic community carry a reputation of less than
adequate. Moreover, curricularists' would-be
clients in schools often think of curriculum as
dry and boring, largely due to its association
with curriculum guides and similar documents.
From still another domain, one scarcely needs
reminders about the public criticism that riddles
the entire educational establishment from the
nursery to the graduate school. Surely, curricularists are not immune to this phenomenon.

Clearly, there is no small hiatus between the
ideal that motivates curriculum scholars and the
worth of work attributed to them by colleagues,
clients, and the public. A major problem, then,
is to generate increased regard for the work of
the curriculum professoriate. An important step
can be made by applying curriculum inquiry to the
wider domain from which it has grown, i.e., to a
holistic concern for the journey from birth to
adulthood. Hopefully, this concern which became
professorial through the thrust of universal
schooling was only diverted and not expurgated
by its necessary preoccupation with schooling.
Today, I suggest that broader applications of curriculum inquiry are needed to include and go beyond
schooling. I refer to one example as non-school
curricula and to another as a theory within
persons.

346

Non-School Curricula

Curriculum books almost invariably attest to the near universal emphasis on schooling by curriculum authors. Extricated from its social and cultural context, curriculum becomes addressed as only one of many forces in the journey that enables children to understand, function in, and contribute to adult life. That one force is schooling. Most any teacher will readily admit that forces beyond the control of schooling and outside of its purview have monumental influence on the child's view of the world. Quite obviously, homes, peer groups, formal youth organizations, jobs, and media profoundly influence children and youth. I submit that these are curricula in their own right and should be studied as such by curriculum scholars.

Compared to the cumulative effect of these non-school curricula, the impact of school curriculum itself is dwarfed. It is doubtful that curriculum can be studied meaningfully today apart from full attention to the interdependent character of life's curricula. Each curriculum influences conceptions of self and others, hopes, ambitions, fears, insights, values, roles, rules, power hierarchies, etc. The curriculum professoriate has accumulated a repertoire of analytic categories for investigation of school curriculum. I suggest that these or similar categories can be used to map features of the journey of children and youth through the curricula of media, peer groups, jobs, organizations, and homes, i.e., major domains of non-school curricula.

A "Theory" Within Persons

The non-school and school curricula shape a "theory" or world view within children and youth. It is a theory that they are, a living theory that guides their functioning, that embodies their information and misinformation about the world, how

it works, and how to relate to it. Without knowledge of student knowledge,[10] how can curriculum
developers defensibly determine what is needed for
subsequent stages of the journey of children and
youth toward adulthood? It is such knowledge of
the journey that shapes human character and builds
human ideals that must be addressed, in my estima-
tion, if the spark that ignited perennial curriculum interest is to be kept alive. It was a
similar spark that Jaeger sought to find as he
described paideia, "the shaping of Greek character" (p. ix),[11] He described the unique purpose
of his classic work as follows:

> Although many scholars have under-
> taken to describe the development
> of the state, the society, the
> literature, and religion, and the
> philosophy of the Greeks, no one
> seems to have attempted to explain
> the interaction between the histori-
> cal process by which their character
> was formed and the intellectual pro-
> cess by which they constructed their
> ideal of human personality.
> (Jaeger, 1945, p. ix).

Characterizing paideia in every culture is, I
suggest, important to any scholarly domain, foreign
to none, and essential to the work of curriculum
scholars. As we assert a tighter grasp on the
essence of our own paideia,we acquire a position
from which we can more defensibly create curricular
extensions of the journeys on which our children
and youth continuously embark.

Notes

[1]This observation was influenced by a viewpoint portrayed by Philip Jackson in a paper on
values imposed on education by psychology. The
paper was given at Session 4.14 of the Annual
Conference of the American Educational Research
Association, San Francisco, April, 1979. He

emphasized that the most important influences of psychology on education were not conveyed by overt values alone; instead, they were more subtle, pervasive, and diffuse.

[2]A sizable portion of the conclusion is drawn from the following paper: Schubert, W.H. Frames of Curriculum Knowledge Production: Historical Review and Recommendations. Presented to the Annual Conference of the American Educational Research Association, San Francisco, April, 1979. (Delivered in Session 16.26 to a Symposium entitled Occupational Characteristics of the Curriculum Professoriate, organized by Stephen Hazlett.)

[3]Schubert, W.H. and Posner, G.J. Toward a Genealogy of Curriculum Scholars. Presentation to the Society for the Study of Curriculum History, San Francisco, April 8, 1979. The research was also presented by: Posner, G.J. and Schubert, W.H. A Genealogy of the Curriculum Field. Paper for the Annual Conference of the American Educational Research Association, San Francisco, April 12, 1979, Session 33.10. A further elaboration of this work is scheduled for publication: Schubert, W.H. and Posner, G.J. Origins of the Curriculum Field Based on a Study of Mentor-Student Relationships. The Journal of Curriculum Theorizing, 1980, 2(2).

[4]Readers will recall that Schwab (1970) criticized the epistemological base of educational research, labeled it theoretic, and advocated a move to the practical or quasi-practical. Similarly, Pinar (1975) criticized educational research of the social science ilk, labeled it conceptual empiricist, and advocated a move to reconceptualization and emancipation.

[5]J. Fodor exemplifies the need to engage in serious speculation in a book-length essay that embraces psychology, linguistics, and philosophy of mind. See Fodor, J. The Language of Thought. New York: Crowell, 1975. The quotation was taken from p. vii.

[6] This was a central purpose of a series of sessions at the 1979 Annual Conference of the American Educational Research Association, San Francisco, April, culminating in Session 12.01 chaired by Joseph Schwab, entitled: Values Imposed by the Behavioral and Social Disciplines: Implications for Education Research and Development Policy. (This session culminated six sessions: 1.24, 4.14, 6.11, 8.17, 9.106, 11.30. It was organized by Hendrik Gideonse and Robert Koff).

[7] This challenge was communicated by Michael Scriven in his 1979 Presidential Address at the Annual Conference of the American Educational Research Association, San Francisco, April 10, 1979.

[8] Broudy, H.S. What Do Professors of Education Profess? Annual De Garmo Lecture to the Society for Professors of Education, Chicago, February 28, 1979. (Subsequently published by The Society.)

[9] Kaplan, A. In Pursuit of Wisdom. London: Glencoe Press, 1977.

[10] I briefly discussed this idea in: Educational Knowledge about Student Knowledge. Insights. December, 1978, 15(2), pp. 3-4. The non-school curriculum and theory within persons are current subjects of several pieces that are at different levels of preparation.

[11] Jaeger, W. Paideia: The Ideals of Greek Culture (Volume I). New York: Oxford University Press, 1976 reprint of 1945 text, p. ix.

Epilogue

Any attempt to be inclusive and thoroughly accurate in a book such as this is bound to fall short. Therefore, I would be most grateful for suggestions, corrections, additions, and other ideas. It is through cooperation that curriculum literature and its study can be best furthered. Thus, the real epilogue for this book must be a cooperative venture of all who care about curriculum problems. I wish you well in your curricular pursuits. Thank you.

William H. Schubert

University of Illinois at Chicago Circle

College of Education Box 4348

Chicago, Illinois 60680

INDEX

Prefatory Comments

The index is limited to the following: authors of books included in the bibliographical sections of this book; authors noted in discussions of curriculum literature; and topics listed in discussions of curriculum thought and literature. The Contextual Reminders sections are not indexed; these sections are provided for their impressionistic impact rather than primarily for detailed reference. Bibliographical sections are indexed for authors only, not for topics. Titles of curriculum books are not indexed for two reasons: (1) curriculum books tend to be known by their authors more than their titles, and (2) titles are so similar that it would be difficult to efficiently use an index based on them.

Finally, topical entries are limited to Curriculum Thought and Literature sections. Categorizations of books and ideas frequently place a given book into several categories. It is fully acknowledged that most curriculum books treat many topics; nevertheless, it is beyond the scope of this index to provide classifications that are more detailed than topical categorizations discussed in commentary sections of the chapters of this book. I assert that these topics reflect many of the central sub-areas of curriculum inquiry over the years; however, they are not offered as definitive categories of contributions.

Aikin, W.M., 102, 114
Alberty, E.J., 140, 157, 179, 201
Alberty, H., 108, 118, 121, 137, 151, 179, 201, 332
Alcorn, M.D., 143, 153, 159
Alexander, W.M., 132, 139, 154, 179, 180, 185, 189, 191,
    205, 215, 216, 220, 248, 272, 284, 289, 302, 330
Allen, D.W., 206
Allen, E.D., 220
Alpren, M., 180, 216
Amalgamation of schools of curriculum thought, 35, 50-51,
    68, 100, 105, 135-136, 145, 174-175, 193-194, 251,
    330 (see also Synoptic texts)
Ambrosetti, R.J., 263, 279, 289
American Association of School Administrators, 43, 56, 138,
    151, 185, 187, 203, 211
American Council on Education
    American Youth Commission, 99, 112,
American Educational Research Association, xiii, xv, xviii,
    7, 80, 83, 189, 195, 196, 203, 216, 223, 245, 274,
    348, 350
    Special Interest Group on the Creation and
        Utilization of Curriculum Knowledge, xv, xviii
Ammerman, H.L., 255, 279
Anderson, D.W., 187, 209, 270, 303
Anderson, R.H., 142, 159, 181, 184, 196, 204
Anderson, V.E., 140, 155, 185, 186, 192, 205, 209, 223
Anderson, W.G., 216
Andrus, R., 72, 86
Apperceptive mass, 20, 21
Apple, M.W., 238, 244, 246, 258, 267, 320, 341
Aristophenes, 2
Aristotle, 2
Armentrout, W.W., 261, 284
Association for Childhood Education, 107, 119
Association for Student Teaching, 139, 151
Association for Supervision and Curriculum Development, 9,
    105, 108, 116, 118, 134, 139, 140, 141, 142, 143,
    148, 150, 153, 154, 155, 156, 158, 182, 183, 184,
    185, 187, 189, 192, 193, 195, 198, 201, 203, 205,
    209, 216, 224, 242, 244, 253, 255, 266, 279, 284,
    299, 331
Augustine, Saint, 2
Axtelle, G., 74, 87

Bacon, F., 2, 254-255
Bagley, W.C., 9, 22, 24, 27, 47, 50, 55, 327, 328
Bailey, S.K., 212

Curriculum (continued)

Curriculum (continued)

Davies, I.K., 262, 269, 309
Davis, A.M., 136, 151
Davis, C.O., 43, 49, 57
Davis, O.L., 266, 306, 309
Davis, R.A., 185, 203
Davis, R.B., 217
Dearden, R.F., 191, 221
DeCarlo, J.E., 272, 295
DeGarmo, C., 20, 327, 332, 335, 340, 350
de Grazia, A., 185, 207
De Keijzer, A.J., 264, 311
Della-Dora, D., 299
Democracy and curriculum, 33, 68, 74, 75, 99, 100, 103,
        105, 136, 137, 138, 253, 258, 267, 335
Denemark, G.W., 203
Dennison, G., 237, 275
Denver Public Schools, 57
Department of Elementary School Principals, 91
Department of Health, Education, and Welfare, xiv, 173
Derr, R.L., 257, 295
Descartes, R., 2, 332
Dewey, J., 4, 9, 21, 22, 23-24, 27, 33, 34, 36, 42, 43, 49,
        66, 68, 71, 73-74, 75, 77, 80, 81, 89, 100, 109, 134,
        143, 173, 175, 181, 183, 189, 240, 241, 243, 244, 246,
        247, 252, 254, 255, 270, 275, 276, 277, 323, 327,
        328, 331, 335, 340, 344
Deyoe, G.P., 71, 83
Dickens, C., 2, 333
Dickenson, E., 2
Dickson, G.E., 249, 300
Dillon, E.J., 280
Dix, L., 91
Dixon, K., 261, 289
Doane, D.C., 104, 114
Dodd, C., 28
Doll, R.C., 138, 152, 185, 205, 207, 248, 249, 270, 280,
    295, 300, 317
Doll, W., 267
Donne, J., 2
Dorsey, B., 182, 200
Dostoyevski, F., 2, 333
Dottrens, R., 201
Douglass, H.R., 108, 119, 140, 156, 179, 180, 207
Downey, L.W., 196
Drag, F.L., 108, 119

Goggans, S., 100, 112
Goodlad, J.I., 142, 159, 184, 185, 187, 188, 195, 204, 208,
    212, 243, 249, 258, 259, 296, 300, 304, 320
Goodman, S.M., 108, 119
Gordon, P., 318
Gorrell, R.M., 199
Gosin, B., 266, 293
Gow, D.T., 269, 309
Gower, R.R., 269, 313
Gracey, H.L., 266, 269, 290
Graham, B.G., 112, 279
Gran, E., 269, 314
Grant, N., 293
Gray, E.D. McQ., 32, 36
Gray, W.S., 32, 43, 60
Great Britian Schools Council, 190, 218, 221, 259, 296, 305,
    309
Green, A., 276
Greene, G.G., 259, 268, 296
Greene, M., 238, 254, 261, 317, 341
Greer, C., 276
Gress, J.R., 248, 318
Grobman, H.G., 191, 192, 221, 225, 257, 281, 290
Gross, R., 10
Grossman, R.H., 218, 269, 306
Grumet, M.R., 244, 245, 311, 332
Guttchen, R.S., 180, 193, 225
Gwynn, J.M., 103, 116, 132, 138, 146, 179, 192, 197, 225, 330

Haan, A.E., 182, 199
Habermas, J., 244
Hagaman, N., 204
Hagen, O.A., 249, 288
Haigh, G., 253
Haines, P.G., 210, 305
Hall, G.S., 21, 327, 335
Hall, K.H., 57
Halverson, P.M., 180, 212
Hamilton, D., 257-258, 259, 273, 309, 314
Hamilton, N.K., 180, 192, 225
Hamilton, O.T., 45, 57
Hammock, R., 113
Hampson, D.H., 195, 307
Hand, H.C., 134, 137, 149
Haney, R.E., 188, 212

Hidden curriculum, 184, 192, 246, 335
Hildreth, G.H., 109, 119
Hill, P.S., 42, 53,
Hillestad, M.C., 191, 220
Hillson, M., 271, 286
Hines, H.C., 43, 54
Hirst, P.H., 262, 305
Hissong, C., 73, 82
History of Education Society, 265, 286
Hoban, C.F., 88
Hobbes, T., 254, 326
Hockett, J.A., 151
Hollaway, O., 243, 305
Holley, B.J., 257, 302, 303
Holloway, W.J., 59
Holly, D., 243, 253, 261, 300
Holmes, B., 264, 296
Holt, J., 237, 275
Holt, M., 250, 318
Homer, 2, 333
Hook, S., 262, 305
Hooper, R., 271, 286
Hopkins, L.T., 43, 48, 49, 60, 67, 69, 70, 74; 88, 89, 101, 109,
        113, 138, 144, 153, 270, 329
Hoppe, A., 140, 156, 157, 263
Horace Mann School, 28, 34, 36, 37, 42, 48, 104
Horn, E., 50
Hotter, L., 301
House, J.E., 299
Houston Texas, Independent School District, 71, 79
Houston, W.R., 280
Howson, G., 281
Hoyle, E., 249, 291
Huebner, D.E., 180, 186, 187, 208, 242, 244, 341
Hug, W.E., 255, 305, 320
Hughes, P.W., 269, 297
Hull, C., 344
Humanistic curriculum, 70, 183-184, 190, 191, 192, 194, 242,
        243, 244-247, 252, 253, 254, 331, 342
Hunt, F.J., 286
Hurley, B.J., 140, 157
Hyman, R.T., 271, 286, 297

Ibsen, H., 2
Ickes, H.L., 85

Illinois, Western Illinois University, 147
Indiana, Department of Public Instruction, 60, 116
Inlow, G.M., 188, 212, 248, 297
In-service programs and curriculum, 142
Intellectual Traditionalists, School of Curriculum Thought,
    xii, 6, 16, 17-18, 19, 24, 26, 34-35, 41, 49-51, 66, 69,
    70, 73, 105, 135, 174-175, 194, 246, 247, 251-252, 326,
    328, 329, 335, 337, 339
International Bureau of Education, 197
International Curriculum Conference (Second), 213
International Educational Assessment, 239
International Kindergarten Union, 43, 53

Jackson, D.M., 140, 156
Jackson, P.W., 192, 221, 246, 274, 277, 348
Jacob, T.N., 71, 82
Jaeger, W., 348, 350
James, H.T., 192, 225
James, W., 18, 340, 344
Jameson, M.C., 180, 197
Janzen, H., 264, 281
Japan, Department of Education, 181, 197
    National Commission for UNESCO, 199
Jarvis, O.T., 188, 189, 213, 221
Jaspers, K., 338
Jefferson, T., 100
Jelinek, J.J., 243, 263, 318, 320
Jenkins, D.R., 248, 257, 261, 273-274, 291, 302, 309, 314
Jenkins, J.M., 243, 249, 253, 284
Jersild, A.T., 107, 118, 132, 147
Jobe, E.R., 147
John Dewey Society, 74, 91, 139
John, W.C., 85
Johnson, H.T., 191, 221
Johnson, M., Jr., 182, 200, 262, 264, 269, 302, 314
Johnston, A.M., 257, 281
Joint Committee on Curriculum of the Department of Supervisors
    and,
    Directors of Instruction of the National Education
    Association and the Society for Curriculum Study, 88
Jones, A.J., 68, 91
Jones, D.M., 249, 314
Jones, G., 70, 72, 85
Jones, H.L., 180, 192, 225
Jones, L., 150

Nelson, M., 267, 318
Nelson, M.R., 111
Nerbovig, M., 253, 282
Neskora, T.W., 263, 314
Netherlands Workshop on Curriculum Research, Vierhouten,
     Netherlands, 264, 297
Neufeld, K.A., 282
Newfield, J.W., 269, 306
Newfoundland Teachers Association, Curriculum Seminar, 218
Newlon, J.H., 71, 72, 82
Newman, F.M., 263, 306
Newton, J.E., 263, 310
New York City Department of Education, 104, 108, 116, 121
New York State University, 85, 154
Nicholls, A., 248, 269, 292, 318
Nicholls, H., 248, 269, 292, 318
Nietz, J.A., 182, 200
Nisbet, S.D., 141, 157, 191, 222
Noar, G., 108, 120
Non-school curriculum, 7
Normal Schools, 22
North Central Association of Colleges and Secondary Schools,
     71, 76, 83
North Carolina, 67, 71, 84, 85
Northern Ireland, 71, 80
Norton, J.K., 77, 87, 100, 330
Norton, M.A., 77, 87, 100, 330
Nowak, A.T., 280
Number of curriculum books by decade, 8, 10-11

Oberholtzer, E.E., 68, 89
Objectives, purposes, goals and aims, 43, 46, 49, 68, 74, 75,
     99, 104, 109-110, 132, 140-141, 142, 145, 175-176, 177,
     178, 181-182, 185, 187, 189, 191-192, 253, 257, 260-
     261, 266, 267
Offner, H.L., 105, 116
Ogletree, C.J., 255, 298, 320
Ohio State University, 103, 108, 121, 154
Ohliger, J., 226
Oho, H.J., 198
Oliver, A.I., 186, 210, 248, 250, 287, 315
Olsen, E.G., 138, 153, 243, 254, 315
Olson, A.V., 259, 268, 292
Olson, W.C., 142, 157, 265, 287
Ontario Association for Curriculum Development, 189, 214, 222, 301

Pinck, D.C., 180, 188, 213
Plato, 2, 173, 345
Platt, E.T., 80
Ploghoft, M.E., 185, 204, 248, 270, 283, 316
Plutarch, 2, 333
Pold, K., 222
Ponder, G.A., 9, 306
Pope, A., 2
Popham, W.J., 192, 226, 255, 259, 294
Posner, A., 264, 311
Posner, G.J., 269, 319, 349
Postman, N., 269, 321
Potter, G.L., 204
Prescott, W., 305
Pring, R., 267, 273, 311
Pritzkau, P.T., 143, 159, 282
Professors of Curriculum, 9
Progressive education, 23, 42, 43, 48-51, 70, 73-74, 99,
    102, 109, 111, 135, 172, 175, 176, 183, 194, 244
Progressive Education Association, 21
Project method, 33, 47, 48-49, 67, 68-69, 73
Promfret, A., 304
Prosser, C.A., 71, 91
Provus, M., 259
Pugno, L., 175, 185, 207
Purpel, D.E., 248, 263, 293, 318

Quadrivium, 17
Quintillian, 2

Rado, M., 267, 317
Ragan, W.B., 136, 138, 139, 153, 179, 189, 198, 214, 270,
    287, 315, 330
Raup, B., 85
Raynor, J., 293
Razik, T.A., 255, 293
Recommendations for curriculum scholarship, 341-351
Reconceptualists, 144, 242, 244-246, 252, 350
Regan, E.M., 249, 301
Reid, W.A., 238, 242, 249, 254, 257, 258, 261, 272, 303,
    306, 319, 321, 341
Reisner, E.H., 72, 76, 79
Review of Educational Research, xvi, 48, 73, 193
Review of Research in Education, 274
Revised and reprinted editions of curriculum texts, 132,
    137, 178-179, 268, 270

379

Sachs, B.M., 215, 249
Sacramento Curriculum Conference, 210
Salisbury, E., 43, 49, 54
Sand, O., 215
Sands, L.B., 223
Sanguinet, E.H., 71, 73, 84
Santa Barbara (California) Schools, 104, 114
Sartre, J.P., 244, 338
Saxe, R.E., 300
Saylor, J.G., 101, 114, 139, 154, 179, 180, 189, 215,
    225, 248, 284, 293, 302, 330
Schaffarzick, J., 174, 195, 258, 267, 272, 307, 321
Schenk, Q., 138, 150
Schill, W.J., 208
Schiro, M., 262, 265, 319
School consolidation, 144
School Health Education Study, 219
School Review, 241
Schools, 2, 3, 17, 19, 21, 32, 34, 72, 108, 130, 133,
    136, 137, 138, 141, 172, 174, 183, 186, 192, 194,
    238, 239-240, 250, 251-252, 254, 266, 267, 268, 270,
    273, 275, 323, 324, 328, 329, 330, 333-336, 339, 340,
    343, 344, 346-347,
Schools Council, 219, 302
Schools Council for Curriculum and Examinations, 263, 287
Schools of curriculum thought
        see Amalgamation; Experientialist;
        Intellectual traditionalist; and
        Social behaviorist
Schubert, A.L., i, iii, 389
Schubert, W.H., xviii, 276, 349, 351, 389
Schwab, J.J., 74, 78, 144, 193, 226, 238, 241-242, 244,
    261, 276, 282, 319, 331, 339, 341, 344, 349, 350
Science, Conceptions of, and curriculum, 6-7, 16, 19-20,
    32, 33, 45, 46, 49-50, 68-69, 173, 177-178, 182, 190,
    194, 237-238, 240, 241-243, 246, 254-255, 256, 258-
    259, 260, 271-272, 328-329, 331, 335, 337-341, 343-
    345, 350
Scobey, M.M., 179, 182, 191, 200, 223, 279
Scott, L.F., 218, 269, 306
Scott, M.B., 269, 313
Scott, W.E., 115
Scottish Council for Research in Education, 81
Scottish Education Department, 147
Scriven, M., 189, 215, 216, 259, 344, 350

Snyder, E.R., 181, 198, 283
Social Behaviorist, School of Curriculum Thought, xii,
        6, 16, 19-20, 24, 32, 34, 41, 44, 49-51, 66, 69, 73,
        100-101, 105, 135, 142, 174-175, 176, 177-178, 182,
        183-184, 190, 194, 238, 242-243, 246, 247, 252, 254-
        259, 326-327, 328, 329, 331, 335, 337, 340
Social efficiency movement, 20, 44, 49-50
Society for Curriculum Study, 71, 76, 90
Society for Professors of Education, 350
Society for the Study of Curriculum History, 7-8, 111,
        266, 277, 349
Sociological, political, and ideological perspectives, 44,
        237-238, 240, 245, 257, 258, 266-267, 268
Sockett, H., 269, 273, 312
Sohn, D.A., 185, 207
Sophocles, 2
South Dakota, 71, 79
Sowards, G.W., 179, 180, 182, 191, 200, 205, 223
Sparrow, F., 311
Spears, H., 71-72, 89, 99, 108, 113, 120, 136, 142, 149,
        157, 330
Speiker, C.A., 266, 269, 302, 312, 316
Spencer, H., 19, 25, 34-35
Spessart, K.H., 181, 196
Spring, J., 276
Springer, U.K., 192, 227
Sputnik, 141, 172
Stake, R., 192, 259, 260, 341
Staley, S.C., 70, 72, 85
Standing Joint Committee of the Headmaster's Conference
        and Incorporated Association of Preparatory Schools,
        71, 86
Stanford Education Conference, 84
Stanley, W.O., xiii, 130-131, 134, 138, 140, 147, 157, 186,
        265, 330
Staples, I.E., 269, 307
Stearns, F.K., 211
Steeves, F.L., 180, 223, 248, 319
Stegeman, W.H., 183, 202
Steimer, W., 9
Steinbeck, J., 2
Steiner, R., 193
Stendler, C.B., 139, 179, 198, 214
Stenhouse, 248, 249, 257, 259, 307, 341

ABOUT THE AUTHOR

William Schubert is coordinator of the graduate program in Instructional Leadership: Programs
for Schools and Institutions in the College of Education at the University of Illinois at Chicago
Circle. Currently an assistant professor, he received a Ph.D. from the University of Illinois at
Urbana-Champaign in 1975, an M.S. from Indiana
University in 1967, and a B.S. from Manchester College in 1966.

Presently the chairperson of the American Ed-
ucational Research Association Special Interest
Group on the Creation and Utilization of Curriculum
Knowledge, Schubert is active in: Professors of
Curriculum, the John Dewey Society, the National
Society for the Study of Education, the American
Educational Studies Association, the Association
for Supervision and Curriculum Development, the
Society for Professors of Education, and was a
founding member of the Society for the Study of
Curriculum History. His publications have appeared
in Educational Researcher, Educational Studies,
Studies in Educational Evaluation, the Journal of
Curriculum Theorizing, Curriculum Review, and the
Journal of Teacher Education.

Formerly an elementary school teacher for seven
years in Downers Grove, Illinois, the author now
consults with Chicago area schools on curriculum,
instruction, evaluation, and learning environments.
His teaching and research focus on these general
areas, and more specifically, on curriculum theory,
research orientations, design, and implementation.

Ann lynn Schubert, who assisted in the preparation of this book, taught for three years in the
Chicago Public Schools and is presently a Doctoral
candidate in Public Policy Analysis at the University of Illinois at Chicago Circle. She and her
husband often write, conduct research, and consult
together.